Pope, Swift,
and Women Writers

Pope, Swift, and Women Writers

Edited by
Donald C. Mell

WITHDRAW.

DELAWARE

Newark: University of Delaware Press
London: Associated University Presses

Associated University Presses
440 Forsgate Drive
Cranbury, NJ 08512

Associated University Presses
16 Barter Street
London WC1A 2AH, England

Associated University Presses
P.O. Box 338, Port Credit
Mississauga, Ontario
Canada L5G 4L8

The paper used in this publication meets the requirements
of the American National Standard for Permanence of Paper
for Printed Library Materials Z39.48–1984.

Library of Congress Cataloging-in-Publication Data

Pope, Swift, and women writers / edited by Donald C. Mell.
  p.   cm.
 Includes bibliographical references and index.
 ISBN 0-87413-590-7 (alk. paper)
  1. English literature—18th century—History and criticism.
 2. Women and literature—Great Britain—History—18th century.
 3. English literature—Women authors—History and criticism.
 4. Swift, Jonathan, 1667–1745—Political and social views.   5. Pope,
Alexander, 1688–1744—Political and social views.   6. Swift,
Jonathan, 1667–1745—Characters—Women.   7. Pope, Alexander,
1688–1744—Characters—Women.   8. Authorship—Sex differences—
History—18th century.   9. Verse satire, English—History and
criticism.   10. Women in literature.   I. Mell, Donald Charles.
 PR448.W65P67   1996
 820.9′0082—dc20   96-16288
                                                                CIP

Contents

Preface

ALEXANDER Pope's and Jonathan Swift's writings and satire have aroused intense hostilities in women readers and feminists, both in their own day and in ours, for their allegedly unsympathetic treatment of women. They have been accused of indifference to the plight of eighteenth-century women in a patriarchal society and even of exhibiting sexist and misogynistic attitudes in the case of the eighteenth-century woman writer. Despite Pope's satirical depictions and often contemptuous treatment of a whole range of what he called the "variegations" of the female sensibility, he clearly enjoyed the company of women and placed high value on female friendships during his life. And regardless of Swift's habitual lashing out at "fair-sexing" and at the fulsome gallantries with which women are condescendingly depicted in periodicals like the *Spectator* and in amatory verse, and in spite of his insistence that women be treated intellectually and socially on a par with men, not exploited as sex objects, and even though despite the tender realism and sincerity characterizing the verse addressed to Esther Johnson (Stella) and the good-natured raillery often found in the Market Hill poems written to Lady Acheson, feminists find evidence in such works as *Gulliver's Travels* and the "scatological" poems of fierce and deep antagonisms that seem to defy rationalization. Indeed, the very language and phrasing that the two men employed when expressing their praise of women—for example, Pope's "softer Man," in reference to Martha Blount, and Swift's "Friendship and Esteem" to describe the ideal marriage relationship—seem only to make matters worse. According to their detractors, such expressions are sexist and deny possibility of an independent female identity. It is a case of damning with the wrong kind of praise.

The eleven essays in *Pope, Swift, and Women Writers* contribute to a growing number of critical studies that challenge such antifeminist stereotypes. These essays employ a variety of interpretive strategies, which combine recent modes of critical inquiry with traditional historical and formalist readings. The essayists have discovered not so much a difference or otherness separating Pope,

9

Swift, and the women writers under consideration as the presence
of unremarked-upon similarities in literary attitudes, belief sys-
tems, and social and political outlook, as well as a certain shared
status as alienated, displaced, excluded, victimized, and even self-
divided outsider figure.

Nine of the eleven essays in this volume originated in the form
of papers read at three successive annual meetings of the American Society for Eighteenth-Century Studies (ASECS) in Pittsburgh (1991), Seattle (1992), and Providence (1993). The topic
for these seminars was "Pope, Swift, and Women Writers," which
accounts for the book's title. The essay by Carole Fabricant was
commissioned for this volume; the essay by Nora Crow was read,
in an earlier version, during the Third Münster Symposium on
Jonathan Swift, which took place 31 May–1 June 1994 at the
Ehrenpreis Center for Swift Studies, located at Westfälische
Wilhelms-Universität, Münster, Germany. All but two focus on the
literary, social, political, and cultural worlds in which Alexander
Pope and Jonathan Swift moved and wrote and on the women
writers of the day who were their acquaintances or even collabora-
tors in the literary enterprise. One of these two essays challenges
the claim that Swift and the late-eighteenth-century feminist
Mary Wollstonecraft were ideological opposites; the other deals
with an unnoted kinship between Swift and the twentieth-century
satirist Dorothy Parker, whose writings arguably share with Swift
a similar ironic wit and satiric style. All the essays have been
lengthened, amplified, reconsidered, and thoroughly revised for
inclusion in this collection. The scholarship has been updated,
new materials added, and new perspectives and viewpoints developed. Some parts of Barbara McGovern's essay appeared in different form elsewhere (*Anne Finch and Her Poetry: A Critical
Biography*, 1992). For permission to use these materials the editor
thanks the University of Georgia Press. Claude Rawson's essay on
Swift's *Cadenus and Vanessa* was first published in *Connaissance
et création au siècle des lumières: mélanges Michel Baridon*, ed.
Frédéric Ogée and others, a special number of *Interfaces: Images
Texte Langage* 4 (1993): 19–35. It was delivered at a conference
in honor of Michel Baridon, at the Université de Bourgogne, Dijon,
France, in the summer of 1991.

As for the book's organization, the first four essays discuss both
women in Pope's poetry and Pope and women poets of his period;
the fifth essay focuses on Pope, Swift, and other literary figures,
male and female; and the remaining six deal with Swift's personal
and literary relationships with women writers both in his day and

later on, as well as account for his special attraction for feminist critics. The introduction, intended as a guide to reading the essays, provides a broad survey of the subjects discussed and a description of the themes explored.

Many people both in and out of academe have been very helpful during the gestation of this collection. It is impossible to acknowledge all of them. I do, however, want to single out the program committees for the three annual meetings of ASECS previously mentioned. Their generous and unusual decisions to approve three seminars on a single topic provided an early forum for the essays in this volume and made possible this enterprise.

I am in tremendous debt to my Delaware colleagues J. A. Leo Lemay and James Dean, to whose offices I continually beat a well-worn path during the editing process. Where editorial expertise and sound scholarly advice are involved, they are without compare. Whatever successes are deemed for this volume owe much to their thoughtful editorial suggestions; the faults and blunders are of my own making. I also appreciate the support and various suggestions from Jerry Beasley, Charles Robinson, Elaine Safer, and Bonnie Kime Scott of the Delaware English faculty; George Miller and Carl Dawson were department chairs during the period when this collection was being edited, and I thank them for approving a number of grants and research funds to aid publication.

Deborah Lyall deserves praise for her expert managing of computer files and handling of the voluminous correspondence connected with publication. Richard Duggan, campus information technology associate, and Suzanne Potts, English department administrative assistant, patiently answered my interminable questions about computer capabilities and word-processing procedures, and I appreciate their interest in this project. They have made the entire editing process more accurate and efficient.

Mark Netzloff, my research assistant during the preparation of this volume, earns accolades not only for his thorough checking of references, notes, and documentation, but also for his thoughtful and scholarly critiques of the essays for style and content. The volume is stronger for his careful attention to detail and Swiftian common sense.

I especially appreciate the encouragement of Elizabeth Reynolds, editor of the University of Delaware Press, whose diligent and intelligent copy-editing of the manuscript was a crucial factor in the publication of this volume. She continually brought to bear her editorial expertise on the project and took special interest in guiding the book through publication. She incorporated my numerous last-minute changes and revisions with cheerful forbearance.

Finally I thank the contributors for the patience and unfailing support over the months, even years for some, while this volume was being put together. This applies especially to the academic year 1993–94, when I was working in the Division of Research Programs at the National Endowment for the Humanities. My duties there as a program officer meant delaying all but the most routine of editorial activities for the duration of the assignment. I appreciate their trust in me as editor as well as their confidence that this book would be brought to a successful completion.

The volume is dedicated to Charles Bohner, Hans-Peter Breuer, and Thomas Calhoun, distinguished colleagues in the English department at the University of Delaware, exemplary scholars, and longtime friends.

Abbreviations and Short Titles

Ehrenpreis	Ehrenpreis, Irvin. *Swift: The Man, His Works, and the Age*. 3 vols. Cambridge: Harvard University Press, 1962–83.
Mack	Mack, Maynard. *Alexander Pope: A Life*. New York and New Haven: Norton and Yale University Press, 1986.

Editions of Pope's Works

Pope, *Corresp.*	*The Correspondence of Alexander Pope*, ed. George Sherburn. 5 vols. Oxford: Clarendon Press, 1956.
TE	*The Twickenham Edition of the Poems of Alexander Pope*. Edited by John Butt et al. 11 vols. New Haven: Yale University Press, 1939–69. References are to volume and page number.

Editions of Swift's Works

Swift, *Corresp.*	*The Correspondence of Jonathan Swift*. Edited by Harold Williams. 5 vols. Oxford: Clarendon Press, 1965–72.
Rogers	*Jonathan Swift: The Complete Poems*. Edited by Pat Rogers. Harmondsworth: Penguin, 1983.
JS	*Journal to Stella*. Edited by Harold Williams. 2 vols. Oxford: Clarendon Press, 1948.
Swift, *Poems*	*The Poems of Jonathan Swift*. Edited by Harold Williams. 2d ed. 3 vols. Oxford: Clarendon Press, 1958. References are to

volume and page number.

Swift, *Prose* *The Prose Works of Jonathan Swift*. Edited by Herbert Davis et al. 14 vols. Oxford: Blackwell, 1939–74.

Swift, *Tale* *A Tale of a Tub*. Edited by A. C. Guthkelch and D. Nichol Smith. 2d ed. Oxford: Clarendon Press, 1958.

Introduction

DONALD C. MELL

Both Alexander Pope and Jonathan Swift have been lightning rods for feminist hostility in not only our own age, but in the eighteenth century as well. This hostility manifests itself in different and sometimes contradictory ways (which has recently provoked vigorous rejoinders from equally impassioned "defenders of the orthodox critical faith").[1] Such poems as Anne Ingram's "An Epistle to Mr. Pope" and the unidentified Miss W——'s "The Gentleman's Study, In Answer to The Lady's Dressing-Room" give evidence of both being read as misogynistic in their own day. And Lady Mary Wortley Montagu's "The Reasons That Induc'd Dr. S[wift] to write a Poem call'd the Lady's Dressing Room" and her "P[ope] to Bolingbroke" demonstrate that both satirists could be viewed as antifeminist by a contemporary.[2] Swift himself refers to accusations "of abusing the Female Sex" in his prefatory letter from Gulliver to Cousin Sympson, dated 1727 but added to George Faulkner's 1735 edition of Swift's *Works*. Faulkner also warns readers of the poetry that "the Ladies may resent certain satyrical Touches against the mistaken Conduct in some of the fair Sex."[3]

In our time Pope's best-known twentieth-century biographer, Maynard Mack, can argue that "the poet's own profound and delicate appreciation of women . . . and also that quality of his sensibility that some critics have called feminine" most likely have resulted from womanly influence both in his household and through his many female friendships while Ellen Pollak asserts that Pope indeed codifies an antifeminist tradition in the eighteenth century by creating a world of "sterile fetishism" in his *Rape of the Lock*, in which "female sexuality is a material property over which man has a natural claim."[4] For Laura Brown, Swift's "misogyny is appropriately understood in the context of mercantile capitalism"; Margaret Doody asserts that Swift's satire acts as "a useful and liberating model" for the woman author. And she further explains that in the eighteenth century, "for every female

15

voice raised against Swift there are several to speak for him."[5] To complicate matters further, Katharine M. Rogers, epitomizing these ambivalent attitudes, regards Swift at one point as a misogynist only to make a 180-degree turnabout, viewing him later as a proleptic feminist—and on essentially the same evidence and documentation.[6] These conflicting critical opinions would suggest, then, that when gender matters are at stake interpretive difficulties abound. Pope spoke well for both himself and Swift—and their modern commentators, it would seem—when he remarked in the *Epistle to a Lady*: "Woman's at best a Contradiction still" (*TE*, 3.2:270).

When women writers are the targets of such satire, according to a number of the more determined feminists, the attacks can be especially misogynist, virulent, and perverse. "Female writers are maligned as failures in eighteenth-century satire," write Sandra Gilbert and Susan Gubar, "precisely because they cannot transcend their female bodily limitations: they cannot *conceive* of themselves in any but reproductive terms." The "debased arts" of the female writer come then to symbolize failure of the creative imagination as well as the materialism, dilettantism, hypocrisy, and professional vanity—all matters of corruption, folly, and vice the male satirist is powerless to change and reform.[7] According to this argument, the male satirist, in a display of uncontrolled masochism, apparently "attacks *in others* the weaknesses and temptation that are really *within himself*," as Kenneth Burke once described the dynamics of satire.[8] Thus Pope's good-natured dismissal of female writers as "Sapphoes wee admire no more" in his "Impromptu" addressed to Anne Finch, who had chided him for his antifeminist "scoffing rhimes"; his scurrilous depiction of Eliza Haywood, in *The Dunciad*, as first-prize award for the winner of a urinating contest; Swift's dismissal of Delariviere Manley by depicting her "cooking" his suggestions into a sixpenny pamphlet on Robert Harley's stabbing; the strange mixture of satire and ironic self-referentiality in the depiction of Manley in his poem *Corinna*—all would then in fact exemplify a form of male self-satire.

Happily, three of the contributors to this volume, Carole Fabricant, Ellen Pollak, and Valerie Rumbold, have been noteworthy for their purposeful yet cautious and nuanced feminist writings on Pope and Swift, and while not approaching the writings of Pope and Swift from an exclusively feminist perspective, they have continually provided effective challenges and needed correctives to the often tendentious, reductive, and narrowly ideological approaches that sometimes characterize feminist treatments of the satires of Swift and Pope and the circle of women writers in which these two male satirists moved. I do not mean to imply that they (or other contributors to this volume) would deny the presence of sexism in the writings of Pope and Swift or that they rationalize and disregard instances of misogyny, exploitation, or bad-faith motivations in their satirical attacks on women. What they and the other contributors do is consider such issues in the context of the generic traditions of antifeminist satire and in light of the formal devices and rhetorical practices employed by satirists in the process of creating their satiric fictions.

Although formalist assumptions consistently inform the analyses of the essays in this volume, the contributors do not neglect historical contexts and political background. They take into account the impact of the dominant cultural politics and ideological concerns of the age on the writings of Pope and Swift. They conclude that the involvements of Pope and Swift with women writers of the period are far more complex than had been previously understood. And in her essay on women scholars and Swift, Nora Crow explores the implications for Swift studies of this ongoing feminist/antifeminist debate over Swift's attitudes toward women, both in the eighteenth century and the present. She concludes that although women, for culturally determined reasons, bring to interpretations of Swift "certain gender-specific advantages over men," they do not supplant male opinion, only complement it.

The essays on Pope and Mary Leapor, Judith Cowper, and Mary Chandler share similar critical methodologies. The authors treat Pope's life, his poetic themes and imagery, and his couplet style and creation of varied fictive identities as a mirror image for the female poets that contributes to their own self-fashioning and attempts to create an individualized poetic identity.

In the first essay of the collection, Caryn Chaden explores Mary Leapor's impact on Pope's poetry and finds "not just a model for writing poetry, but a model for viewing herself as a poet." Chaden emphasizes how Leapor shares Pope's attention to social commentary, appropriating his critical perspective of the outside observer. Both poets represent themselves in their poetry as objects of attack, wrongly besieged by lesser poets and jealous critics, a parallel most explicitly evident in Leapor's *The Libyan Hunter, A Fable*. But some essential differences exist between the poets: Leapor's poetry often describes the difficulties specific to a working-class woman writer. Thus, while the second *Mira to Octavia* evinces verbal and thematic references to Pope's *Of the Characters of*

Women, each similarly concluding with a "reaffirmation of Christian humanist values," her poem specifically advises that women seek an alternative to marriage. Although Leapor works within the same conventions as Pope—the Horatian portrait, for example—her works subvert the content of Pope's poems, more adequately addressing the relation of money and power to marriage and definitions of female virtue. A poem like *Crumble Hall* further demonstrates how Leapor, unlike Pope, concludes her poetry with a "retreat from social practices she finds oppressive," emphasizing the endemic societal inequalities that persist regardless of personal failings. Although one cannot label Leapor a "feminist," as critics have attempted, Chaden concludes that Leapor challenges the tradition represented by Pope "to live up to its own ideals and apply its values universally."

According to Valerie Rumbold, Judith Cowper's brief and small poetic output resulted not so much from opposition to her work or personal pressures as from an inability to balance her roles as poet and "attractive and well-connected young woman." Moreover, Cowper inherited from Pope, her ostensibly benevolent mentor, both a gendered and hierarchical conception of poetry; consequently, she consistently characterizes poetry as a masculine endeavor. Not only does she depend upon gendered metaphors and state a preference for "manly" genres like epic and history painting, but she also accepts as benign the poetic status of women as objects rather than as the active "Sacred Source" of poetic expression. Despite her early derivative apprentice pieces and later feeble attempts at satire, Cowper's final spurt of poetic activity—the love poems inspired by "Lysader" (her future husband, Colonel Martin Madan)—demonstrates her ability to assume a masculine poetic voice in her passionate contemplation of her husband, placing herself in the "forbidden role of a desiring woman" as she writes about her beloved as male poets have traditionally written about women. Overall, however, Cowper seems most comfortable in a gendered role of both celebration and deference. Naively assimilating herself within a male poetic tradition, Cowper is denied the authority necessary to challenge the terms of her exclusion.

For Linda Troost language and structural organization in Mary Chandler's *A Description of Bath* establish a decidedly feminized landscape of spherical and cyclical images and metaphors that contrast the linear, phallic imagery characteristic of her mentor, Pope. Among the many similarities between the poets is topographical poetry that privileges retirement over the activity of the city. But despite Chandler's acknowledged debt to Pope, she diverges from his models like *Windsor Forest* in her own topographical poem. Troost argues that "Chandler avoids the linear organization of space," working principally in circular romance structures or "feminized" patterns. Conversely, Pope often employs circular images to represent narrow, selfish, and solipsistic vision, preferring hierarchical, linear metaphors—"scales of reason, chains of love, streams of time." For Troost, these metaphors reflect Pope's indebtedness to gendered hierarchies conventional to poetry, tropes in effect reversed by Chandler's poem. Chandler's poem "breaks down a central site of power distribution in Augustan poetry: the relationships among the poet, the patron, and the muse." As a female poet, Chandler has both a female muse and patron, but she significantly maintains her independence from both, extending her gender role reversal to a reversal of power distribution as well. Troost concludes that Chandler herself becomes the contemplative creative spirit: "she shapes history, geography, and even Ralph Allen's garden into her feminine ideal, a pattern of cycles instead of phallic lines, of containment instead of active expansion."

Peter Staffel shifts the critical focus of the three previous essays on the reciprocating influences among Pope and specific women poets to consideration of the internally genderized dialectic among such figures as Belinda, Thalestris, and Clarissa within *The Rape of the Lock* itself. Staffel's reexamination of Pope's *Rape of the Lock* situates the central conflict within the poem not in the war between the sexes, but among the women, specifically Thalestris's and Clarissa's competition for influence over Belinda. As Staffel argues, "Clarissa claims to defend honor as virtue, but in practice . . . defends feudal submissiveness to male authority—woman as object of man's gaze and his desire, and tool of his power. Thalestris, on the other hand, defends a world where virtuous reputation rather than true virtue equates with honor." Staffel further develops the opposition between Clarissa and Thalestris through his application of Julia Kristeva's "paradigm of oppositional female societies within a dominant patriarchy": one group, like Clarissa, "succeeds in gaining access to the power structure and is in turn absorbed by the dominant culture and employed as an instrument of its hegemony"; the other group, representatives of "more radical feminist currents" and demonstrated in the poem by Thalestris, construct a countersociety in opposition to the former group's acquiescence to patriarchal control. Thus Thalestris would urge Belinda to exert her power "to draw or attract every man's gaze and desire, recognize it, and then reject it." As a manifestation of the image of the amazon figure in the eighteenth century, Thalestris embodies a transgressive force that deflects "criticism of basically indefensible male actions," linking the monstrous image of the termagant with the frighteningly subversive demand for sexual equality.

In her essay Barbara McGovern introduces the figure of Swift into configurations of Pope and the female poets analyzed by Chaden, Rumbold, and Troost, treating this tripartite interaction as a complex self-discovery process that places Finch in a self-reflexive posture vis-à-vis Pope and Swift, and situates the two male satirists in a similar self-reflexive mode vis-à-vis Finch.

The marginal social positions shared by Finch, Pope, and Swift furthered their support of each others' poetry, McGovern asserts. Swift encouraged Finch to publish after her return to London, aiding her inclusion in the sixth of Jacob Tonson's *Poetical Miscellanies* by writing "Apollo Outwitted. To the Hon. Mrs. Finch" in her honor and introducing her to other writers; she in turn felt a sympathetic identification with him because both were forced into exile for political reasons. In the case of Pope, Finch's shared literary relationship was more substantive, and she maintained a polemical though good-natured debate with him over the role and quality of women writers. Despite his frequent, deprecatory comments on this issue, Pope highly respected Finch, elicited her opinion on revisions of *The Rape of the Lock,* and even compared her to Queen Anne in "Impromptu, to Lady Winchilsea." Finch did not allow Pope's compliments to efface the condescension of his "gallantry," though. Rather, in poems like "The Answer [to Pope's Impromptu]" and "An Epilogue to the Tragedy of Jane Shore," Finch "quarrels with a distinctly patriarchal view of women," one furthered both through Rowe's representation of his heroine and Pope's satirical jab at the actress Anne Oldfield in his rejected epilogue to the play. Finch nevertheless remained a close personal and literary friend of Pope, a writer similarly marginalized because of his ideological and religious beliefs, defending him from attack in her poems and reciprocating the support he gave to her work.

Taken together, the essays by Melinda Rabb and Carole Fabricant on Delariviere Manley show how Swift's interaction with this fascinating and controversial female antagonist and political propagandist can educe widely different, sometimes contradictory critical readings. Manley functions as a two-sided mirror in cases of these authors, reflecting for Rabb an affinity or "congeniality" between the two satirists, and providing for Fabricant a glimpse into the ambivalence, anxieties, and self-divisions that are the result of harshly conflicting ideological, political, cultural, and gender orientations.

Rabb approaches Manley as a political satirist, not as a figure in the rise of the novel. Using as her critical springboard the glass of satire trope found in both Swift and Manley, Rabb explores its implications as an indication of an unremarked "congeniality between the two authors": both were propagandists; both created satiric fictions in which anarchic energies outran and confounded their ostensible moral purposes; both were marginalized and alienated politically and materially by the fall of the Tory ministry; both are concerned with the body and sex, and both were aware of the contradictions they embodied as writers. Rabb analyzes Manley's themes and narrative structures in the *New Atalantis,* the *Examiner* (a collaborative effort of Swift and Manley), and *A True Narrative of what pass'd at the Examination of the Marquis De Guiscard* to show similarities with Swift's narrative strategies and argumentative methods in *A Tale of A Tub, Gulliver's Travels,* as well as instances in the *Examiner* and elsewhere where "the body becomes the ultimate text of the human condition." But it is in the "spirit of *menippea*" that Rabb ultimately locates the deeper literary and political affinities between Manley and Swift, namely the similar uses of Bakhtinian "carnivalesque," concern with the topical and local, the generating of ironic disjunctions, abrupt shifts in plot, tone, and style, the fashioning of utopias, and the creation of various fictional identities and personae. Finally, Rabb finds the most profound similarity between Manley and Swift in their problematic positioning of the satirist in the text, Manley's the result of obstacles facing a woman writing in a male satirical tradition and Swift's created by the multiple rhetorical perspectives reflecting elusive and often contradictory states of mind.

Where Rabb finds "congeniality" as operative dynamic in the relationship between Manley and Swift as satirists, Fabricant sees a crystallizing of anxieties in both Swift's and Manley's life and writings that result from their implicit threat to Augustan moral and literary values and standards and the dangers of contamination and promiscuous commingling of gender differences, class and cultural distinctions, and popular and elitist literature. Her essay shows how exceedingly difficult and elusive is the task of discriminating between "hack" status and Augustan high seriousness—a case in point being the futility of distinguishing between Manley's and Swift's contributions to the *Examiner.* For Fabricant, Swift's reluctant praise of Manley reveals his own ambivalent ties to the journalistic world of the political propagandist, which she has come to embody, and the creative tensions produced by Swift's dual status as a satirist of a universal human nature above the parochial and topical and as a writer intensely concerned with the tangible affairs of a country in crisis. Her inquiry also offers Fabricant the chance to investigate the ideological contradictions generated by being in the position of a popular Tory writer. Her essay concludes with a discussion of Manley's "feminism" in relation to other "progressivist" women authors of the age who were Tories and suggests a model of ideological consciousness more complicated than was formerly believed.

Swift's poem *Cadenus and Vanessa* (addressed to Esther Vanhomrigh) is one of his most problematic and recalcitrant productions. It has been described as an inconclusive attempt to reconcile the demands of love and friendship, a "convoluted and straightforward, cryptic and open" poetic failure brought on less by Swift's "personal pathology" and misogyny than by an antifeminist impasse that is culturally and linguistically generated.[9]

Claude Rawson generally agrees with this predominantly negative assessment of the poem, but on different grounds. For him *Cadenus and Vanessa* is flawed in tone and fails as an exercise in "raillery." He sees this poem as distinctly autobiographical and, unlike Swift's famous satirical mirror, "wherein Beholders do generally discover every body's Face but their Own," in this case reflecting matters having to do "with Swift's relations with himself, and which inevitably bear on his relations with others: with women of course, and lovers, but also with readers and that animal called man." Dismissive of feminist critiques of the poem and of biographical critics' concern with Swiftian psychology, Rawson focuses instead on Swift's fashioning of a special brand of irony (also found in other autobiographical poems), "a coy self-derision . . . frequently referred to as 'raillery'" that "proclaims anger by denial." Rawson laments the absence of a critical vocabulary that can account for Swift's complex mediation between Horatian and Juvenalian satire and his habit of creating intensities and rage in language seemingly devoid of these qualities, despite his stated preference for Horace and for satire that provides "the least Offence" (*Intelligencer* No. 3). Swift's raillery often consists of a "*dis*avowal of 'lofty style,' of 'rage,'" an ironic stance that has produced misreadings of Swift as either a misanthrope or as a "sobersided moderate from the Land of the Golden Mean." Rawson also asserts that Swift utilizes an excess of rage, a "sophisticated defense" against "appearing emotionally overcommitted" that especially characterizes the scatological verse. *Cadenus and Vanessa* similarly exemplifies how Swift sets up "a front designed to disguise or neutralize embarrassment at poetic acts of self-celebration or self-justification," an awkward position resulting from Swift's "posture as both the retailer of [Vanessa's] feelings *and* the object of her passion." Swift's self-deprecating and self-exposing stance not only invites the reader's speculation through teasingly opaque autobiographical details, but also characterizes the ironic play between poet and persona. In summary, Rawson writes that "in the atmosphere of self-regarding obliquity that disfigures this poem, it is not women who are at issue, but Swift's own sense of himself."

The next two essays—those by David Venturo and Ellen Pollak—add further complexities to earlier discussions of relations of Pope, Swift, and women writers in their close-knit and elitist literary and political circle of early eighteenth-century England. Venturo compares the writings of Swift on women with those of Mary Wollstonecraft of a later generation to argue for surprisingly similar viewpoints on the matter of female education and the dignity of women, as well as a shared endorsement of "a rationalist feminist position" (Rawson's phrase). Pollak reaches across the Atlantic to compare Swift's satiric temperament with that of Dorothy Parker, the twentieth-century American journalist and famous member of the Algonquin Round Table, who in fact may have never actually read Swift.

Challenging the tendency of previous studies to portray the two writers as ideological opposites, Venturo instead underscores ways "the supposedly neat ideological division between Wollstonecraft and Swift is narrower and more complicated than scholars commonly assumed." Despite Wollstonecraft's critique of Swift in the *Vindication of the Rights of Woman,* which complains of the harshness of the satire, Venturo argues that her main targets are sentimentalists like Rousseau and Dr. James Fordyce, who advise women to gain power through "emotional and sexual manipulation." Even though the Anglican Swift never subscribed, as Wollstonecraft later did, to the casuistical emphasis on environment as the main determinant of character, a position more characteristic of Dissenters, "both firmly believed in holding men and women to a uniform code of private conduct," an emphasis on reserve, moral and public virtue, and education that transcends sex. And while Swift may not have shared Wollstonecraft's vision of equal access to education across gender lines, largely endorsing a role for women within companionate marriages, he did admire and

help further Esther Johnson's economic independence and intellectual talents.

In a wide-ranging and speculative comparison of a twentieth-
century satirist with the best-known eighteenth-century prac-
tioner, Ellen Pollak traces ways in which Dorothy Parker uses
Swift "as an operative point of reference in 'The Professor Goes
in For Sweetness and Light,'" her satirical review of Yale professor
and public-opinion booster William Lyon Phelps's *Happiness*. Although she makes no specific reference to Swift, Parker appropriates the Swiftian form of mock-defense to critique the social
and intellectual biases of the Ivy League elite, those who had
elevated modern hacks at the expense of figures like Swift. She
satirizes the arrogance (and ultimately the ignorance) of Phelps's
hypocritical stance, which was equally dependent upon Arnoldian
elitism and ethnocentric glorifications of an exclusively Puritan
and Anglo-Saxon American cultural tradition, a form of "Ku Klux
Kriticism" similar to the intolerance evinced by the contemporane-
ous trial of Sacco and Vanzetti. Through her narrator, the mask
of a "deferential" and "inept" female American tourist, Parker may
also "masquerade as a blissfully myopic 'little lady'" and "articulate
her own problematic status as a woman writer positioned simultaneously inside and outside the historically male-dominated traditions of literary criticism and satire." Pollak argues that Parker
and Swift found themselves similarly situated to "major sites of
cultural power." Both writers possessed multiple and conflicting
loyalties and were ultimately locked out of the inner circles of
cultural privilege to which they both once had access. And like
Swift, Parker dons and abandons authorial masks, hiding herself
with tantalizing hints of autobiographical detail. Through this
process Parker heightens "our sense of the illusory or invented
nature of even her 'real' identity, itself always already mediated
by culturally constructed versions of womanhood" and attempts
to establish a "public" literary criticism that extends "across lines
of class, ethnic, gender, and educational privilege."

In the volume's concluding essay, marked by generous quotations and useful references to writings of a number of the other
contributors and to some of the previous essays in this collection,
Nora Crow offers an explanation of the peculiar fascination of
Swift for women writers and critics, past and present. For her, it
is rooted in Swift's "protean sensibility," an "empathic knowledge"
of women that results in the suppression of his own male ego and
enables him to imagine women from the inside, to "inhabit the
body of another being of his own creation." Of course, it is vintage

Swift and a characteristic strategy of his satire to assume masks and create multiple personae and fictional identities. But when the process involves not just acting out a role, but "revealing the woman within him," the result, according to Crow, can often be cause for considerable confusion, discomfort, vexation, and sometimes outright hostility in feminist or antifeminist alike. Further, Swift's capacity for empathy does not, however, mean a suspension of moral judgment. Empathy without approval, as evidenced in such works as the scatological poems, for example, strikes Crow as an especially "cruel maneuver," and partly explains the critical controversy and conflict that beset Swift studies. Crow sees "fluidity" of sexual identity as a two-way street: Swift himself embodies this male/female duality at the same time that he projects this ambivalent identity onto women. Thus occur the curious gender ambiguities of a Stella, Vanessa, or the young woman being advised on marriage. Despite a long history of belittlement of Swift's women friends and the persistent questions raised about his own masculinity, beginning with his first biographer, Lord Orrery, Crow points out that Swift rose above the prejudices of his age, especially regarding women's education, and provided a brief moment of freedom from cultural restrictions. Thus he remains "a primary subject of study" for women scholars who respond passionately to his life and art. Their diverse and often contradictory views do not supplant those of male critics. They complement them in the ongoing Swiftian critical enterprise.

In their introduction to *The New Eighteenth Century,* Felicity Nussbaum and Laura Brown credit feminist critics for engaging in archival retrieval of women's texts obscured "by ideologies of gender at work in the 'major writers' of the period."[10] A number of essays in this volume clearly further this important scholarly activity by bringing to light hitherto neglected writings of women authors. And in his essay "Pope and the Social Scene," revised for publication in a collection entitled *Essays on Pope* (1993), Pat Rogers calls recent feminist writing "the liveliest area of Popeian studies." While few of the contributors to this collection would feel particularly comfortable with the label "feminist critic," it nevertheless is the sensitivity to and concern with issues of gender in the broad and inclusive sense shared by all the contributors that serve ultimately to shape the critical inquiry pursued throughout this volume and give it authority and relevance. Rogers argues that feminist readings "have opened up wider areas of Pope's mind and art for our consideration."[11] These diverse and often innovative treatments of the lives and art not only of Pope but of Swift and the women writers as well bear witness to the cogency of Rogers's claim, and they represent an advance in our understanding and appreciation of these particular authors likely to inform and mold future critical thinking. *Pope, Swift, and Women Writers* challenges received opinion, gives new insights, and makes a valuable contribution to women's studies while at the same time providing a more complete picture of the eighteenth-century literary world and its relevance to our own age.

Notes

1. See Robert Markley, "Beyond Consensus: *The Rape of the Lock* and the Fate of Reading Eighteenth-Century Literature," *New Orleans Review* 15, no. 4 (1988): 68–77; reprinted in *Critical Essays on Alexander Pope*, ed. Wallace Jackson and R. Paul Yoder (New York: G. K. Hall, 1993), 69–83. Markley summarizes the interpretive disputes that have resulted from Marxist, feminist, and deconstructionist readings of Pope and other eighteenth-century figures. The implications of his "metacritical" critique, however, go far beyond specific controversies over interpretations of Pope's *Rape* and address "fundamental ideological divisions within eighteenth-century studies and within academe at large" and their relation to the process of literary evaluation in humanities studies generally. See also Penelope Wilson, "Feminism and the Augustans: Some Readings and Problems," *Critical Quarterly* 28 (1986): 80–92. In a perceptive critique Wilson points out that "both Pope and Swift represent positions which are properly inimical to a modern feminist consciousness" (83–84); nevertheless, she argues that in their attempts "to free readings from the pall of misogyny, there are acute problems for feminism in these uncongenial waters": to wit, the ideological and political motives often fueling such correctives can compromise their usefulness "as a critical tool," especially in Augustan satire, which is "perhaps uniquely adept at constructing the terms of its own criticism and at pre-emptive disablement of the opposition" (82).

2. See *Eighteenth-Century Women Poets: An Oxford Anthology*, ed. Roger Lonsdale (New York: Oxford University Press, 1989), 150–51; 130–34, and *Lady Mary Wortley Montagu: Essays and Poems*, ed. Robert Halsband and Isobel Grundy (Oxford: Clarendon Press, 1977), 279–84 and 273–76.

3. Swift, *Prose*, 11:xxxv; George Faulkner, *The Works of Jonathan Swift, D.D., D.S.P.D., in 4 vols.* (Dublin, 1735), 2:i–ii.

4. Mack, 29; Ellen Pollak, *The Poetics of Sexual Myth: Gender and Ideology in the Verse of Swift and Pope* (Chicago: University of Chicago Press, 1985), 97.

5. Laura Brown, *Ends of Empire: Women and Ideology in Early Eighteenth-Century English Literature* (Ithaca: Cornell University Press, 1993), 199; Margaret Anne Doody, "Swift among the Women," *Yearbook of English Studies* 18 (1988): 91, 70.

6. Katharine M. Rogers, *The Troublesome Helpmate: A History of Misogyny in Literature* (Seattle: University of Washington Press, 1966), 166–74; *Feminism in Eighteenth-Century England* (Urbana: University of Illinois Press, 1982), 58–62.

7. Sandra M. Gilbert and Susan Gubar, *The Madwoman in the Attic: The Woman Writer and the Nineteenth-Century Literary Imagination* (New Haven:

Yale University Press, 1979), 32; Susan Gubar, "The Female Monster in Augustan Satire," *Signs: Journal of Women in Culture and Society* 3(1977): 389.

8. Kenneth Burke, *Attitudes toward History*, 3d ed. (Berkeley and Los Angeles: University of California Press, 1984), 49.

9. Doody, "Swift among the Women," 75; Pollak, *Poetics of Sexual Myth*, 129.

10. *The New Eighteenth Century*, ed. Felicity Nussbaum and Laura Brown (New York: Methuen, 1987), 15.

11. Pat Rogers, *Essays on Pope* (Cambridge: Cambridge University Press, 1993), 166.

Pope, Swift,
and Women Writers

Mentored from the Page: Mary Leapor's Relationship with Alexander Pope

CARYN CHADEN

AFTER generations of neglect, working-class poet Mary Leapor (1722–46) has received enough critical attention in recent years to spark some controversy over her relationship to the canon and, in particular, her views of Alexander Pope. Donna Landry offers the most radical reading; although she acknowledges that "Leapor's most obvious poetical debt is to Pope," she emphasizes the ways in which Leapor subverts Pope's patriarchal stances towards class and gender. Landry concludes that of the poetry produced by laboring-class writers in the first half of the eighteenth century, Leapor's is "the body of work most easily assimilable to what we commonly describe today as 'radical feminism,' with its polemics against patriarchy, male violence, and heterosexist containments of economies of desire."[1] In contrast, both Betty Rizzo and Richard Greene agree that Leapor takes strong positions against social injustices—especially those concerning gender and class—but see her as fundamentally conservative, accepting the traditions that she learned, in large part, from Pope. Greene writes that "Leapor's attitude toward Pope very much reflects her tendency to respect the intellectual, social, and religious traditions of her society while arguing bravely against specific ideas or practices which she believes are oppressive. Leapor's passionate admiration of Pope's work is matched by a robust independence of mind."[2] Rizzo goes even further, arguing that Leapor, like other "primitive poets" of the day, "had to catch up, make up for lost time, follow Pope and learn to write like him. She was overwhelmed with an anxiety, not the anxiety of influence but the anxiety *for* influence. As a result her poetry, like that of [Stephen]

I would like to thank DePaul University for giving me a 1993 Summer Research grant to complete this project.

31

Duck, could scarcely be more conventional, but of course was never as accomplished as that of Pope, Young, Otway or Rowe."[3]

The one point on which these critics agree is Pope's inescapable presence in Leapor's work.[4] Thus, to assess the degree to which Leapor's work can be described as either "radical," "conventional," or something else, we need to look more closely at her views of Pope—what she learned from him, how she applied those lessons, and where her views depart from his. Leapor's reading was not restricted to Pope, of course. Margaret Doody sees Swift's influence in "The Mistaken Lover" and "Strephon to Celia. A Modern Love-Letter,"[5] and Greene persuasively argues that Leapor read much more widely than her patron Bridget Freemantle might have wanted potential subscribers to believe.[6] But while Leapor learned specific ideas and techniques from other writers, and while she received the most direct support from Freemantle and another patron, Susanna Jennens,[7] it is Pope whom she describes as her "favourite";[8] it is Pope from whom she imbibed a vocation. What she gained from reading his *Essay on Criticism, Essay on Man, Epistle to Dr. Arbuthnot, The Dunciad,* and even *Of the Characters of Women* was not just a model for writing poetry, but a model for viewing herself as a poet. This model, with its emphasis on social commentary and the critical perspective of an outside observer, shapes both the form and content of Leapor's poetry. And ultimately, this model shapes Leapor's critique of Pope as well.

As Greene remarks, "Pope's verse has for Leapor a significance second only to scripture."[9] Indeed, despite their differences, her view of Pope reflects the ideal he presents in *An Essay on Criticism* of someone

> . . . who Counsel *can* bestow,
> Still *pleased* to *teach,* and yet not *proud* to *know*[;]
> Unbiass'd, or by *Favour,* or by *Spite;*
> Not *dully prepossest,* nor *blindly right;*
> Tho' Learn'd, well-bred; and tho' well-bred, sincere;
> Modestly bold, and Humanly severe[.]
>
> (*TE,* 1:310–11, ll.631–36)

What Leapor sees in Pope is a man not only blessed with poetic talent and genius, but also one who shares her Christian values. Perhaps more important, Pope shares her struggles as a writer, occupying a similar position both as an outsider and as a person attempting to live a pious life. In "On Mr. Pope's *Universal Prayer*" (1 : 142–44) she addresses her mentor directly—"To thee a Stranger, to thy Lines a Friend"—and looks to his work for guidance: "O teach my Soul to reach the Seats divine, / And praise her maker in a Strain like thine" (1 : 9–10). It is interesting to note that *The Universal Prayer* is the only poem of Pope's that Leapor explicitly mentions by name in her own poetry. A personal article of faith all-embracing in its sense of a universal deity and free of allusions to particular people or events, "On Mr. Pope's *Universal Prayer*" is the poem with the most direct connection to the circumstances of Leapor's life and the internal struggles she faces daily. Perhaps most tellingly, Pope asks his God to

> Save me alike from foolish Pride,
> Or impious Discontent,
> At ought thy Wisdom has deny'd,
> Or ought thy Goodness lent.
>
> (*TE*, 6 : 148, ll.33–36)

Leapor was no stranger to emotions that could be characterized as "impious"; discontent, in particular, is the topic of numerous poems from her own work.[10] What impresses her most about Pope's poem is not simply the ease with which his "Numbers flow" but the purity of his sentiments, a purity more striking to her for the way it stands in the face of any criticism that he, as a Catholic, might receive from the Protestant "Enthusiasts" to whom she directs these lines:

> Ye careless Ones, who never thought before
> Read this grand Verse, then tremble and adore:
> Let stern Enthusiasts here be taught to know,
> 'Tis from the Heart true Piety must flow:
> Here Hope, Content, and smiling Mercy shine;
> And breathe celestial through the speaking Line:
> From the still Mind its guilty Passions roll,
> And dawning Grace awakes the fervent Soul.
> Let angry Zealots quarrel for a Name,
> The good, the just, the virtuous are the same:
> Grace to no Sect, nor Virtue is confin'd;
> They blend with all, and spread amongst the kind;
> And the pure Flame that warms the pious Breast:
> Those cannot merit who condemn the rest.
>
> (1 : 11–24)

In this call for religious tolerance, Leapor outlines the qualities that she considers universal marks of virtue—hope, contentment, mercy, justice, piety—that is, the values of Christian humanism. And while her specific focus here is the way these qualities "spread amongst" religious sects, elsewhere she extends her argument across class lines: "If we consider the Behavior of Mankind, from the Prince to the Peasant," she writes in an early letter, "we shall find the Seeds of the same Passions, the same Virtues and Vices, in all ranks and Degrees of People" (2:303–4). What most interests Leapor are those qualities that "blend with all," and so make differences in circumstance irrelevant. Where Leapor finds common ground with Pope is in the pursuit of a virtuous life in the face of hostility. Hence she concludes the poem with one more plea for guidance:

> Teach me between the two Extremes to glide,
> Not brave the Stream nor swim with ev'ry Tide:
> But more with Charity than Zeal possest,
> Keep my own Faith, yet not condemn the rest.
>
> (2:49–52)

In this poem, the eighteenth-century adage that poetry should delight and instruct becomes both personal and concrete, as the persona engages in a kind of literary apprenticeship, allowing Leapor to pay homage to her teacher with the same humility that Pope shows in his address to God, and thereby learning from Pope's work how to approach her own dual task of writing and living well. It is the loss of this relationship that Leapor most laments in "On the Death of a Justly Admir'd Author" (1:252–54): "Ah! who shall now our rustick Thoughts refine / And to grave Sense and solid Learning join / Wit ever sparkling, and the Sweets of Rhyme?" (1:37–39).

Leapor identifies with Pope most strongly as an object of critical attack, a position demonstrated in "The Libyan Hunter, A Fable" (1:153–62), which she has "Inscribe'd to the Memory of a late admir'd Author":

> Old Story tells us, on an earthly Plain
> Once *Jove* descended wrap'd in golden Rain:
> Now Fate permits no such familiar Powers,
> But Shoals of Criticks fall in leaden Showers;
> These gaze at Wit, as Owls behold the Sun,
> And curse the Lustre which they fain wou'd shun;
> These Beasts of Prey no living worth endure,

> Nor are the Regions of the Dead secure;
> Yet shall the Worthy o'er their Spite prevail;
> Here lies the Moral—follows next the tale.
>
> (1:5–14)

Leapor extends the inscription's references to Pope within her description of "the Worthy," a figure who ultimately prevails over a gang of envious, predatory "Criticks." These "Beasts of Prey" reach even into the grave to satisfy their destructive cravings. What follows is the story of "happy Sylvius": an accomplished hunter, a strong yet graceful poet of nature, and "A well-known Fav'rite of the Prince of Day" (1:18). Although struck down by jealous muses, Sylvius is ultimately resurrected by Phoebus and mysteriously taken away. In the place where Sylvius's body had lain, new life appears in the form of a bush: "Now the gay Shrub each happy Climate knows, / by all admir'd, and 'tis call'd the Rose" (1:131–32).

In this fable, Leapor demonstrates complete sympathy with the view that Pope presents of himself in *An Epistle to Dr. Arbuthnot* and the other Horatian Imitations, that of a superior poet wrongly besieged by hacks.[11] In the end, Leapor argues, vile envy can do nothing to destroy Sylvius's spirit or the beauty he has left behind. This argument serves Leapor equally well when she applies it to her own work. In "To Grammaticus" (1:122), "Advice to Myrtillo" (1:167), "The Complaint" (2:88), "Timon" (2:280), "Minutius. Artemisia. A Dialogue" (2:285), and "The Visit" (2:290), among others, Leapor adopts a stance similar to Pope's as she writes of herself—either in the first-person or third-person accounts of "Mira," her name for herself—withstanding assaults from self-absorbed, superficial critics who would rather point out errors in punctuation or penmanship than understand her poems.[12]

The most sophisticated poem from this group is "An Epistle to Artemisia. On Fame" (2:43–54), a poem that echoes both the sentiments and the cadences of Pope's *Epistle to Dr. Arbuthnot*. Having already gathered subscribers with one volume,[13] Leapor had achieved a measure of fame in her village at the time of this poem's composition, and it appears that she found the consequences of this success mostly negative. Thus, like Pope to Arbuthnot, Leapor addresses her most trusted friend and asks, "Say, Artemisia [her name for Freemantle], do the Slaves of Fame / Deserve our Pity, or provoke our Blame?" (2:1–2). And while Artemisia, unlike Arbuthnot, remains silent, Leapor uses dialogue with other characters to establish her own voice as a poet.

As Leapor "count[s] the Patrons of [her] early Song" (2:69) we find that most of them, like those Pope describes in the first hundred lines of *Arbuthnot*, are not really interested in her poetry. While Leapor cannot provide the favors that Pope could, her visitors similarly seek a connection with someone "famous" to make themselves feel important, and the facts of Leapor's circumstances only make their solicitations more ridiculous. In her portrait of "Cressida," for example, Leapor describes a small-town Sporus, similarly self-absorbed as she flits from one activity to the next:

> A decent Virgin, blest with idle Time,
> Now gingles Bobbins, and now ponders Rhime:
> Not ponders—reads—Not reads—but looks 'em o'er
> To little Purpose, like a thousand more.
>
> (2:87–90)

Cressida's interest quickly turns from Leapor to herself: "I've read the-like, tho' I forget the Place: / But, Mrs. *Mira*, How-d'ye like my Lace?" (2:103–4). As her visit drags on, the poet begins to sound more and more like Pope asking John Serle, his gardener, to bar the door:

> Afflicted *Mira*, with a languid Eye,
> Now views the Clock, and now the Western Sky.
> "The Sun grows lower: Will you please to walk?
>   "No, read some more."
>   "But I had rather talk."
> "Perhaps you're tired."
>   "Truly that may be."
> "Or think me weak."
>   "Why, *Cressy*, Thoughts are free."
> At last we part, with Congees at the Door:
> "I'd thank you, *Mira*; but my Thanks are poor.
> "I wish, alas! But Wishes are in vain.
> "I like your Garden; and I'll come again.
> "Dear, how I wish!—I do, or let me die,
> "That we liv'd near"
>   —Thinks *Mira*, "So don't I."
>
> (2:106–16)

Mira is indeed "tired" of Cressy's company; but as she demonstrates her skill in shaping dialogue out of whip-cracking heroic couplets, her comments glide right by her visitor's "weak" mind. Hence Leapor, like Pope, fuses form and content to affirm her own superiority as the afflicted poet.

"Epistle to Artemisia" provides Leapor the opportunity to reaffirm her commitment to her craft and to document the sacrifices she has made in its service—in her case, through lectures at home and dismissal from work:

> *Parthenia* cries, "Why, *Mira,* you are dull,
> "And ever musing, till you crack your Skull;
> "Still poking o'er your What-d'ye-call—your Muse:
> "By pr'ythee, *Mira,* when dost clean thy Shoes?"
>
> Then comes *Sophronia,* like a barb'rous *Turk:*
> "You thoughtless Baggage, when d'ye mind your Work?
> "Still o'er a Table leans your bending Neck:
> "Your Head will grow prepost'rous, like a Peck.
> "Go, ply your Needle: You might earn your Bread;
> "Or who must feed you when your Father's dead?"
> She sobbing answers, "Sure I need not come
> "To you for Lectures; I have store at Home.
> "What can I do?"
>   "—Not scribble."
>   "—But I will."
> "Then get thee packing—and be aukward still."
>
> (2:149–63)

Landry has shown Leapor's debt to Pope's "First Satire of the Second Book of Horace" in these lines, for his "refusal to stop writing, despite the advice of his friends . . . enables Leapor's defiance."[14] But these lines are also informed by *An Epistle to Dr. Arbuthnot* in that they provide autobiographical material that establishes the poet's claim to the craft. The two poets take opposite journeys, of course. While Pope argues that his position is entirely natural—he "lisp'd in Numbers, for the Numbers came," he received recognition from writers he respected, and made money selling his work (*TE,* 4:104–6, ll. 125–46)—Leapor documents the sheer determination required of a working-class woman, no matter how talented she may be, who dares to pursue her craft. And while Pope ends his poem confident in his position, Leapor still has doubts: "Methinks I feel this coward Bosom glow: / Say, *Artemisia,* shall I speak, or no?" (2:179–80). But Leapor continues to speak despite her doubts, using Pope's model to create her own self-portrait. Indeed, this poem serves a purpose in her work similar to that served by *Arbuthnot* in Pope's: it offers us an account of her life as a poet—in her case, a life cut short before such lingering reticence might have been outgrown. And while

Pope wrote *An Epistle to Dr. Arbuthnot* later in his career when his talent was universally recognized, Leapor writes to stake her claim, to show that the poems that gave her fame in her village were not passing fancies but products of a talent that would endure.

"On Mr. Pope's *Universal Prayer*," "The Libyan Hunter, A Fable," and "Epistle to Artemisia" establish the basis for understanding Pope's influence on Leapor, demonstrating both their shared religious values and their similar stances as poets. Leapor, like Pope, uses her position as an outsider to speak what she sees as the truth. When we examine these poems, now widely recognized as responses to Pope, we find that she borrows procedures that help her apply those values universally. Where she departs from his procedures, she does so in order to reaffirm values that he has only selectively applied.

We can see most clearly Pope's presence in Leapor's developing sense of herself as a poet by comparing the two "Mira to Octavia" poems (1 : 258–61; 2 : 100–110). In both poems, Leapor attempts to persuade Octavia not to marry her attractive but penniless suitor. Critics agree that the version published in volume 2 is a more general critique of eighteenth-century marriage conventions than the volume 1 version.[15] In the first poem, Leapor suggests the sedate but secure Dusterandus as a responsible alternative to "Florio witty, young, and gay" (1 : 7); in the second, she argues that honorable men "are extremely rare" (2 : 154) and so advises Octavia to retain her liberty: "I fear your Shackles will be found / Too dearly purchas'd with a thousand Pound" (2 : 156–57).

Significantly, Leapor establishes her authority as an advisor to Octavia in each poem, subsequently building her case, a process accomplished in the first four lines of the earlier poem:

> Fair One, to you this Monitor I send;
> *Octavia,* pardon your officious Friend:
> You think your Conduct merits only Praise,
> But out-law'd Poets censure whom they please:
> Thus we begin . . .
>
>   (1 : 1–5)

Here Leapor apologizes for what she suspects might be taken as an intrusion, suggesting that poets operate outside the bounds of social graces, and therefore, may "censure whom they please." In the second poem, Leapor is both more thorough and more precise in establishing her authority:

> Pardon my Fault, in off'ring to advise
> A thinking Virgin, like *Octavia* wise:
> Fate knew your Worth, and did her Fav'rite raise
> Above my Censure, and beyond my Praise:
> But out-law'd Poets scorn the beaten Rules,
> And leave Distinction to the Forms of Fools;
> Can make e'en *Jove* descend in golden Show'rs,
> And form new Statues on *Olympian* Bow'rs:
> Or, shiv'ring by the Side of rural Springs,
> At Courtiers rail, and satirize on Kings.
> Of these am I, who with presumptuous Pen,
> Subscribe myself the fair *Octavia*'s Friend . . .
>
> (2:8–19)

Mira's request for forbearance is the same here, but now she is more specific about whom she claims the right to criticize—her social superiors. Outside the "beaten Rules" of social engagement, Leapor suggests, distinctions in class and circumstance become irrelevant, thus enabling her to speak her mind to gods and kings alike. And while she may remain "shiv'ring" outside the seats of power, that perspective is precisely what enables the poet to speak without inhibition.

Leapor's care to establish a platform from which she can "scorn the beaten Rules" of class distinction invites comparison with Pope's description of his stance as a poet in *An Epistle to Dr. Arbuthnot*:

> Not Fortune's Worshipper, nor Fashion's Fool,
> Not Lucre's Madman, nor Ambition's Tool,
> Not proud, nor servile, be one Poet's praise
> That, if he pleas'd, he pleas'd by manly ways;
> That Flatt'ry, ev'n to Kings, he held a shame,
> And thought a Lye in Verse or Prose the same[.]
>
> (*TE*, 4:120, ll. 334–39)

Pope's emphasis differs from Leapor's: whereas her passage reveals her sheer exuberance at her ability to cross class boundaries and speak her mind, his emphasizes the honor of his ideas, unsullied by material concerns. Nonetheless Leapor shares with Pope the stance of an outside observer, a position that enables them to speak what they see as the truth, in spite of their audience. And while Pope may describe that stance as "manly," Leapor has made it a woman's as well.

A central assumption behind such a position is that truth is unchanging and universal. Hence Pope's arguments, like Horace's, often include a series of portraits that apply the principle at hand to a variety of characters. *An Essay on Man, Of the Characters of Women, The Dunciad,* and *Epistle to Bathurst,* among others, all follow this procedure.[16] When Leapor makes her more limited argument in the first "Mira to Octavia" poem, she simply contrasts the likely outcomes of the prospects at hand and then asks her friend to choose:

> Say, would you in [Dusterandus's] hapy [*sic*] Mansion reign
> Roast of the Village and the rural Plain?
> . . . .
> Or cold and hungry writhe your tired Jaws
> And dine with *Florio* upon Hips and Haws,
> In troth I think there's little room to pause.
>
> (1:56–62)

But in the second "Mira to Octavia," where Leapor makes the broader argument that marriage to nearly anyone is too risky, she not only follows Pope's procedure but announces her intention: "round us first an Audience let me call: / Draw near, and listen, O ye Maidens all. / Of Wives I sing, and Husbands, not a few: / Examples rare! some fictious, and some true" (2:26–29). The four portraits that follow illustrate a variety of ways that marriage becomes a trap for women, as the husband turns out to be a fool, a tyrant, a profligate, or a drunk, thereby building an empirical basis for her argument.[17]

Had Leapor unequivocally followed Pope's lead, she would have offered at this point in the poem a contrasting portrait illustrating the qualities Octavia should seek in a husband. Such a move would uphold the virtue of the institution despite its abusers, as Pope accomplishes in the conclusions of *An Essay on Criticism, Of the Characters of Women,* and *Epistle to Burlington,* to name a few. Leapor nods in that direction with the following qualifier:

> Yet, not a Rebel to your *Hymen*'s Law,
> His sacred Altars I behold with Awe:
> Nor Foe to Man; for I acknowledge yet
> Some Men have Honour, as some Maids have Wit.
> But then remember, these, my learned Fair,
> Old Authors tell us, are extremely rare.
>
> (2:148–53)

These lines echo the end of *Of the Characters of Women (TE,* 3.2:70–72, ll. 269–93), where Pope's portrait of Martha Blount establishes the ideal against which all the other women he has portrayed can be judged.[18] But rather than providing a corresponding portrait of an honorable husband, Leapor promotes an alternative—spinsterhood—in which Octavia could live out a virtuous and happy life and still retain control of her money and her home:

> Then be the charming Mistress of thy Gold;
> While young, admir'd; and rev'renc'd, when you're Old.
> The Grave and Sprightly shall thy Board attend,
> The gay Companion, and the serious Friend.
> Let meagre Wits a kind Acceptance find,
> And boast they lately with *Octavia* din'd.
> Let hungry Orphans there redress their Woes;
> Pity for these, let *Mira* plead for those.
> So may your Days in Halcyon Moments run,
> Happy at rising and declining Sun!
> Still may *Octavia* bless the infant Day,
> And still with Smiles behold its parting Ray!
> Till those gay Roses bid your Cheeks adieu,
> And your brown Locks shall take a silver Hue.
> Then, calm as weary Infants seek Repose,
> *Octavia* shall her beauteous Eye-lids close.
>
> (2:158–73)

Critics disagree about the extent to which Leapor advocates spinsterhood over marriage in this poem.[19] But clearly the absence of a portrait that would bring life to the abstract idea of an honorable man suggests that, for Leapor, such examples are so "extremely rare" that spinsterhood is the safer choice. Leapor's modification of Pope's procedure is instructive. Like him, she concludes her poem with a reaffirmation of Christian humanist values; yet in order to uphold those values, she suggests, women must seek an alternative to marriage itself.[20]

Similar moves occur at the end of "An Essay on Woman" and "Crumble Hall," two poems that have received a good deal of critical attention for the way they imitate the form but subvert the content of Pope's poems.[21] In "An Essay on Woman" (2:64–67), Leapor responds to Pope's contention in *Of the Characters of Women* that "Most Women have no Characters at all," examining instead the way that they are treated by men:

> Woman—a pleasing, but a short-live'd Flow'r,
> Too soft for Business, and too weak for Pow'r:
> A Wife in Bondage, or neglected Maid;

> Despis'd, if ugly; if she's fair—betray'd.
> 'Tis Wealth alone inspires ev'ry Grace,
> And calls the Raptures to her plenteous Face.
>
> (2:1–6)

A man is not interested in a woman's "character," Leapor suggests: he is interested in her money. Once he obtains it in marriage, then in his eyes, "mighty *Hymen* . . . sweeps her Charms away, / And turns the Goddess to her native Clay" (2:15; 18–19). After Leapor has summarized her argument, she again offers a series of examples, this time to illustrate "What small Advantage Wealth and Beauties bring" in a world where neither women's wit, wisdom, nor vibrancy are honored, and where no money is ever enough to satisfy a "Thirst of Gold . . . Instill'd by Nature, or a careful Sire" (2:20; 40). A woman may retain her integrity, Leapor concludes, only by separating herself from (male) society:

> If this be Wealth, no matter where it fall;
> But save, ye Muses, save your *Mira*'s Walls:
> Still give me pleasing Indolence, and Ease;
> A Fire to warm me, and a Friend to please.
> Since, whether sunk in Avarice, or Pride;
> A wanton Virgin, or a starving Bride;
> Or, wond'ring Crouds attend her charming Tongue;
> Or deem'd an Idiot, even speaks the Wrong:
> Tho' Nature arm'd us for the growing Ill,
> With fraudful Cunning, and a headstrong Will;
> Yet, with ten thousand Follies to her Charge,
> Unhappy Woman's but a Slave at large.
>
> (2:49–60)

As in the second "Mira to Octavia," Leapor reverses Pope's conventional method of closure: the suggestion that individuals fail to uphold society's ideal of "virtue." Instead she argues in her conclusion that women's faults naturally serve to protect them against an oppressive society, a society that forces women into private retreat to retain any integrity at all.

"Crumble Hall" (2:111–22), modeled on Pope's *Epistle to Burlington*, provides the final example of the way Leapor modifies Pope's amelioristic method of closure to conclude an argument more critical of the social order than her mentor's. Critics agree that this poem offers a laborer's perspective on the English country house, as Leapor notices spiderwebs near the ceiling (2:46–47), mice running through passages (2:52), and newly polished armor (2:51; 61), even describing the lives of servants Roger and Ursula rather than the masters of the house (2:121–55). Yet while Greene acknowledges that "the absence of panegyric ... sets Leapor's poem apart from earlier country house poems," he contends that "the underlying values ... are not that far removed from the basically conservative view of society advanced in those poems."[22] Landry, in contrast, argues that the poem "seeks to demystify the values of the gentry, whose social power in large part depends upon the deference—and the continued exploitable subservience—of servants and laborers."[23]

Landry's argument gains support when examining "Crumble Hall" in light of Leapor's procedure in the second "Mira to Octavia" and "An Essay on Woman." The poem's conclusion similarly rejects Pope's ideal. Like Pope's extended portrait of ostentatious and greedy Timon (*TE*, 3.2:142–49, ll. 99–176), Leapor's poem develops a single example. After leading her readers through the house, where the absent master's belongings—emblems of a less-than-glorious past (2:40–43), unread books (2:90–94), old shoes (2:99), old farm equipment (2:101)—do little to glorify him and the servants are exhausted and overworked, Leapor leaves the confines of the house for the hope of freedom in the grove, but is disappointed:

> But, hark! what Scream the wond'ring Ear invades!
> The *Dryads* howling for their threaten'd Shades:
> Round the dear Grove each Nymph distracted flies
> (Tho' not discover'd but with Poet's Eyes):
> And shall those Shades, where *Philomela*'s Strain
> Has oft to Slumber lull'd the hapless Swain;
> Where Turtles us'd to clap their silken Wings;
> Whose rev'rend Oaks have known a hundred Springs;
> Shall these ignobly from their Roots be torn,
> And perish shameful, as the abject Thorn,
> While the slow Carr bears off their aged Limbs,
> To clear the Way for Slopes, and modern Whims;
> Where banish'd Nature leaves a barren Gloom,
> And awkward Art supplies the vacant Room?
> Yet (or the Muse for Vengeance calls in vain)
> The injur'd Nymphs shall haunt the ravag'd Plain;
> Strange Sounds and Forms shall teaze the gloomy Green;
> And Fairy-Elves by *Urs'la* shall be seen:
> Their new-built Parlour shall with Echoes ring:
> And in their Hall shall doleful Crickets sing.
>
> (2:165–84)

While Greene rightly points out that "this landscape represents safety and refuge for the poet," he incorrectly argues that "it is a natural landscape corresponding to a natural and secure social order."[24] The nymphs and dryads that Leapor imagines to live there stand outside society altogether and are visible only to another outsider: the poet. In any case, the prospect of self-centered landowners who intend to fell trees and destroy the natural landscape in favor of artificial slopes and a "new-built Parlour" threaten the pastoral setting that conventionally nurtures both poetry and wildlife. Greene and Landry agree that Leapor "goes beyond Pope's criticism of Timon in her attitude towards changes at Crumble Hall."[25] Landry adds that Leapor "reverses the praise that Pope had offered Burlington for his use of the forest in the service of building, commerce, and imperial exploits."[26] Pope apostrophizes Burlington's example as a civic-minded landowner

> Whose rising Forests, not for pride or show,
> But future Buildings, future Navies grow:
> Let his plantations stretch from down to down,
> First shade a Country, and then raise a Town.
>
> (*TE*, 3.2 : 150, ll. 187–90)

As in the second "Mira to Octavia" and "An Essay on Woman," Leapor supplants Pope's concluding reaffirmation of idealized social convention with a reaffirmation of values that require a rejection of those conventions, illustrated in this case by the practice of "improvement": "Then cease, *Diracto,* stay thy desp'rate Hand; / And let the Grove, if not the Parlour, stand." Even if Leapor acknowledges that the country house once represented generosity and hospitality to visitors, as Greene argues,[27] she also emphasizes the labor required to provide such bounty, as well as the corruption of the masters who benefit from that labor. Nowhere does she offer an economically and aesthetically harmonious example of a country house; instead, as in the second "Mira to Octavia" and "An Essay on Woman," she alternatively presents a retreat from social engagement, a retreat in this instance into a threatened grove.

Taken together, the second "Mira to Octavia," "An Essay on Woman," and "Crumble Hall" reveal both Leapor's sophisticated handling of the models she adopted from Pope and the limits of her ability to envision alternative models. In all of them she follows Pope's procedure just as long as he criticizes abuses in society; and in all of them, at the very moment when Pope consistently changes direction and leaves his readers with images of the social order and economic prosperity, Leapor takes her arguments to their logical conclusion and promotes a retreat from the social practices that she finds oppressive. The overall effect of her illustrative portraits is thus the opposite of Pope's: whereas his final support for the social order places responsibility for improper behavior and improvement solely on the individual, her final retreat from oppressive conventions suggests that the abuses she describes are not simply the result of individual failings. Rather, these abuses are endemic to a society where wives are, legally, their husband's property and property is all too often the standard measure of an individual's worth: Christian virtues hardly reign here. While the limited attention given to those retreats and their placement at the end of her poems suggests their nascent quality in Leapor's thinking, they also suggest a direction in which her work may have been heading when measles claimed her at the young age of twenty-four.

Nonetheless, Leapor was hardly on her way to abandoning Pope as a model when she died. On the contrary, the values of hope, contentment, mercy, justice, and piety that she promotes for husbands as well as wives, employers as well as laborers, men as well as women in "Mira to Octavia," "An Essay on Woman," and "Crumble Hall" are the same values that she promotes in "On Mr. Pope's *Universal Prayer*." Leapor's constant concern is to see that Christian values are indeed universally applied. And when Pope or any other representative of what she describes in "The Enquiry" as "grave-fac'd Wisdom" fail to live up to these standards themselves, she challenges their views, encouraging her readers to engage in a similar reexamination.

To the extent that these values may be considered "conventional," Leapor is indeed a conventional poet. And to the extent that the forms she borrows from Pope shape her arguments in ways that assume unchanging truths and a God-given order to the universe, her poetry is conventional as well. But Leapor's poetry demonstrates that the tradition of social commentary which she learned from Pope can be used to call for positive change, just as well as it can harken back to a golden age. Landry goes too far when she associates Leapor's views with contemporary "radical feminism," for Leapor shares more with Pope than that description allows. But Leapor also does more than "write like [Pope]," as Rizzo asserts, or even "[argue] bravely against specific ideas or practices which she believes are oppressive," as Greene concludes.[28] Instead, she calls on the tradition represented by Pope to live up to its own ideals and apply its values universally. Like any student with her mentor, Leapor initially seeks guidance from Pope and follows his example to establish her own claim to her craft. Indeed, she learns her lessons so well that she ultimately uses the authority that she attributes to "out-law'd poets" to challenge her mentor himself. Such a challenge honors mentor and student alike.

Notes

1. Donna Landry, *The Muses of Resistance: Laboring-Class Women's Poetry in Britain, 1739–1796* (Cambridge: Cambridge University Press, 1990), 119.

2. Richard Greene, *Mary Leapor: A Study in Eighteenth-Century Women's Poetry* (Oxford: Clarendon Press, 1993), 182.

3. Betty Rizzo, "Molly Leapor: An Anxiety for Influence," *The Age of Johnson: A Scholarly Annual* 4 (1991): 332.

4. See Greene, *Mary Leapor*, 180–82, for a list of Leapor's poems containing allusions to Pope. I gratefully acknowledge Richard Greene's generosity in sending me the manuscript of his book before it came into print. He saved me from several serious mistakes about Leapor's biography.

5. Margaret Anne Doody, "Swift Among the Women," *The Yearbook of English Studies* 18 (1988): 68–92.

6. Greene, *Mary Leapor*, 163–85.

7. See Ibid., 13, and Rizzo, "Molly Leapor," 321–23.

8. Leapor, *Poems on Several Occasions*, 2 vols. (London: J. Roberts, 1748; 1751), 2:309; all citations to Leapor's poetry are from these volumes.

9. Greene, *Mary Leapor*, 182.

10. See, for example, "The Moral Vision" (1:65), "Essay on Happiness" (1:54), "Essay on Hope" (1:60), "On Discontent: To Stella" (1:70), "On Patience: To Stella" (2:1), "Mopsus" (2:11), "Advice to Sophronia" (2:54), and "The Consolation" (2:81). For a discussion of Leapor's use of her poetry to "quiet her anxieties and longings with philosophy," see Rizzo, "Molly Leapor," 333–35. Also see Greene, *Mary Leapor*, 196–98.

11. Greene further suggests that "Leapor projects on Pope her own resentment against those who belittle her writing," *Mary Leapor*, 182.

12. For a discussion of Leapor's biting comments on male literary critics, see Landry, *Muses*, 99–102.

13. See Greene, *Mary Leapor*, 18–22.

14. Landry, *Muses*, 102.

15. See ibid., 87–88, and Greene, *Mary Leapor*, 61–65.

16. Of course, Pope is not the only poet to follow this procedure, but it is Pope's use of it that impacts Leapor most strongly. See Ralph Cohen, "The Augustan Mode in English Poetry," *Eighteenth-Century Studies* 1 (1967): 3–32.

17. Greene sees this procedure as "the less offensive course of a generalized commentary," offered because the first poem "was evidently not well received" (*Mary Leapor*, 62). Whether or not it is "less offensive," it is designed to carry more authority by placing the immediate situation in the context of other examples and by following a traditional model in doing so.

18. For a discussion of the problematic nature of Pope's portrait of Blount, see Landry, *Muses*, 88 and Ellen Pollak, *The Poetics of Sexual Myth: Gender and*

Ideology in the Verse of Swift and Pope (Chicago: University of Chicago Press, 1985), 123–27.

19. See Greene, *Mary Leapor*, 63–64 and Landry, *Muses*, 88.

20. Greene correctly points out (*Mary Leapor*, 64–65) that celibacy is no panacea for Leapor either, but I think he overstates the case when he says that "repeatedly in her work she offers examples of marriages which could bring a woman some kind of satisfaction," 74. There is a far greater number of examples in her work showing just the opposite.

21. See ibid., 137–44; Landry, *Muses*, 107–19.

22. Greene, *Mary Leapor*, 138.

23. Landry, *Muses*, 107.

24. Greene, *Mary Leapor*, 141.

25. Ibid., 142.

26. Landry, *Muses*, 118–19.

27. Greene, *Mary Leapor*, 139–40.

28. Rizzo, "Molly Leapor," 332; Greene, *Mary Leapor*, 182.

The Poetic Career of Judith Cowper: An Exemplary Failure?

Valerie Rumbold

Judith Cowper, in her youth a competent and enthusiastic writer of verse, a correspondent of Pope and member of a family distinguished both in politics and literature, lived from 1702 to 1781; yet despite the promise of her early verse (most of it surviving only in manuscript), she virtually abandoned the writing of poetry in her early twenties.[1] In 1722, moreover, at the age of twenty, she had been personally encouraged by Pope, who had expressed approval of her writings and offered suggestions for further projects. While this might have been expected to stimulate further growth towards poetic maturity, within two years her voice as a poet was virtually silenced.

The explanation offered by Judith's chronicler Falconer Madan, that "the cares of a growing family occupied her whole attention and diverted her thoughts from poetry," is hardly likely to strike modern readers as fully adequate; for even when one takes into account the demands on her time and energy made by the nine children born to her between 1725 and 1742, one can still think of other women who in comparable circumstances left evidence that writing remained important to them: Hester Thrale, for instance, wrote her *Thraliana* despite pregnancies, children's lessons, and infant deaths; and later in life, with more time to herself, she moved on to more ambitious works for publication.[2] Granted, Cowper had limited time and energy for private pursuits in the first two decades of her marriage (she married in 1723), but the intensity of the contrast between her early productivity and her later near-silence demands an explanation that takes account of internal dynamics as well as changing personal circumstances. It is only necessary to look at her conception of what it meant to be a poet, and to set that conception against her social role as an attractive and well-connected young woman (in the terms of the age, both a "lady" and a "beauty"), to see that the role of poet was

48

at odds with any self-image that she could comfortably maintain. The encouragement she received from Pope and others—however well meant—was in fact so constructed as to reinforce the tensions that ultimately silenced her.

Cowper's notions of poetry and of poets emerge clearly from the poems she wrote in response to her reading, for a high proportion of her early poems are devoted to the praise of contemporary and near-contemporary writers, including Waller, Dryden, Rowe, Hughes, Addison, and Pope. It is significant that, except for a brief reference to Sappho, she neither refers to any female tradition nor manifests any dissatisfaction at the absence of her own sex from the canon she celebrates. Furthermore, her numerous definitions of excellence in poetry unquestioningly exalt those qualities conventionally gendered as masculine. Notably, she uses a complex of images related to fire: there is the "fire" of genius itself and its ability to "fire" the emotions of the reader; and this is in turn related to the image of the sun and its deity, Phoebus Apollo. The animating power of the sun is thus her primary metaphor for creativity of all kinds, evident in a multitude of allusions to heavenly "smiles" and "warmth." Thus she aligns creativity with the conventionally masculine sun, or with the Aristotelian notion of the masculine heat that guarantees the primacy of the male in reproduction.[3] The metaphorical language of heat and light is hardly unusual—versions can be found, for example, in Pope's *Essay on Criticism,* a key source for Cowper's thinking about poetry—but in Cowper's work it appears with unusual density and emphasis.[4]

In her pioneering progress poem, "The Progress of Poetry," for example, Cowper frames her quest for origins in terms of the question "where, Great Source of Verse! thou Phoebus first arose?"[5] Real poetry, she insists, cannot be written without the "warmth" figured by his association with the sun:

> Where Nature warmth & genius has deni'd,
> In vain are Art's stiff languid Pow'rs apply'd,
> Unforc'd the Muses smile, above Controul,
> No Art can tune th'Inharmonious Soul,
> Some Rules 'tis true unerring you may cull,
> And be like D——is[6] regularly dull,
> Correctly flat may flow each studi'd Line,
> And each low Period indolently chime;
> A Common Ear perhaps, or vulgar Heart,
> These Lays may please, the Labour'd Work of Art;
> Far other Strains delight the polish'd Mind,

> The Ear well judging, & the Tast refin'd;
> To blend in Heav'nly Numbers, Strength & Fire,
> An *Addison* will ask, a *Pope* require,
> Genius alone can force like theirs bestow,
> As Stars unconscious of their Brightness glow.

The true poet is a star, a sun, radiating heat and light out of his or her essential being without any of the laborious contrivance that Cowper here associates pejoratively with "Art." Yet while she appropriates Pope's expressions of scorn for "regularly dull" versifying (compare particularly *Essay on Criticism, TE*, 5:267, ll. 239–42) and singles out Dennis as an uninspired follower of the rules, she is unresponsive to Pope's contention that poetic apprenticeship to a great model, as exemplified in Virgil's study of Homer, effectively reconciles the claims of nature with the rules (ll. 130–40). This is problematic for a young poet engaged, as Cowper is, in imitation of an admired original; for her rigorous notions of poetry as authorized only by inspiration systematically devalue such deliberate application. Whereas Pope can concede that "True Ease in Writing comes from Art, not Chance, / As those move easiest who have learn'd to dance," Cowper, even while she follows his example so closely, withholds any explicit acknowledgment that verse is a discipline to be studied (ll. 362–63). Genteel decorum is evidently part of the problem for this well-connected amateur, as her casual use of "common" and "vulgar" suggests: a laborious apprenticeship in the technicalities of verse—which for Pope, the son of a tradesman, seems to have posed no particular problems of identity—might have seemed an embarrassing lapse from aristocratic ideals of easy accomplishment.

Cowper's theory of inspiration extends even to the longest and most complex literary works. Her conception of Homer's *Iliad* is patently conditioned by Pope's preface to his translation, in which he had characterized Homer, in terms highly congenial to Cowper, as distinguished by "unequal'd Fire and Rapture"; and in her response to Homer she represents his plan as a "rising Wonder," bursting forth with spontaneous, godlike authority:

> There the Great Bard the rising Wonder wrought,
> And plan'd the *Iliad* in his boundless Thought,
> By no mean Steps to full Perfection grew,
> But burst at once refulgent on the View.

By implication, there would have been something "mean" about a compositional process that proceeded by "Steps." Ironically, the closest that Pope—a craftsman deliberate both in the planning and the revising of his work—was to come to this language of bursting refulgence was in the spurious sun and stars of the theatrical new heaven and new earth of *The Dunciad Variorum*: "Thence a new world, to Nature's laws unknown, / Breaks out refulgent, with a heav'n its own."[7] For all her adulation, Cowper's rhetoric of quasi-divine spontaneity alienates her, to her cost, from some of her master's most characteristic concerns. Only a beginner convinced of her own innate genius could have been encouraged by the theory of poetry Cowper had adopted, a theory that left her without encouragement even to apply herself to the learnable skills of verse. Moreover—and this is a motif that recurs throughout the dead ends of her writing career—her writing never articulates the problem. She lavishes praise on the genius of her masters, but gives no sign of recognizing that her belief in the necessity of genius excludes her from worthwhile creativity.

Another aspect of this problem is that Cowper's conception of genius is implicitly gendered as masculine, and although she never articulates any explicit perception that gender limits her scope as a writer, her pliability to the polarizing tendency of the heroic couplet highlights contrasts loaded with implications of gendered subordination. Her earliest extant poem, an appreciation of Waller written when she was only fourteen or fifteen, already shows an insistent and value-laden patterning of this kind:

> To charm ye Soul, & Captivate ye Mind,
> Here softest Verse, & manly Sence are Joyn'd.[8]

She chooses the epithet "manly" for "Sence" and marks out "the Mind" as its province, framing its complement as "softest Verse" and designating its realm as "ye Soul." For her, meaning is evidently masculine, and it is meaning that stands supreme in the accepted theory of poetry. Meaning undoubtedly needs a medium, in this case "softest Verse," but as the epithet "soft" (routinely applied to women) suggests, meaning needs its medium only in the way that, in the traditional Aristotelian account of human generation, the warm, formally creative male seed needs the inert, unorganized matter provided by the female.

The implications of a taxonomy of poetic effect that implies a gendered hierarchy are developed further in "To Mr Pope," a direct address to the principal object of her admiration and imitation:

> O Pope by w^{ht} commanding wond'rous Art
> Dost Thou each Passion to each Breast impart?
> Our beating Hearts wth sprightly measures move,
> Or melt us wth a Tale of *Hapless Love,*
> Th'elated Mind's impetuous starts controul,
> Or gently sooth to Peace the troubled Soul,
> Graces till now y^t singly met our View
> And singly charm'd, unite at once in you.[9]

At first sight, it may seem that Pope is praised simply for effecting an equal marriage of strong with soft, the "sprightly measures" that impart energy against the melting effect of amorous woe, the disciplining of the "elated Mind" against the comforting of "the troubled Soul." On the other hand, it is the strong that in each couplet precedes the soft; and Cowper reserves the climaxes of her praise for those aspects of Pope's work in which she discerns the authoritative strength of the sun god:

> With Energy divine each Period swells,
> And all the Bard th'Inspiring God reveals.

In effect, the capacity of Pope's genius to appropriate the feminine merely underlines its comprehensive masculine potency.

"To Mr Pope" was written in 1720, as a response to his collected *Works* of 1717. From 1722 Cowper and Pope became correspondents, initiating a relationship that reinforced Cowper's all-pervading construction of aesthetics in gendered terms.[10] In October 1722 she received a poem in which Pope evidently intended to compare her favorably with Lady Mary Wortley Montagu:

> Tho' sprightly Sappho force our love and praise,
> A softer wonder my pleas'd soul surveys,
> The mild Erinna, blushing in her bays.
> So while the sun's broad beam yet strikes the sight,
> All mild appears the moon's more sober light,
> Serene, in virgin majesty, she shines;
> And, un-observed, the glaring sun declines.[11]

Cowper represents the disapproved Sappho, the best-known female poet of antiquity, as the sun: her beam is "broad"; she "strikes the sight"; she can "force" a response from her (male) audience.

Cowper is the lesser-known Erinna, and she qualifies for Pope's approval by blushing for the assertiveness she has shown in aspiring to the "bays." She is the moon, "mild," "sober," "serene," "virgin": the verbs of which she is subject are muted in comparison with Sappho's ability to "force" and "strike," for Erinna only "appears" and, at her most assertive, simply "shines." The poem thus defines Cowper by denying her precisely those characteristics that she most fundamentally associates with poetic excellence.

These lines, more familiarly reworked in the conclusion of *Epistle to a Lady: Of the Characters of Women*, present as axiomatic a proposition about ordinary human experience that is generally untrue. For when there is a "glaring" sunset, the eye is usually drawn to it, rather than to the pale moon rising. The simile is typical of those prescriptions that seek to keep women out of male preserves by claiming that the limited sphere ordained for women is really the more valuable. But if the world does not behave according to such "real" values, the justification is effectively an empty one. We can imagine a world in which people instinctively stare at the pale rising moon and habitually ignore flaming sunsets, but we know we do not live in it. In these lines it has apparently been Pope's achievement to obscure the fact.

Just how contrary to ordinary feeling and experience this handling of the sunset image is, and how untenable as a self-image for Judith Cowper as poet, is demonstrated in her elegy on John Hughes, written in 1720.[12] It closes with an image of the sunset, used to meditate on the irony that Hughes's last and best play was acted for the first time only on the night of his death:

> So when the Sun to Worlds unknown retires,
> How strong! how boldly! shoot his parting Fires,
> Larger his setting Orb our Eyes confess;
> Eager we gaze, & the full Glory bless,
> As o'er the Heavens sublime his Course extends,
> Wth equal State the radiant Globe descends,
> Sinks in a Cloud of gold & Azure bright,
> And leaves behind gay Tracks of Beamy Light.

This stress on the enthusiasm people feel for sunsets ("Eager we gaze, and the full Glory bless") shows by contrast the tendentiousness of Pope's assertion. What is generally admired is the energy that culture has appropriated as masculine, not the speciously recommended feminine ideal offered as its opposite term.

A brief allusion to Sappho in "The Progress of Poetry," the only reference to a female writer in Cowper's verse, suggests the way that a hierarchically gendered conception of poetic effect made it difficult for Cowper to confront her own gender. Cowper portrays Sappho—whom she presumably knew only through the versions presented by Ambrose Philips in *Spectator* nos. 223 and 229[13]— solely as the poet of amorous softness:

> Mark Muse the conscious Shade & vocal grove
> Where *Sapho* tun'd her melting voice to Love.

As a poetic mother, Sappho directs her daughter to the amorous, not the epic, to the soft rather than the fiery, to the lower genre rather than the higher. In the light of such a perception, the enthusiastic Cowper's apparent lack of interest in any quest for foremothers is readily comprehensible.

At this early stage in her writing Cowper was still concentrating on eulogy and commendatory verse, reworking her subjects' themes and effects without challenge or criticism. The extent to which she is able to immerse herself in a masculine poetic culture is perhaps most strikingly illustrated in the way that "To Mr Pope" responds to epic values and in particular to Pope's translation of Homer:

> Now War & Arms thy mighty Aid demand
> And Homer wakes beneath thy pow'rfull Hand,
> His Vigour, genuine Heat & manly Force
> In Thee rise worthy of their Sacred Source,
> His Spirit heighten'd yet his Sence Intire,
> As Gold runs purer from the trying Fire.[14]

Cowper presents the familiar language of "heat," of the transmission of the "Sacred Source" from poetic father to poetic son. The implicitly masculine "Force" is made explicitly "manly." Pope's role as translator is represented as that of a refiner's fire; but because Cowper probably knew no Greek, her estimate of Pope's fidelity to his original is presumably based on the borrowed judgment of a man who did know Greek. Yet there is nothing grudging or resentful in her response to the intellectual and creative authority of men: she accepts it without question in order to celebrate the poetry she loves.

Such is the supremacy of epic in Cowper's estimation that she refers to Pope's Homer translation at the climax of her praise of the variety and appropriateness of his style. She obviously has in mind the celebrated sequence of effects with which Pope had illustrated his precept that "The *Sound* must seem an *Eccho* to the *Sense*" (*Essay on Criticism, TE,* 1 : 281, l. 365); but it is evident from her treatment of the theme, as compared with her original, that she is especially concerned to rank poetic modes and to insist on the preeminence of the epic. In an age that was to find the epic at best an impressive impossibility, at worst a glorification of violence out of keeping with civilized modern values, this preference might appear a mere gesture of sterile pedantry were it not for the evident passion that enlivens her recollected reading:

> O for a Muse like Thine, while I rehearse
> Th'Immortal Beauties of thy Various Verse,
> How light as Air th'enlivening Numbers move,
> Soft, as the downy Plumes of Fabled Love,
> Gay, as the Streaks yᵗ stain the Gaudy Bow,
> Smooth as Meander's Chrystal Mirrors flow;
> But when Achilles panting for the War
> Joins the fleet Coursers to the whirling Car,
> When the warm Hero wᵗʰ Coelestial might
> Augments the Terror of the raging Fight,
> From his fierce Eyes refulgent Light'nings stream,
> As Sol emerging darts a Golden Gleam,
> In rough, hoarse verse we see th'Imbattled Foes,
> In each loud Strain the fiery onset glows,
> With Strength redoubled here Achilles shines,
> And all the Battle thunders in thy Lines.

As she evokes battle under the influence of Pope's own language (notably "The *hoarse, rough verse*" of *Essay on Criticism,* l. 369) she consistently resorts to imagery very close to that which she uses for poetry and poets: the warrior Achilles is "warm" and "refulgent," bursting on the eye with the impact of the sun itself, "As Sol emerging darts a Golden Gleam." In another context, when praising Homer in *The Progress of Poetry,* Cowper similarly celebrates the moving power of his representation of "all that Fires the Hero's Soul to War." In a remarkable instance of a mind learning to imagine as if it belonged to the other sex, she seems untouched by any doubt of the universal validity of warrior values or of the poetic supremacy of the epic that expresses those values. Although she had begun her praise of Pope's versification in "To Mr Pope" with allusions to his lighter effects, including extended praise of his pastoral mode, the enthusiasm generated by her reading of his epic translation sufficiently demonstrates her commitment to the traditional hierarchy of genres.

Cowper's celebration of the traditional hierarchy of genres does

not stop here, however, but develops into an extended analogy
with the art of painting. This is a particularly interesting allusion,
since her acquaintance with Pope seems to have begun when he
found her sitting for her portrait to his friend Charles Jervas, from
whom he had himself taken lessons in painting.[15] Pope, who was
particularly concerned both as amateur painter and as collector of
paintings with portraiture as a commemoration of friendship, had
in effect initiated their closer acquaintance by begging the portrait
for himself.[16] On the other hand, he had also encouraged Jervas
not to limit himself to the private and personal realm of "such silly
stories as our faces tell of us," but also to "do something for the
Publick" by extending his ambition to history painting, traditionally considered the highest kind of art; and it is in line with this
hierarchical approach to art that Cowper's poem, passing over the
relatively lowly art of portraiture, focuses on the wider claims to
authority implicit in landscape and history painting.[17] Cowper
does not underrate the ordering implicit in landscape as constructed by "the bright Magick of the Painter's Hand," for she
deploys the balancing potential both within and between lines and
couplets in a careful rendering of the painter's repertory of harmo-
nizing and contrasting techniques. It is only in history painting,
however, that she finds a force and authority parallel to that which
she reveres in epic:

> But when the Artist does a Work design,
> Where bolder Rage informs each breathing Line,
> When the stretch'd Cloath a rougher Stroke receives
> And *Caesar* awfull on the *Canvas* lives,
> When Art like lavish *Nature*'s Self supplies
> *Grace* to the Limbs & *Spirit* to the Eyes,
> When ev'n the *Passions* of the *Mind* are *seen*
> And the *Soul* speaks in the exalted *Mien,*
> When all is *Just,* & *Regular,* & *Great,*
> We own the Mighty *Master*'s Skill as boundless as compleat.

As in her depiction of the epic, Cowper presents history painting
as a strongly masculine depiction of male business, emphasizing
the "awfull" presence and "exalted Mien" of the subject and the
"bolder Rage," "rougher Stroke," and animating power of the artist. Ironically, in looking to traditional authority to tell her what to
admire, Cowper commits herself to ideals that are problematic not
only for her as lady and potential poet, but also for the male artists
who still proclaimed such values: in an age effectively characterized by portraiture and the novel, Cowper accepts from her men-

tors a commitment to history painting and epic that even they were to find creatively unworkable.

If Cowper seems less than alert to the strain imposed on male writers by unrealistic privileging of the masculine connotations of traditional literary values, she shows herself equally unprepared to confront issues of gender as they affect her own participation in literary tradition, and makes no explicit reference to her sex as presenting any kind of difficulty. Thus she can accept as benign the conventional role of women in poetry as objects under the assessing gaze of men. Her poem on Waller, for example, opens by admiring his praise of Saccarissa:

> Great Waller matchless Saccarissa sung,
> In verse that still keeps Saccarissa young.

There is no acknowledgment here that Cowper is trying to participate in a tradition in which the role of her sex is to be written rather than to write. Similarly, in the reference to the Lodona episode in *Windsor Forest* in "To Mr Pope," with its complimentary echoes of Pope's pastoral phraseology, she accepts as unproblematic the male poet's traditional privilege of immortalizing the female object:

> In mighty Pope's Immortalizing Strains
> Still shall she grace & range the Verdant Plains,
> By him selected for the Muse's Theme
> Still shine a Blooming Maid, & roll a limpid Stream.

It is in a compliment to her cousin Lady Sarah Cowper that she comes closest to facing the conflict set up by her view of poetry as an amorous art in which woman is immortalized, though even here she seems to evade the issue that she so pointedly raises.[18] Lady Sarah has evidently said that she wishes *she* could write poems like her cousin, who responds by turning Sarah's lack of talent to compliment by reinterpreting the story of Apollo's pursuit of Daphne. Behind this reworking stands Swift's *Apollo Outwitted*, a witty compliment to the poet Anne Finch, which portrays the god as philanderer and the poet as a respectable lady shrewd enough to employ the muse he has given her as a chaperone. But Cowper's Phoebus is so affronted by Daphne's rejection that he bears all pretty girls a grudge for her sake, and absolutely denies them the assistance of the muses:

> In vain, fair Nymph, you beg the Muses Aid,
> Phoebus presides o'er each harmonious Maid
> . . . .
> Daphne in you reviving strikes his view,
> And he resolves, like Him, you vainly shall pursue
> . . . .
> E'er since that fatal Day, the God, averse,
> To Beauty still denies the Aid of verse.

The compliment is ingenious, but problematic. If verse and beauty are mutually exclusive, what can it mean for a poet who is also seen by society as a beauty to tell another that *her* beauty sufficiently explains her incompetence in verse? Cowper is thus forced into the false modesty of disclaiming beauty by her need to negotiate a workable relation with the mythology of her art. By putting aside the social role of beauty, she maneuvers herself by the end of the poem into a position from which she can console Lady Sarah for her lack of poetic voice by dedicating her own art to her cousin's praise, a gesture she has learned from male poetry. Pope, for instance, was to close his *Epistle to a Lady: On the Characters of Women* by delivering himself to Martha Blount as a present sent to her by Phoebus. It is characteristic of Cowper's ambiguous relation as poet to her own gender that this maneuver, which raises so many awkward questions, passes undiscussed, its necessity unchallenged.

The real difficulties that lie behind these evasions, the difficulties of a patriarchal society's response to a poet of "the fair sex," are amply demonstrated by poems written in Cowper's praise. An anonymous verse compliment in the British Library shows just how far focus on the woman as beauty can compromise attention to the woman as poet.[19] The writer begins by addressing Pope as a moral paragon who bestows honor on those he honors with friendship:

> Amongst those few, a Sprightly Nymph appears
> In Judgm^t ripe, and Wit beyond Her years.
> Tis lovely Cowper! that Inspired Fair!
> Apollo's Darling, & the Muses Care,
> Whose Beauteous shape! Delightfull to behold,
> Was surely cast in Nature's finest Mould.
> Such Symmetry of parts! Majestick Air!
> And blooming Youth! must ev'ry heart ensnare.
> Who can behold the Lustre of her Eyes!
> And not become a willing Sacrifice?

> To this Bright Form, compleatest of its kind,
> The Heavenly Pow'rs have given a perfect Mind.

Poetry, as far as the woman poet is concerned, is assimilated to sexual allure, and the patronage of Phoebus (she is his "Darling," whereas Pope is his "Son") is read as amorous. Furthermore, the rhetoric of gallantry demands an excess that makes it hard to take seriously any claims made for the woman poet's achievement. Although the poem contains a specific and plausible tribute to her power over the emotions in *Abelard to Eloisa,* any hope of sober evaluation disappears as the author moves into realms of irresponsible hyperbole, ranking Cowper's modest youthful accomplishments alongside the achieved art of Pope:

> Take up thy Lute, thy Heav'nly voice prepare,
> And chaunt the Praises of this tunefull Fair!
> No Muse but thine can keep her flight in view;
> She soars too High for any one but you.

For this writer Cowper's poetry is so irradiated by her rank and beauty that gallantry, not literary criticism, seems the obvious response; and his closing compliment eclipses the would-be poet in a fantasy of sexual irresistibility:

> Might I presume to Council Phoebus's Son,
> The sight of this Bright Nymph you ought to Shun:
> Admire, like us, the Beauties of her Mind,
> Her pregnant Wit, and fancy unconfin'd;
> But don't approach—or fatally you'll Prove,
> No Heart's secure against the Force of Love.

In comparison with this preposterous gallantry, Pope's response to Cowper is comparatively balanced and helpful, at least in intention. Compared with his earlier correspondence with Lady Mary Wortley Montagu, his letters to Cowper are friendly rather than amorous, hardly rising above the minimum level of gallantry that politeness demanded: "If you can Overlook an Ugly *Body* (that stands much in the way of any Friendship, when it is between different Sexes) I shall hope to find you a True & Constant Kinswoman in Apollo."[20] In fact, he seems to have enjoyed the correspondence for the access it allowed to some of the more difficult areas of his own creativity, notably genres and mental states associated with disorder and disproportion. What made this possible was not only that Cowper was a woman, but also that she suffered badly from depression. Pope advises Cowper to use her poetry as a creative focus to fight her condition, but he seemed to assume—we do not have her side of the correspondence—that although she could produce descriptive passages, she was held back by an inability to give her work the form it needed. He suggests to her an allegorical vision, a genre of relatively low status in the period. Yet Pope's suggestion is not disingenuous, insofar as he confesses that he too is attracted by such a project:

> I could wish you tryd something in the descriptive way on any Subject you please, mixd with Vision & Moral; like the Pieces of the old Provencal Poets, which abound with Fancy & are the most amusing scenes in nature. . . . I have long had an inclination to tell a Fairy tale; the more wild & exotic the better, therfore a *Vision*, which is confined to no rules of probability, will take in all the Variety & luxuriancy of Description you will. Provided there be an apparent moral to it. . . . If you did but, at leisure, form descriptions from Objects in nature itself which struck you most lively, I would undertake to find a Tale that shoud bring em all together.[21]

Whether confided by Cowper herself, or assumed by Pope, this inability to form matter into poetry is a serious charge. Like the cold Aristotelian female, Cowper is seen as bringing inert matter—mere description—to receive the dynamic heat of male form. If this is really her perception of her condition, she is in effect declaring her inability to be a poet, a dead end all too understandable in terms of the masculinity of her conception of Phoebus and his warming, fertilizing power. Despite his helpful intentions, Pope's offer to organize and connect Cowper's descriptions implies that the higher reaches of creativity are not for her. His advice points her not towards authoritative independence as a poet, but to a lesser position of genteel amusement, which may indeed have been his genuine reaction to her efforts. He proposes writing as therapy for her depression; yet the writing is assumed to partake of the disorder that produces it, since it falls into the category of description—for Pope, an element very low in the hierarchy of the poet's skills—and hence requires the imposition of legitimating form from outside.[22] This is a kind of help that, however kindly meant, reinforces dependence: Pope's comparison of Cowper as writer to the moon, although intended to show how much he esteemed her, remains enmeshed in notions of female passivity that are hard to reconcile with the role of authoritative poet.

By her midtwenties Cowper had worked her way through a variety of essentially parasitic apprentice pieces, for nearly all her longer poems respond in some fairly simple way to a text or texts. Not only does she typically elaborate a formal skeleton provided by the male tradition, but she also, in the majority of cases, celebrates that tradition explicitly, so that her poems are for the most part doubly unassertive. Growth into poetic maturity would have required not only a capacity to generate original formal ideas and to carry this impetus through units longer than the couplet, but also the confidence to speak with a more independent and incisive voice.

An indication of Cowper's difficulties in gaining an independent and critical voice is the relatively muffled impact of her few attempts at satire. In her attack on Ambrose Philips, who had published a garbled text of one of her poems, she imagines Philips racked with anxiety as the first night of his forthcoming tragedy *The Briton* approaches.[23] Thus, like Cowper and the other victims of his editing, Philips will know how it feels to be a vulnerable author. There are some effective touches: Philips rests his head uncomfortably on his own periodical publications while his play, the "Dear, Dull Product of a twelvemonth's Spleen," disturbs his sleep with "visionary Catcalls," nightmares that "sketch in broken Sleeps thy woes to come." Yet overall the satire is not sustained, and a characteristic tendency to diffuse, repetitive formulations leads her to exchange length for impact. Moreover, she seems unable to express negative feelings forcefully. "Wit & Humour," appearing "wth blended Grace," are ludicrously unfrightening apparitions, even if they are, logically, Philips's "Eternal Foes"; and the vague gesturing of personified "Works," "Graces," and "Lines," even if *"Murder'd"* and "Mangled" through Philips's editorial shortcomings, does not even begin to produce the comic horror required. Altogether the effect is weak in comparison with the ringing tones Cowper achieves in the more congenial task of celebration.

The last major phase of Cowper's active career as poet takes up a completely new direction, although not one that is ultimately to prove enabling. Having written in her poem on her birthday in August 1723 that she was "Not apt to Love, tho' sacred Friendship's Slave," she was to experience a sudden conversion: the next month she writes a quite new kind of verse, lamenting her hopeless love for "Lysander."[24] Henceforth she is a poet of love, and moreover, of happy love: the obstacles she initially feared were soon overcome, and in December of the same year she married her "Lysander," Colonel Martin Madan. In the poems prompted by this relationship, love, like all that is creative and powerful, is for Cowper a fire, but "a gentler Fire" than the poetic ardor that had previously possessed her.[25] Cowper's final burst of poetic activity culminates in a poetry of tender, gentle, and softly compelling emotion, developing only the "feminine" element in the balance between strength and softness that she recognized in the greatest poets. Even in her first poem to Lysander, presenting the "Pangs" inflicted by "Lysander's killing Form," and her attempts to resign herself to the "Duty" of forgetting him, love is rendered predominantly in terms of the "soft," the "gay," the "languishing," and the "melting."[26] Form and language express a relinquishing of rigor in this phase, as lighter forms—rhymed quatrains and octosyllabic couplets—predominate over the previously habitual heroic couplets. Yet the view of love expressed in this softening and lightening of tone contrasts significantly with the evidence of Lady Mary Wortley Montagu's satiric verse epistle "Miss Cowper to ——," in which the courtship is presented as a far from comfortable time.[27] Her courtship letters too—which evoke an insecure, unhappy, and demanding personality—and her recurrent depressive episodes testify to darker aspects of the experience that find no place in her poetry.[28]

For Falconer Madan, writing in the 1930s, these poems showed "Judith at her best."[29] Madan's judgment results partly from the value he set on personal emotion in poetry: "these later love poems, though artificial in form, exhibit natural feeling of the right kind, gracefully and tenderly expressed." But "feeling of the right kind" suggests another reason for the preference: that conjugal affection is woman's proper fulfillment, leading naturally to the motherhood that "diverted her thoughts from poetry." But one does not have to accept either the evaluation or the reasoning to recognize the significance of this new direction: for the first time, Cowper invents the fable of her poems for the occasion, taking the subjects directly from life. In addition, these poems present an intriguing attempt, unusual among women poets in the eighteenth century, to write about happy, consummated love, and, in particular, to evoke the physical charms of the beloved.

For her husband's first birthday after their marriage she writes of how Venus had distinguished him at his birth:

> Where Young Lysander slumbring lay,
>   The bloomy goddess watchfull stands,
> Each Grace officiously obeys,
>   With duteous Hast her mild Commands.

One to his Eyes their killing Fires
    Temper'd wth melting Softness gives,
While one his air, his Mein inspires,
    Coelestial Bloom, another breaths,

The Cyprian Queen their Art approves
    And gently crowns the pleasing Toil,
She plants a thousand laughing Loves,
    In ev'ry gayly dimpled Smile,

Pleas'd wth her Work compleat, She crys,
    So shone Adonis, Heav'nly Fair,
So dazzling bright his speaking Eyes,
    Such his maturer Bloom & Air!

But Heaven a milder fate prepares,
    On Thee kinder Planets shine,
Successful Love's transporting Cares,
    Happy Darling Boy be Thine![30]

Perhaps it is excessive to call such a poem erotic, but in comparison with the general reluctance of women in this period to celebrate the male body, Cowper's enraptured contemplation of her husband probably deserves the epithet. Characteristically, Cowper ignores the clash between her female identity and the male tradition in which she works: she writes about a man very much as male poets have written about women. In another poem from the first year of their marriage, she reproves her husband for stealing his breath from the flowers, his voice from the nightingale, and his kisses from the bee:

In budding Spring when Phoebus' Ray
Bids every Flower its Pride display,
From Plant to Plant the Spoiler goes,
First of its Fragrance robs the Rose;
Nor can the Vi'let's lovely Blew,
Impearled with drops of early Dew,
The unrelenting Rifler stay,
But all its Sweets he bears away,
And soon conceals them in his Breath,
Nor heeds the Vegetable Death.
When Philomel in yonder Grove
In gentle Plainings told her Love,
While listning Echo caught the Sound,
Rewarbling to the Woods around,
Beneath a Shade *Lysander* lay,

And stole each softest Note away.

. . . .

Nay, not content with this is he,
But next pursues the thymy Bee:
His balmy, humid Treasure steals,
And on his Lips the Theft conceals.[31]

Madan's note to this poem is somewhat embarrassed: "It may be
doubted whether Capt. Martin Madan recognized his own portrait
in these lines. He was more at home in the Camp than among
the Muses." The problem is not, however, with poetry in itself
(after all, soldiers have been poets), but with the kind of poetry
that Cowper writes about her husband. In effect, he is feminized;
for Cowper's procedure is one usually associated with poems that
fashion women as lovely objects of desire. Cowper characteristically overlooks the implications of the switch of genders: Martin
is in life a soldier, ranging the world in his campaigns, having
command over other men, exercising the profession of arms that
Cowper presents as the theme of the noblest poetry in her celebration of Homer; yet in her love poetry he is as narrowly defined by
sexual allure as any woman. This is not, however, the conscious
subversion it could so easily be in an avowedly feminist discourse,
even though it places Cowper herself, however mildly, in the forbidden role of desiring woman. In her love poems, as elsewhere,
she avoids striking opportunities to draw attention to the negotia-
tions, transfers, and inconsistencies entailed in working within
the male tradition.

Any attempt to interpret Judith Cowper's career must take into
account the limitations of what she did write and the fact that by
her midtwenties all her explorations seem to have become dead
ends. To think along these lines unavoidably raises the question
of evasion. After all, one of the implications of her doctrine of the
unequal union of the fiery with the soft, an implication underlined
by the value she sets on epic, is that the poet must measure up
to what is vigorous, demanding, and painful, as well as respond
to what is attractive and comforting. Her depressive episodes, the
anxieties of her courtship, and the intensity of her unhappiness
during her husband's regular absences on military duty indicate
central areas of personal difficulty that her poetry never either
explicitly or even implicitly engaged. More significant, however,
is that she gives no sign of recognizing that there is anything
problematic about her trying to work in a tradition made by and
for men. This refusal of potential challenge and confrontation re-

flects a personality happiest and most fluent in celebration and deference: Cowper was never prepared to take her writing out of the realm of what was safe and authorized. Whereas Pope can enjoy the ambiguity and wavering of his Eloisa, contriving the coda to his poem to foreground expressiveness and exemplary passion, Cowper answers his poem with an anxious but unconvincing assertion by Abelard that moral victory is both possible and necessary.[32] Her anxiety for moral closure is arguably more an act of self-persuasion than a felt rejection of Pope's subtlety. Perhaps it is to her credit that in these circumstances she virtually ceased to write poetry. Neither poetry nor marriage had solved her problems, and in later life she became a zealous Methodist: what little verse she composed after her conversion expresses, for the most part, exclamatory delight in the promises of her religion.

To speak of Judith Cowper as a poet, to think of her verses in terms of a career, is not to overlook the shortcomings of what she wrote and is certainly not to claim for her a particularly high place among the women poets of the eighteenth century. Her significance lies less in achieved texts than in her exemplary status as baffled female poet. Accepting the gendered polarities of sun and moon, soft and fiery, passive and dynamic, she was unable to proceed by the way of challenge, like her bolder, perhaps less typical contemporaries. She was, in Pope's image, precisely a moon, trained to esteem herself for the qualities that denied her the authority to identify and challenge the terms of her exclusion.

Notes

1. Judith Cowper's father, Spencer Cowper, was a judge; his elder brother William was the Lord Chancellor Earl Cowper. Her aunt by marriage, Mary Countess Cowper, and her paternal grandmother, Sarah Cowper, were both considerable diarists; her daughter Maria published poetry and her son Martin became notorious for his anonymously published *Thelyphthora; or, A Treatise on Female Ruin* (London, 1780), in which he advocated polygamy (see Virginia Blain, Patricia Clements, and Isobel Grundy, *The Feminist Companion to Literature in English* (London: Batsford, 1990), entries for Judith Madan, Mary Cowper, Sarah Cowper). Her brother Ashley was a competent versifier (see examples of his work in his commonplace book, British Library Add. MS 28101); the poet William Cowper was the son of her brother John.

2. Falconer Madan, *The Madan Family and Maddens in Ireland and England: A Historical Account* (Oxford: Clarendon Press, 1933), 270; William McCarthy, *Hester Thrale Piozzi: Portrait of a Literary Woman* (Chapel Hill: University of North Carolina Press, 1985).

3. For the implications of Aristotelian accounts of gender in this period, see Valerie Rumbold, *Women's Place in Pope's World* (Cambridge: Cambridge University Press, 1989), 7–9, 22–23.

4. For examples, see *Essay on Criticism, TE,* 1:240–62, ll. 13, 21, 58, 70–71, 195.

5. Text from Ashley Cowper's commonplace book, BL, Add. MSS 28101, fols. 154–57. I am grateful to Gerald Maclean for his help in placing this poem in the tradition of progress poems.

6. Presumably John Dennis.

7. For Pope's planning, including the use of prose drafts, see Joseph Spence, *Observations, Anecdotes, and Characters of Books and Men,* ed. James M. Osborn, 2 vols. (Oxford: Clarendon Press, 1966), 1:nos. 302, 310, 343; for his techniques of revision, see, for example, 1:nos. 203, 391, 402. For the spurious new world, see *The Dunciad Variorum, TE,* 5:3.177, ll. 237–38.

8. Autograph, Bodl. MS Eng. poet. d.196, fol. 1.

9. From Ashley Cowper's commonplace book, British Library Add. MS 28101, fols. 149–50. I am grateful to Donna Landry for pointing out that "To Mr Pope" was later printed among other commendatory poems in Pope's *Miscellany Poems,* 2 vols. (London, 1732).

10. For an outline of Cowper's contacts with Pope, see Rumbold, *Women's Place in Pope's World,* 145–50.

11. *TE,* 6:306, ll. 1–7; 308.

12. From Ashley Cowper's commonplace book, BL, Add. MSS 28101, fol. 136.

13. *The Spectator,* ed. Donald F. Bond, 5 vols. (Oxford: Clarendon Press, 1965), 2: 365–69, 390–93.

14. See Carolyn D. Williams, *Pope, Homer and Manliness* (London: Routledge, 1993), for a wide-ranging account of the role of classical studies in the inculcation of manliness in the eighteenth century; and particularly p. 62, on Homeric "fire" as mediated by Pope.

15. Pope, *Corresp.,* 2:139 and n. 1.

16. For Pope's studies and tastes in painting, see Morris R. Brownell, *Alexander Pope and the Arts of Georgian England* (Oxford: Clarendon Press, 1978), 10–15.

17. For Pope's exhortation to Jervas, see Pope, *Corresp.,* 1:377.

18. From Ashley Cowper's commonplace book, BL, Add. MSS 28101, fol. 142.

19. BL, Add. MSS 4456 (Birch Collection: Poetical Fragments I), fol. 97.

20. Pope, *Corresp.,* 2:138.

21. Ibid., 2:202–3.

22. For the subordinate status of description, see Spence, *Observations,* vol. 1, nos. 380, 384.

23. From Ashley Cowper's commonplace book, BL, Add. MSS 28101, fol. 106.

24. "On her birthday," 1723, printed in Madan, *The Madan Family,* 100.

25. Autograph in Bodleian MSS, Eng. lett. 284, fol. 105.

26. "When first Lysanders killing Form I viewd," autograph in ibid., fol. 13.

27. *Essays and Poems and Simplicity, a Comedy,* ed. Robert Halsband and Isobel Grundy (Oxford: Clarendon Press, 1977), 216–24.

28. Letters between Cowper and Martin Madan are preserved in Bodleian MSS, Eng. letter, c. 284.

29. Madan, *The Madan Family,* 269–70.

30. "July the First. 1724," from Ashley Cowper's commonplace book, BL, Add. MSS 28101, fol. 160.

31. Printed in Madan, *The Madan Family,* 101.

32. Printed in *Poems by Eminent Ladies,* ed. G. Colman and B. Thornton, 2 vols. (London, 1755), 2:137–43.

Geography and Gender: Mary Chandler and Alexander Pope

Linda Veronika Troost

IF one were to ask a poet of the eighteenth century to name the most influential topographical poem, Sir John Denham's *Cooper's Hill* (1642) would lead the list. Constantly alluded to by later poets and seen as the model for eighteenth-century topographical poetry, Denham's poem works very much in the tradition of Virgil, Ausonius, Claudian, and Drayton.[1] Denham's particular contribution to the genre, however, lies in fusing to the topographical poem features from the epigram, the georgic, and the meditation.[2] Even Samuel Johnson recognized that Denham had created "a new scheme of poetry": "*local poetry,* of which the fundamental subject is some particular landscape, to be poetically described, with the addition of such embellishments as may be supplied by historical retrospection, or incidental meditation."[3] Denham inspired Pope's *Windsor Forest* (1713), and Pope's poetry in turn served as a model for Mary Chandler's *A Description of Bath* (1733). Like Pope and Denham before her, Chandler fused together many sources. Her work combines elements of Roman literary forms— the journey poem, the town poem, country-house poem—with distinctly English forms such as the meditative local poem and the satiric spa poem. Hers is also the first work to choose the city of Bath as its subject.

Mary Chandler had much in common with her contemporary, Alexander Pope, who "complimented" her poem on Bath for its "good sense and politeness."[4] She was born in 1687, a year before Pope, and died in 1745, the year after him. Like Pope, she was not raised in the established church: he grew up Roman Catholic and she grew up Presbyterian, the eldest daughter and sister of dissenting clergymen. Both Pope and Chandler were largely self-educated, Chandler's family not having quite enough money to educate the girls. Both earned their own livings. Pope became a professional writer and editor; Chandler ran a millinery shop in

Bath from the age of eighteen, publishing her first verses while in her forties.

Pope and Chandler shared other similarities: neither poet married, each cultivated an interest in landscape gardening through association with the aristocracy, and both befriended other poets.[5] They admired Ralph Allen, Dr. William Oliver,[6] and Dr. George Cheyne, creator of the milk-and-vegetable diet designed to strengthen nerves weakened by back problems. In fact, ill-judged medical advice hurried both poets to their deaths. Both also had been hunchbacked since youth. Unlike Pope, however, Chandler's deformity resulted from a childhood injury that did not gradually incapacitate her in the way that tuberculosis of the spine progressively disabled Pope.[7]

Given their affinities in coming from marginalized backgrounds and sharing intellectual interests, it seems inevitable that Chandler would have chosen Pope as a model in both life and work.[8] Pope's influence shows strongly in her first published work, *A Description of Bath,* as well as in her later lyrics, not only in the heroic-couplet form but in the Horatian tone. Significantly, both wrote poetry that privileged retirement over social bustle. Chandler's poem on Bath and Prior Park, however, exploits a paradox between her active and contemplative worlds. Although she laughs at social foibles and praises the quiet life of retreat and poetry, she manages to make a constrained, feminine existence active and more empowering than one might expect.

Chandler's poem was highly successful, especially for a first publication. Editions appeared in 1733 and 1734, with six more appearing over the next thirty-three years. The three editions appearing between 1736 and 1741 included some reflective verses and poems written for friends. The sixth edition (1744) added another favorite, "A True Tale," a versified account of a marriage proposal she received (and refused) from a man who read and admired her Horatian poem "The Wish." Chandler claims to have included this work in the sixth edition only to avoid the tediousness of transcription: "my chief Motive for Printing now any thing besides this New Edition of the *Bath* Poem, was, to put an End to the troublesome Employment of writing out Copies, without disobliging my Friends."[9]

The first edition of *A Description of Bath* is couched as an anonymous "letter to a friend," although Chandler drops the epistolary pretense with the second edition. The poem's structure can be summarized as follows: after an invocation, Chandler opens with a brief history of Bath in pre-Roman times and then describes the healing powers of the waters. This description leads directly to an ode on the virtues of temperance and health. Next she describes the scenery visible from Bath, with a digression on Thomas Burnet's history of the world as an explanation for the area's hilly terrain. About a third of the way through the poem, she moves into the center of town—Bath Abbey—to begin the expected tour.

After touring the monuments and giving readers the history of Bath Abbey from the dark ages of Catholicism to the enlightened age of Protestantism, she exits to the street, visiting a variety of sights: the Pump Room, the Baths, the West Gate, and the Royal Residence of the Princess Amelia (George II's sister). Next she admires some Roman statuary unearthed in the previous decade, the Orange Grove, and the monument to the Prince of Orange. She gives four lines to Richard Nash, master of ceremonies, and several more to the amusements at Mrs. Lindsay's assembly rooms. She then compliments her publisher, James Leake, strolls down the lime tree walk to Harrison's Banqueting House, and admires the river Avon.

The final section of the poem devotes itself to Ralph Allen: benevolent postmaster, post-office reformer, road-builder, Bath Corporation member, mayor, and member of Parliament.[10] Chandler praises the new road and Allen's machinery for transporting Bath stone inexpensively from the quarry. The sight of construction leads her metonymically to Prior Park, the new house Allen was planning. Because he had not yet built or landscaped his estate, Chandler must invent the details. The poem concludes with a short celebration of Allen's accomplishments in the post office and quarrying business.

Chandler's encomiastic poem of 322 lines follows a well-established tradition of topographical poetry. Ausonius's *Mosella* (A.D. 371), a 483-line poem describing the Rhine and Moselle, nicely displays several of the genre's topoi. The poet salutes the two rivers and human activity, cataloguing wholesome edibles (in this case, fish) and imagining the antics of nymphs and satyrs. Indulging in a modicum of mock-epic similes, he then describes rural sports (hunting and fishing), admires the region's architecture, and concludes with a political panegyric.[11] *Cooper's Hill* and *Windsor Forest* contain variations on these themes and probably served as Chandler's real models. Similarly, she salutes the spa water, catalogues the virtues of (moderate) consumption, imagines the antics of beaux and belles, invokes mock-epic similes, describes urban sports (gambling), admires the architecture of the old Pump Room, and praises the House of Hanover.

Several classical writers created poetic journeys through the countryside or the town. For example, Horace's *Satire* 1.5 (ca. 30 B.C.) consists of an anecdotal journey to modern-day Brindisi and Juvenal's *Third Satire* (ca. A.D. 110) on the city of Rome sets the satirical tone for many town poems written in Restoration and eighteenth-century England. Traces of this tradition show up in Mary Chandler's critical comments on frivolous and irreligious Bath society. But not all town poems are caustic. Decimus Magnus Ausonius, a Gallo-Roman poet, develops an alternative approach to Juvenal's. *Ordo urbium nobilium* (ca. A.D. 380) apostrophizes twenty famous cities, providing the reader with both a generalized description and background of each locale. His native Bordeaux, for example, is noted for its excellent wine, mild climate, and nicely laid-out streets. Pope's *Windsor Forest* and Chandler's *A Description of Bath* both fit squarely into this mode with their respective praises of London and Bath.

Even spa poetry has classical antecedents. The principal model for these poems appeared early in the fifth century in Claudian's one hundred-line *Aponus* (ca. 400), which praises the mineral springs of Abano, Italy. This serious poem provides a detailed geographical description of the area, praises the fount, and speculates on the hot spring's source of heat: either Phlegethon is the source or else water and fire have struck a treaty, a *concordia discors*. Most English spa poems before Chandler's take a Juvenalian approach; hers is better characterized as following Claudian's encomiastic voice.

Chandler's imaginative construction of Prior Park and its gardens at the end of her work owes much to country-house poems like Ben Jonson's *To Penshurst* (1616).[12] This genre has classical roots in Chandler's favorite poet, Horace, and his vision of the good life, as well as in Virgil's portrayals of the Golden Age in his *Georgics* and *Eclogues*. Martial, however, provides the favorite model. *Epigram* 3.58 (ca. 90) contrasts the country houses of Faustinus and Bassus. Faustinus's farm near Baiae teems with abundance and hospitality: the plants grow naturally, farm animals frolic, and the grateful rustics bring the master gifts of cheese and capons. Bassus's house, in contrast, leaves its visitors starved and, with its artificially symmetrical gardens, is unnatural and not self-sufficient. Jonson's *To Penshurst* imitates the first part of this epigram, and Bassus's estate reappears in Pope's *Epistle to Burlington* as Timon's villa, a sterile showplace.

Because Allen's country house is not a working estate, Chandler plays down the farm element and enhances the retreat aspect. In the mid-1700s, the country house became less of an economic necessity and more of an escape from urban living, so the country-house poem focused increasingly on the owner's personal virtues instead of his social virtues.[13] In her description of Prior Park, Chandler is conveniently free from adhering to real geography and architecture, so she invents an estate that maps Allen's benevolent soul.

In Chandler's imagination, Prior Park represents an exact inversion of Bassus's house or Timon's villa: "Thy Taste refin'd appears in yonder Wood, / Not *Nature* tortur'd, but by Art improv'd" (17).[14] The landscape is varied and natural instead of symmetrical and artificial, so it serves as a *hortus conclusus* for Chandler, just as Lord Fairfax's Appleton House did for Andrew Marvell. Allen, like his garden, shows variety and unaffected naturalness. In addition, this imagined garden provides the traditional abundance of the earlier country-house poem with a Marvellian image: "Beneath the Load the tender Branch shall bend, / And the rich Juice regale its *Master's Friend*" (17). Allen's fruit trees willingly offer the poet nourishment as Allen in his benevolence gives of himself to others. Although heartfelt, the compliments that Chandler tenders to Allen are conventional in order to put him in the tradition of great patrons.

Chandler's compliments on Ralph Allen's civic virtue and commercial works also lie in the tradition of topographical poetry. The two rivers along which Ausonius organizes *Mosella* serve as commercial routes for Rome, so the classical poet simultaneously praises both personal pleasures and national commerce.[15] Michael Drayton's epic river poem *Poly-Olbion* (1612/1622), Denham's *Cooper's Hill*, and Pope's *Windsor Forest* praise commercial advancement when in the service of "the general good."[16] Although Drayton may criticize human nature and Stuart monarchs,[17] he glorifies England's natural resources, especially those with economic potential: spa water, rivers, and copper mines. Denham praises the king's charity in rebuilding London, and Pope praises the forest for its role in providing wood for ships. Pope's *Epistle to Burlington* (1731) also praises his subject for his public building projects. Although Allen's accomplishments in reforming the post office are on a lesser scale than a king's or an earl's, Chandler emphasizes his altruism and demonstrates that he always works for the general good.

Although she was widely read in the classics (in translation),[18]

Chandler ultimately looked to her contemporary, Pope. For the second edition of *A Description of Bath,* she added a note of praise for the poet who had praised her: "tuneful POPE" (19), along with Pindar, Homer, Virgil, and Horace, appears in a list of the best poets. But Chandler does not follow him slavishly. Pope's poems, like those of Ausonius and Claudian, generally follow a linear structure, with descriptions of goal-oriented action (as in "masculine" epic) and linear spatial arrangements. For example, *Windsor Forest* details both the hunt, an end-directed activity, and local trees transformed into the hulls of ships that will travel the globe and "Bear *Britain*'s Thunder . . . To the bright Regions of the rising Day."[19] His poems, moreover, travel from place to place without returning to a home base. For example, *The Rape of the Lock* opens in Twickenham, moves down the Thames, and concludes at Hampton Court. *Windsor Forest* moves from woods to meadows to river and then to the ocean.

Chandler uses a linear development for some of her arguments, if not her structure. For instance, the waters of Bath form (at least in the second edition, p. 5) a single unit of mineral water only when they surface:

> The flowing Waters, from their hidden Source,
> Thro' the same *Strata* keep unerring Course;
> The floating *Sulphur* meets dissolving *Steel,*
> And heat in *Combat,* till the Waters boil:
> *United* then, enrich the healing Stream,
> HEALTH to the *sick* they give, and to the *Waters,* FAME.
>   Thus oft contending *Parties* rage and hate,
> Malignant both, and push each other's Fate;
> At last, their Fury spent, and cloy'd with Blood,
> They *join* in *Friendship* for the *Publick Good.*

The first edition contains a more cynical metaphor in the final two lines: "Then on some Neighbouring King's Assistance call / Who builds his Empire on both Parties Fall."[20] In other words, both sulfur and iron are subdued by and subsumed into the water. In Chandler's revision, the polarity of battle resolves into a single course of friendship, a trope of synthesis that very strongly echoes Claudian's speculations on whether the Abano's heat results from a treaty drawn between the warring elements of water and fire. Of course, Denham and Pope also exploit the *concordia discors,* perhaps less extensively than Earl Wasserman has argued.[21] The trope appears in topographical poetry composed since Claudian's time, but it is an end-directed image that Chandler rarely employs.

In general, Chandler avoids the linear organization of space even though her imagination seems to move from the city to the country (actually, she herself never leaves town in the poem). She favors, instead, circular or ring structures (typical of "feminine" romance). Instead of passing linearly through the streets of Bath to Prior Park (or traveling south to north as Drayton does in *Poly-Olbion*), she meanders, only to return to where she started. She starts with an imagined view from the south (from the top of Beechen Cliffs), then moves to Bath Abbey in the town center, and looks through the West Gate. But then Chandler moves east to the Orange Grove, travels south again past Leake's bookstore and the banqueting hall, finally crossing the river and traveling southeast to conclude her journey at Prior Park, barely past the Beechen Cliffs where the poem actually began.

Chandler's organization of time sequences in *A Description of Bath* also eschews the linearity of the chronological. She admittedly starts the body of the poem in the past and concludes with a vision of the future, a structure conventional to topographical poetry. The points in between, however, do not follow so neatly. The movement from past to future occurs at least twice in the poem (a repetition evincing yet another circular design). The first half of the poem moves from the pre-Roman days of Prince Bladud to the vision of the Judgment Day. The second half carves out a tighter span within this large one: from the early days of Bath after the Norman Conquest to Prior Park in the coming decades. In contrast, Pope's *Windsor Forest* seems relatively chronological. There are several historical flashbacks, admittedly, but each one advances in time—from William I to Charles I to Anne—and the poem concludes with a vision by Father Thames of the future greatness of both London and England.[22]

Chandler's passage on the Abbey appears to be a simple chronology, but it, too, contains a circular structure. The description of the Abbey opens in the old days of "Gothic Darkness" (9), a popular theme in topographical poems of the eighteenth century:[23]

> When *living Saints* for *true Devotion* bled;
> And *Rites prophane* were offer'd to the *Dead*;
> When *Idol Images* Devotion drew,
> And *Idol Gods* were worshipp'd as the *true*.
>
> (9)

Chandler's Presbyterian sentiments shine through as she hails the arrival of Protestantism:

Welcome, fair LIBERTY, and LIGHT *divine*!
Yet *wider* spread your Wings, and brighter shine;
Dart *livelier* Beams on ev'ry *British* Soul,
And scatter *slavish Darkness* to the Pole.

(10)

The whiggish sense of religious progress and the images of light beams may suggest a linear pattern, but the poet thwarts our expectations. Instead of being cast out forever, the old idolatrous tendencies have returned to the Abbey in new form:

Ev'n there, by *meaning Looks,* and *cringing Bows,*
The *Female Idol* her *Adorer* knows!
Fly hence, *Prophane,* nor taint this Sacred Place;
Mock not thy GOD, to flatter CAELIA's Face.

(10)

The graven idol of Catholicism is replaced by the idol of the secular spa-world, the heavenly Miss Caelia. Despite the Reformation, worship in Bath circularly reverts to idolatry.

Chandler's critique of the secular world extends further. At Mrs. Lindsay's assembly room, for instance, the guests do not seem different from those at Pope's Hampton Court:

The *ratling Dye* enchants the *Miser's Heir;*
The *hoarded Sums* the *sharking Gamesters* share:
Th' important Bus'ness of the Fair, *Quadrille,*
Employs those Hours which *Dancing* cannot kill;
Or fav'rite *Ombre,* sweetly sung by POPE,
Appalls their *Cheeks* with *Fear,* or reddens them with *Hope.*
There *Miss* soon learns the Language of the *Eyes,*
The *witless Beau* looks soft, and swears he dies;
And who can think so *fine* a *Lover* lyes?

(14)

This elegant satire of high life in Bath owes much to *The Rape of the Lock,* as Chandler explicitly hints. Dapperwit and Sir Fopling have come to Bath to woo Belinda's sisters, and the gaming, dancing, and flirting will continue in an endless cycle. Time will pass, people and fortunes will change, but events repeat endlessly. Each Miss will learn the language of flirtation; each beau will repeat the same old lines.

This conflict of cyclicality pitted against advancement appears in more than just Chandler's poem. Stephen Jay Gould analyzes two similarly contrasting lines in Restoration and eighteenth-century geological thought, which he describes as time the "arrow" (progressive and irreversible) and time the "cycle" (circular and repeating).[24] The Reverend Thomas Burnet (1635?–1715) tried to combine the two opposing views in his *Sacred Theory of the Earth,* published in the 1680s in both Latin and English with popular but short-lived success. Burnet was attacked from many sides for attempting to provide rational explanations for geological matters in biblical narrative (such as the source of water for the Deluge). Religious hardliners saw him as tampering with sacred doctrine. Others, especially in later centuries, laughed at his uses of Aristotelian theories and the Bible instead of confining himself to geological evidence.

Chandler refers to part of Burnet's geological scheme as an appealing meditation in her poem, even if she takes it with a grain of salt.[25] After all, although Burnet's theory defends the inevitability of progress, it also validates the circular structure as generative, one that will establish a newborn world. Near the beginning of her poem, Chandler imagines the view from the highest point near the city, and the many hills around Bath remind her of Burnet's cyclical theory of geology and the evolution of hills:

> Thence view the *pendant Rock*'s majestick Shade,
> That speaks the Ruins conqu'ring *Time* has made:
> Whether the *Egg* was by the *Deluge* broke,
> Or Nature since has felt some other Shock;
> Ingenious BURNET, thine's a pleasing Scheme,
> A gay Delusion, if it be a Dream.
> The shatter'd *Rocks,* and *Strata* seem to say,
> Nature is *old,* and tends to her *Decay:*
> Yet *lovely* in *Decay,* and *green* in *Age,*
> Her Beauty lasts her, to her *latest Stage.*

(8)

For Burnet, the image of time's cycle manifests itself in the pattern of creation and destruction. In the beginning, God created a perfectly smooth world. He destroyed it in the Deluge, which damaged the earth's crust and caused hills and continents to form. Finally, Burnet projected a final conflagration at the second coming that would restore the earth's crust to a smooth surface and reestablish paradise on earth.[26]

Seeing the geological ruins of the antediluvian world (that is, hills) leads Chandler into a meditation on the creation (and subsequent re-creation) of the world:

Wisdom immense contriv'd the wondrous *Ball,*
And *Form* sprung forth, obedient to his Call.
He fix'd her Date, and bid the *Planet* run
Her *annual* Race around the *central Sun:*
He bid the *Seasons, Days,* and *Nights* return,
Till the pent Fires which at the *Center* burn,
Shall the *whole Globe* to one huge *Cinder* turn.
Then, like a *Phoenix,* she again shall rise,
And the *New World* be peopl'd from the *Skies;*
Then *Vice,* and all her Train of Ills shall cease,
And *Truth* shall reign with *Righteousness* and *Peace.*

(8–9)

The two passages teem with images of spheres and recurring cycles of time: the harvest year, the annual rotation of the planets around the sun, globes, the diurnal cycle, the rebirth of a phoenix, decay and rebirth, the (bathetic) image of earth as a spherical egg, the return of the Golden Age. These images imply humanity's current fallen state and also forecast an eventual return to Eden (foreshadowing the creation of Prior Park, too). Nature may be lovely in its ruins (like Romans ruins), but its inhabitants, like those of Roman or Catholic Bath, can look forward to an even better day.

At the same time Chandler was anonymously writing (1733–34), Pope was anonymously publishing a work that also presented a picture of the universe's structure. *An Essay on Man* places humanity at the center of earthly life, just as Chandler's poem puts herself at the center of Bath. As in *Windsor Forest,* Pope's organizing images are linear: scales of reason, chains of love, streams of time, and finally, the most goal-directed of all: "All must be false that thwart this One great End."[27] For Pope, circular images tend to indicate a solipsistic, selfish vision: mere mortals see only the little circular patterns centered on their vain selves. Pope's image of self-love is, in fact, a circle:

Self-love but serves the virtuous mind to wake,
As the small pebble stirs the peaceful lake;
The centre mov'd, a circle strait succeeds,
Another still, and still another spreads,
Friend, parent, neighbour, first it will embrace,
His country next, and next all human race,
Wide and more wide, th'o'erflowings of the mind
Take ev'ry creature in, of ev'ry kind.[28]

For Pope, circles represent the earthbound human that cannot see the larger picture: namely, a linear, hierarchical structure "upheld by God."[29] Lines, therefore, lead directly to heaven.

Chandler, on the other hand, chooses circles and spheres for divinity, elevating the circle where Pope elevates the phallic line.[30] Chandler's poem moves in both chronological and geographical rings, and it contains images of cycles. Even the meditation on the virtues of temperance (added for the second edition) implies a circular structure because it describes a return from sickness to the original state of health and outlines the movement from night to day. From the "*Midnight Feast*" that causes one's veins to boil, one reaches (through the Golden Mean) the "joyful Dawnings of returning Day" (6). The waters of Bath receive the highest accolade through a comparison to holy water, which cleanses the soul of sin: the waters of Bath "wash those numerous Ills" of the "intemp'rate Sinner" (7). Physical health brings one spiritual health and rebirth; physical overindulgence damages the mind and soul:

> Fatal Effects of LUXURY and EASE!
> We *drink* our POISON, and we *eat* DISEASE;
> Indulge our SENSES at our REASON's Cost,
> Till *Sense* is *Pain,* and *Reason's hurt,* or *lost.*

(6)

Chandler, no doubt, was strongly influenced by George Cheyne of Bath, who advocated a change in diet and habits as a way of purging the mind of melancholy and the body of ills.[31] Like Cheyne, Chandler concerned herself with spiritual and physical health, and for her, Bath's spa-water epitomized health as the water of Abano had for Claudian. For Chandler, cyclical motion, including the cyclical nature of water (evaporation to rain and so on), connotes the positive, the whole, the moral. Chandler, much more than Pope, revels in circle imagery, which Pope associates with conceit and confusion. In *Windsor Forest,* for instance, the Pageant of Father Thames specifically avoids the circular in favor of the linear and phallic. All the tributaries feed into and swell the Thames, a river with a mighty goal: it is the conduit to the ocean, and by extension, to British economic power.

The rushing-river image is a popular one in poetry and prose. It dominates *Poly-Olbion* and plays an important role for Denham and Pope as both a literal and a metaphorical vehicle for commerce. Even Burnet uses the image of a river leading to an outlet as a metaphor for the task of the natural philosopher: "there is no greater trial or instance of Natural wisdom, than to find out the Chanel, in which these great revolutions of Nature, which we treat on, flow and succeed one another."[32] Although he sets up ideas of the world as based on cycles, he still acknowledges much of science's desire to see narrative progression and development: hence his return to images of vectors.

Although Chandler's poem contains rivers, streams, and fountains in abundance, all remain within enclosures of various kinds; they do not surge mightily as they do for male poets. Water, an emblem of life, must be contained to be feminine. For example, although the poem centers on a town famous for its hot mineral springs, Chandler always portrays them as calm pools and never as moving water. The river Avon makes only one appearance as "the silent *Stream*" (16) at the base of a pavilion. Perhaps Chandler's pool images echo her own feelings of calm power in her contained, female existence—she can produce an imagined tour of Bath that does not require leaving the walled city. Unlike Denham, Chandler does not even have to climb a hill for a prospect. She also can produce a living for herself, a serious example of power, without leaving her millinery and lace shop in Bath Abbey Churchyard. Nor does she require ships and navigable rivers: her lace comes from Nottingham and her hats from her own workroom.

Chandler has the opportunity to use forceful images of water, but she consciously does not. Ralph Allen built a canal to transport his Bath stone, but Chandler spurns a chance to duplicate the Popelike identification of moving water and advancing commerce. She instead focuses on how the local streams form, not the conventional powerful river, but a small, quiet, hypothetical lake at Prior Park:[33]

> In num'rous Streams the murmuring Waters trill,
> Uniting all, obedient to thy Will;
> Till by thy Art, in *one Canal* combin'd,
> They thro' the *Wood* in various *Mazes* wind;
> From thence the foaming Waves fall rapid down,
> In bold *Cascades,* and lash the rugged Stone.
> But here their Fury lost, the calmer Scene
> Delights the softer Muse, and Soul serene;
> An ample *Bason,* Center of the Place,
> In Lymph transparent holds the scaly Race;
> Its glassy Face, from ev'ry Ruffle free,
> Reflects the Image of each neighb'ring Tree.

(18)

The lake represents a contemplative serenity that negates the brief appearance of the active in the rushing of the foaming waves and the bold cascades. The classical image of the water-mirror, present in both popular topographical poetry and *Paradise Lost,* compounds the picture of fulfillment and completion, free of any taint of narcissism.

Chandler's imagination provides Ralph Allen's Prior Park with a feminized landscape of round pools and quiet groves. Because land is a traditional source and emblem of power, Chandler's imagined landscaping of Allen's garden shows her desire to control the male domain, be it in business, poetry, or land, three areas dominated by men. She has her shop, her poetry, and, in her imagination, she takes control of Allen's land, too. The masculine landscape, however, will win. In the next decade, Pope will help Allen design his gardens at Prior Park, and his plans will emphasize the linear: several thousand pines and elms planted in alleys and on each side of the lawn to set off the length of the garden and the vista to the basin, a waterfall possibly twenty feet high, and a serpentine path through a wood.[34] Although Chandler does not have the authority that Pope will have to reshape Allen's space, she does manage to do so in her verse, and she shapes topography to her own satisfaction, that of a "softer" muse.

Chandler even breaks down a central site of power distribution in Augustan poetry: the relationships among poet, patron, and the muse. Male poets have female muses who, when sufficiently flattered or cajoled, serve them or the patron. The opening of *Windsor Forest* shows such a patriarchal arrangement:

> Be present, Sylvan Maids!
> Unlock your Springs, and open all your Shades.
> *Granville* commands: Your Aid O Muses bring!
> What Muse for *Granville* can refuse to sing?[35]

In the poem, George Granville, Lord Lansdowne, and not the poet, actually controls the muses that Pope coaxes out. Later Granville will preempt the role of poet as well. When Pope hears the sounds of rejoicing in Windsor Forest, he assumes Granville has come to replace Denham and Cowley as poet of the forest and to consort with the Muses on the English Parnassus: "'Tis yours, my Lord, to bless our soft Retreats, / And call the Muses to their ancient Seats."[36] In the final lines of the poem, Pope separates himself from the high-flying lord who can command the Muses by claiming that he, as a mere pastoral poet, has a "humble Muse."[37] In playful humility, Pope switches Muses to avoid comparisons with Granville, allowing the lord to dominate the Nine while he confines himself to lowly pastoral and topographical poetry.

Chandler also claims a humbler muse (as would be decorous in one's first published poem on a topographical subject). But she never pretends to surrender her muse to the patron's control nor does she, as a woman, have the same patriarchal relationship with a female muse that a male poet possesses. The Princess Amelia does not command a semidivine and recalcitrant muse, urging her to "open" to a male patron or poet; in fact, the patron, not the muse, needs to be flattered into helping the poet:

> AMELIA, beauteous PRINCESS, deign to view
> What the *Muse* sings; to YOU the Song is due
> . . . .
> Deign YOU, bright Maid, to hear my artless Lays,
> You'll awe the snarling Criticks into Praise.
>
> (3)

The muse and patron do not have the close association in Chandler's verse that they do in Pope's pastoral: the creative circle contains only poet and muse.

And that muse looks a great deal like Mary Chandler. As she fuses the classical and the neoclassical, conflating the inspirational springs of Hippocrene and Bath, Chandler also conflates the role of muse and poet:

> To sing the Town where balmy Waters flow,
> To which AMELIA's Health the Nations owe,
> My Muse aspires; while conscious Blushes rise,
> And her weak Pinions tremble ere she flies;
> Till drawing Vigour from those living Springs,
> She dares to raise her Voice, and stretch her Wings.
> Not the fam'd Springs which gave Poetick Fire,
> Had nobler Virtues, or could more inspire.
> Too weak my Voice, but Great AMELIA's Name
> Shall raise my Numbers, and defend my Fame.
>
> (4)

The muse may be "weak," Chandler argues, but so is the voice of the female poet. This trope of modesty, conventional both to topographical verse and women's poetry, should not be read literally, however. Chandler has no more sense of real humility than Pope has. Pope pretends to give his patron free reign; Chandler simply expects her patron to accept and praise another woman, not take over the poem.

The end of *A Description of Bath* further demonstrates Chandler's identification with the muse. She imagines Prior Park will become the muse's "haunt": "Here could the Muse for ever spend her Days, / And chant, in humble Rhymes, the Owner's Praise" (18). Because Chandler is actually the one imagining herself at Prior Park and the one writing the praise, she herself becomes the muse in the garden. Furthermore, Princess Amelia, her patron, proves to be of no particular consequence and vanishes early in the poem. Pope used his topographical poem to confer on Granville power over the land of the Nine Muses and the Muses themselves; Chandler takes control of the imaginary landscape of Prior Park and becomes the figure in it. Even in the first edition of *A Description of Bath*, before Chandler received royal permission to dedicate the revised poem to Amelia, Chandler did not relinquish control over her creativity. In presenting the first edition to the world as a verse epistle to a physician friend (probably Dr. Oliver), Chandler never subordinates herself to her dedicatee or suggests any connection other than simple friendship between them or between herself and the muse that inspires her:

> To sing the Town where balmy Waters flow,
> Those sov'raign Springs which chearful Health bestow,
> My Muse aspires,
> . . . .
> Too weak the Voice that now attempts their Praise,
> I sing to please my Friend, nor hope the Bays.[38]

Unable to use a traditional gender or power relationship as a metaphor for her association with the physician, she simply dismisses it and relies on herself to "please" a friend.

The "softer" muse of landscape poetry does not participate in linear power struggles but instead meditates on the city and then retreats (in imagination) to the surrounding country. There, the contemplative muse-poet actively creates the garden in her mind, thereby placing herself on an equal level with the landowner:

> Prophetick here, the Muse shall build thy Seat,
> Great like thy *Soul*, in ev'ry Part compleat.

(17)

In imagining Prior Park as she does, Chandler redefines the creative force as a contemplative-feminine power that she herself represents, rather than as the active-masculine force represented by Allen. She is the still, central point: she shapes history, geography, and even Ralph Allen's garden into her feminine ideal, a pattern of cycles instead of phallic lines, of contemplative containment instead of active expansion.

Apparently the fame of her poem changed her mind on the matter of ambition. The second edition expanded its scope and social status. Chandler added a dedication to the Princess Amelia, passages praising the royal family (including the Prince of Orange, husband to the Princess Royal), and compliments to would-be royals like Beau Nash, the self-appointed "monarch" of Bath.[39] The regularity with which Chandler published until her death eleven years later also suggests a rapid reconciliation to the idea of publicity and popularity. Her paean on Bath became the standard view for quite some time. Parts of the poem embellish the third edition of Daniel Defoe's *A Tour Thro' the Whole Island of Great Britain* (1742), published by Samuel Richardson (brother-in-law of Chandler's publisher, James Leake).[40]

Chandler's verse was notable enough to make her worth including in Robert Shiel's *Lives of the Poets* (1753). Sarah Scott praised her in *The Female Advocate* (1774), but Chandler's verse had by then fallen out of fashion, replaced in the public's imagination by Christopher Anstey's satiric *New Bath Guide* (1766). In 1767, thirty-four years after it first appeared, *A Description of Bath* saw its last edition. Chandler herself had been dead for over ten years. Nash and Allen, key figures in her poem, had been gone for nearly as long.

Moreover, the Bath she described barely existed by this time. The architecture had altered dramatically under the hand of the two John Woods, becoming a city of Palladian squares, crescents, and a circus. The places Chandler satirized were razed and replaced. Most important, however, the spa-poem had moved back into the satirical realm and had little use for the encomiastic manner of topographical poetry. Chandler's poem did its work to popularize the city of Bath and then moved over to make room for the new.

Notes

1. For a discussion of Denham and the classical georgic tradition, see Brendan o Hehir, *Expans'd Hieroglyphicks: A Critical Edition of Sir John Denham's "Coopers Hill"* (Berkeley and Los Angeles: University of California Press, 1969), 13ff.

2. For a more thorough discussion of this generic merging, see David Hill

Radcliffe, "These Delights from Several Causes Move: Heterogeneity and Genre in *Coopers Hill,*" *Papers on Language and Literature* 22 (1986): 352–71.

3. Samuel Johnson, s.v. "Denham," in *The Lives of the Poets,* intro. Arthur Waugh, 2 vols. (1906; reprint, London: Oxford University Press, 1973), 1:58.

4. [Samuel Chandler], s.v. "Mary Chandler," in Robert Shiels, *The Lives of the Poets of Great Britain and Ireland,* rev. Theophilus Cibber, 5 vols. (London: R. Griffiths, 1753), 5:353. All information about Chandler's life derives from this essay, written by her brother. The critical work on Chandler is minimal. See Oswald Doughty, "A Bath Poetess of the Eighteenth Century," *Review of English Studies* 1 (1925): 404–20, 499, and his correspondence with Arthur E. Case in *Review of English Studies* 2 (1926): 343–45. Claudia Thomas devotes a few pages to Chandler's verse in *Alexander Pope and His Eighteenth-Century Women Readers* (Carbondale: Southern Illinois University Press, 1994), 195–99.

5. She was welcome at the estates of Frances Thynne Seymour, countess of Hertford (later duchess of Somerset), and Mrs. Stephens of Sodbury House, Gloucestershire; her poet friends included Elizabeth Rowe and Mary Barber. See Chandler, *Lives of the Poets,* 5:346–47 and 353, and the *DNB.*

6. Dr. Oliver, inventor of the Bath Oliver biscuit, most likely was the one to introduce Pope to Chandler in the autumn of 1734. See Roger Lonsdale, ed., *Eighteenth-Century Women Poets* (Oxford: Oxford University Press, 1989), 152. We also know that Pope read and liked the poem, although Chandler modestly attributes its success to Oliver's incisive critique. In "To Dr. Oliver, Who Corrected My Bath Poem," she writes "Ev'n POPE approv'd, when you had tun'd her Lyre" (in Mary Chandler, *A Description of Bath . . . with Several Other Poems . . . To which is Added A True Tale,* 6th ed. [London: for James Leake, 1744], 22).

7. Marjorie Hope Nicolson and G. S. Rousseau, *"This Long Disease, My Life": Alexander Pope and the Sciences* (Princeton: Princeton University Press, 1968), 8.

8. Thomas, *Alexander Pope,* 195.

9. Dedication to her brother, John Chandler, in the 6th edition.

10. Edith Sitwell, *Bath* (New York: Harrison Smith, 1932), 188–90. For a biography, see Benjamin Boyce, *The Benevolent Man: A Life of Ralph Allen* (Cambridge: Harvard University Press, 1967.

11. Robert Arnold Aubin, *Topographical Poetry in Eighteenth-Century England* (New York: MLA, 1936), 5–7.

12. William A. McClung, *The Country House in English Renaissance Poetry* (Berkeley and Los Angeles: University of California Press, 1977), 8–17.

13. Ibid., 148–49.

14. [Mary Chandler], *A Description of Bath. A Poem Humbly Inscribed to her Royal Highness the Princess Amelia,* 2d ed. (London: for J. Leake and J. Gray, 1734). This edition came out anonymously in late August or September 1734, and it includes a dedication to the Princess Amelia. Unless otherwise specified, I give page references to this edition, which is also available in the microfilm series *The Eighteenth Century* (Woodbridge, Conn.: Research Publications, 1986), reel 1464, no. 4, and from University Microfilms (Ann Arbor, Mich., 1978).

15. Wyman H. Herendeen, *From Landscape to Literature: The River and the Myth of Geography* (Pittsburgh: Duquesne University Press, 1986), 86–88.

16. Radcliffe, "These Delights," 366.

17. Jean R. Brink, *Michael Drayton Revisited* (Boston: Twayne, 1990), 88–89.

18. [Chandler], *Lives of the Poets,* 5:345.

19. *TE*, 1:189, ll. 387–88.

20. [Mary Chandler], *A Description of Bath. A Poem in a Letter to a Friend*, 1st ed. (London: for J. Roberts . . . and J. Leake, and S. Lobb, Booksellers in Bath, [February 1733]), 6. I would like to thank John P. Chalmers for providing me with a photocopy of the imprint in the University of Texas Library.

21. See Earl R. Wasserman, *The Subtler Language: Critical Readings of Neoclassical and Romantic Poems* (Baltimore: Johns Hopkins Press, 1959), 53–88 and 101–58, for discussions of the consistent use of *concordia discors* in Denham and Pope. For a refutation, see Radcliffe, "'These Delights,'" 353–66, and Robert Cummings, "*Windsor Forest* as a Silvan Poem," *ELH* 54 (1987): 63–79.

22. For a different view of Pope's use of time, see Pat Rogers, "Time and Space in *Windsor Forest*," in *The Art of Alexander Pope*, ed. Howard Erskine-Hill and Anne Smith (New York: Barnes and Noble, 1979), 40–51.

23. Aubin, *Topographical Poetry*, 169.

24. Stephen Jay Gould, *Time's Arrow, Time's Cycle: Myth and Metaphor in the Discovery of Geological Time* (Cambridge: Harvard University Press, 1987), 10–11.

25. Chandler is not the first to use Burnet in verse. See Robert A. Aubin, "Grottoes, Geology, and the Gothic Revival," *Studies in Philology* 31 (1934): 408–16. Most particularly, Burnet's ideas come up in William Goldwin's 1712 *A Poetical Description of Bristol* (p. 20) and James Thomson's "Spring" from *The Seasons* (ll. 309–18).

26. Gould, *Time's Arrow*, 42–51.

27. *TE*, 3.1:125, 3.309.

28. *TE*, 3.1:163–64, 4.363–70.

29. *TE*, 3.1:17, 1.34.

30. For a brief discussion of Luce Irigaray's and Jacques Derrida's arguments on "the Phallus and the Logos as transcendental signifiers of Western culture," see Toril Moi, *Sexual/Textual Politics: Feminist Literary Theory* (London and New York: Methuen, 1985), 66–67.

31. The treatise outlining his system, *The English Malady*, appeared in 1733, the same year as the first edition of *A Description of Bath*. Cheyne's earlier work, *An Essay of Health and Long Life*, was published in 1724 by James Leake, the same Bath publisher who brought out Chandler's poem.

32. Thomas Burnet, *The Sacred Theory of the Earth*, (1684–90; 2d ed., 1691), (reprint, Carbondale: Southern Illinois University Press, 1965), 66. Gould's quotation of this passage in another context (42) brought it to my attention.

33. Peter Martin argues that Chandler mentions the lake because it was already in place. Chandler's poem could just as well have predated it. See *Pursuing Innocent Pleasures: The Gardening World of Alexander Pope* (Hamden: Archon, 1984), 209.

34. Ibid., 215–16 and 223–24. By 1769, two naturalistic lakes with a Palladian bridge between them will replace the basin (221).

35. *TE*, 1:148, ll. 3–6.

36. *TE*, 1:174, ll. 283–84.

37. *TE*, 1:194, l. 427.

38. Chandler, *A Description of Bath*, 1st ed., 4.

39. An anonymous work, *Characters at the Hot Well*, "hailed [Nash] as King at Bath, Prince at the Hot Wells, Duke of Tunbridge, Earl of Scarborough, and Lord of Buxton and St. Winifred's Well" (Phyllis Hembry, *The English Spa: 1560–*

1815 [London: Athlone and Rutherford: Fairleigh Dickinson University Press, 1990], 137). For a discussion of Nash as the monarch of Bath, see Peter Briggs, "The Importance of Beau Nash," *Studies in Eighteenth-Century Culture* 22 (1992): 209–30.

40. Dr. Cheyne, as Anita Guerrini has informed me, revised the section on Bath for Richardson's edition of Defoe's *Tour*. Richardson published Cheyne's books during the 1730s and also printed Chandler's poems for Leake, his brother-in-law.

Recovering Thalestris: Intragender Conflict in *The Rape of the Lock*

PETER STAFFEL

UNTIL quite recently much critical writing on Alexander Pope's *The Rape of the Lock* seemed to gravitate around whether Pope liked or disliked his heroine, the "gentle Belle" Belinda. While the poem is a satire of coquettish behavior, surely the oft-quoted couplet from canto 2—"If to her share some Female Errors fall, / Look on her Face, and you'll forget 'em all" (*TE*, 2:159, ll. 17–18)— demonstrates the poet's genuine attraction to the genuinely attractive Belinda. So while there may not be a critical consensus about reading Belinda, she nevertheless offers a rather narrow range for contestation. Therefore, contemporary critics have looked for and found complexity elsewhere—in the sociocultural sphere and also in the minor characters, particularly Clarissa, the last major addition to this continually accreting poem. John Trimble, in "Clarissa's Role in 'The Rape of the Lock,'" [1] was the first to present a Clarissa of considerable depth—a complicated character whose motivations, intentions, and actions challenged the "simple" reading of Clarissa and, concomitantly, of the poem itself. Feminist readings have even further recast once-traditional perspectives on *The Rape of the Lock* (and on the rest of Pope's poetry as well).

This essay will use past critiques of Clarissa as an avenue for further exploration of the riches of *The Rape of the Lock* in three specific areas. First, Pope himself chose to highlight Clarissa's importance for understanding the moral of the poem by declaring as much in a descriptive note published in the 1751 edition of his works; therefore, any attempt to come to terms with the poem must reexamine Clarissa and nudge her ever closer to its center. Clarissa may thus become one of the two primary antagonists who represent the dominant social culture. As its agent, she captures Belinda for this culture or excludes her from it. Second, Thalestris has generally been written off as a simple stereotype, standing for all the hypocrisy and pettiness of the women of the *beau monde*.

Yet for all the negative connotations that the amazon (or warrior woman) held for the eighteenth-century patriarchy, Thalestris, read against the grain, offers a richly rewarding alternative to Clarissa and a powerfully subversive feminist alternative to the patriarchy. Third, a reconsideration of Clarissa and Thalestris enables a rereading of Belinda that produces a not-so-"gentle Belle"—one whom contemporary readers, especially feminists, can claim with less chagrin.

A feminist social and literary critique like Ellen Pollak's examination of what she calls the Myth of Passive Womanhood[2] undermines the critical position that attempts to empower Belinda by subjectivizing her, one that reads her as a truly centered rather than marginalized character. Pollak instead demonstrates how Pope neatly reverses what only appears to be a subjectivized female presence at the center of the text (epitomized by Belinda's toilet and the procession up the Thames to Hampton Court) into an objectivized female

> ideologically . . . situated on the margins of the text. For her visibility in the poem not only signals her nonexistence as a subject, but finally points to the latent and more powerful masculine presence of which she [as object of the male gaze] has been figured as the sign.[3]

Belinda herself is contested ground: no matter which of the primary antagonists—Belinda or the Baron—one places in the center or in the margins, both contemporary and traditional critics have seen the post-rape debate in Hampton Court as a well-delineated struggle for social, emotional, and perhaps even physical control of the assaulted heroine. On the left, the amazonian termagant Thalestris counsels war to defend honor as reputation; on the right, the grave and graceful Clarissa counters with reason and good sense in an attempt to redefine honor more substantively as virtue. But the indeterminate outcome of their opposition, and thus of the poem's conclusion, seems inevitable both as a reflection of historical or anecdotal fact and as the necessary conclusion to Pope's wickedly naughty satire on the fashionable behavior of the *beau monde*. That is, like Clarissa's Iliadic counterpart Sarpedon, whose speech defining martial heroism is parodied by her own speech on honor and virtue, Clarissa goes down to defeat:

> So spoke the Dame, but no Applause ensu'd;
> *Belinda* frown'd, *Thalestris* called her Prude.
> To Arms, to Arms! the fierce Virago cries,
> And swift as Lightning to the Combate flies.
> (*TE*, 2:197, 5.35–38)

Only through the poet's imposition of a *deus ex machina* is the chaos of the melee resolved, albeit rather inconclusively.

Nonetheless, the traditional perspective has clearly favored Clarissa and demeaned Thalestris, seeing the former as the presenter of the literal moral of this poetic drama and the latter as a shrewish virago. In his spirited reinvigoration of the traditional reading of *The Rape of the Lock,* Howard Weinbrot reminds readers that in the 1751 edition of his works, Pope added to his note on Clarissa's famous speech "A new character introduced in the subsequent Editions, to open more clearly the MORAL of the Poem." [4] Weinbrot also discusses the high esteem in which Pope and other classical commentators held Sarpedon.[5] Yet for all Clarissa's apparent charm, good sense, and elegant fluency, she (and particularly her famous speech) is, ironically, still modeled on a defeated hero. Even though Sarpedon is greatly honored by the philandering Zeus, his death is determined by Zeus's divine female opponents, Hera and Athena, the respective champions of monogamous marriage and chastity. Equally important for reading Clarissa's speech is Pope's original note, retained in all subsequent editions, which immediately follows the new clause and closes the sentence: "in a parody of the speech of Sarpedon to Glaucus in Homer." A meticulous writer, Pope surely would have changed "parody" to "paraphrase" or "imitation" if he had desired the literal reading of the moral that Weinbrot espouses. Moreover, the added clause does not specifically identify Clarissa's speech as the moral of the poem; rather, it states that the speech "opens" the moral more clearly.

Various contemporary critics begin their assessment of Clarissa in her role as the arms bearer to Belinda's ravisher, the Baron, and as the instigator of the plot to deflower the unsuspecting Belinda:

> But when to Mischief Mortals bend their Will,
> How soon they find their Instruments of Ill!
> Just then, *Clarissa* drew with tempting Grace
> A two-edg'd Weapon from her shining Case;
> So Ladies from Romance assist their Knight,
> Present the Spear, and arm him for the Fight.
>
> (*TE,* 2:174–75, 3.125–30)

The classical epic, where women are virtually invisible except as booty or property, momentarily gives way to the medieval romance, wherein women are omnipresent but either helpless and passive or active only in a subordinate role to their protector males. Weinbrot throughout much of his defense of Clarissa dismisses as unpersuasive the objection to Clarissa's role in the assault, noting that "in the *Faerie Queene* Una arms the 'clownish' Red Crosse when she still thinks him a country bumpkin unfit for the task." [6] Despite the validity of the example, it ranks as one of the very few exceptions to a consistent romance conceit, and, of course, Una eventually marries Red Crosse once she has helped him become worthy of her. Surely the "simple characterization" that Weinbrot reads in *The Rape of the Lock* could have been easily facilitated by Pope had the poet merely changed, in the five-canto version, the name of the Baron's helper in canto 3, line 127. Instead Weinbrot interprets Clarissa's apparently contradictory actions as "a Friend's kindness. Solid Clarissa knows what the airy sylphs must learn—that the baron and Belinda are appropriate suitors; as an ally she hopes to bring them together *by joining* an apparently harmless trick" [emphasis added].[7] Weinbrot's argument makes perfectly good sense if Pope intended a "simple characterization." Yet, as Geoffrey Tillotson declares in his Twickenham edition of the poem, "The social mockery of *The Rape of the Lock* is not simple, does not make a pat contribution to single-mindedness. The world of the poem is vast and complicated."[8] Or, as Rebecca Price Parkin intimates, "not very far beneath its amusing, lacquered surface lurk graver issues, not ordinarily treated in the mock epic."[9] Weinbrot dismisses this type of complexity, tracing it to a genealogical branch descending from Parkin's 1955 "Ur text," *The Poetic Workmanship of Alexander Pope,* and extending through John Trimble and Ellen Pollak.[10] Weinbrot sees the expanded five-canto poem as a continuation of the original, as well as its intention to repair the rift between two Catholic families. But with the death of Lord Petre (the poem's Baron) from smallpox in March 1712/13,[11] Pope's initial impulse becomes irrelevant, and the world of the poem expands well beyond a simple focus on Belinda. Thus the Parkin branch's version of *The Rape of the Lock* presents a richer and more realistic construction of Clarissa than the traditionalists offer.

John Trimble demonstrates that Pope's language undermines the credentials of the "prudish" Clarissa as the moral center.[12] Thalestris's calling her "prude" might be dismissed as a petty insult from a rival were it not that Pope himself uses the adjective "graver" in describing the prude who "sinks downward to a Gnome," in his catalogue of epic machinery in canto 1, and likewise uses "Grave" to characterize Clarissa in canto 5. Clarissa's prudishness not only changes the tone of her didactic speech to Belinda but might also remind readers that prudes are aging coquettes who are losing their physical charms of attraction and thus their marriageability. But Clarissa holds up matrimony as the proper goal for women and good humor as the appropriate temperament for a successful marriage, even though she herself is unmarried. Clarissa also initiates a practical joke that demands a great deal more good humor of its victim than any coquette of the *beau monde* can reasonably be expected to possess. In addition, she ends her otherwise commendable speech with two couplets sufficiently condescending and mean-spirited to cast her whole position into doubt. Thus the "sisterly" wisdom or advice Clarissa offers becomes suspect because it is subverted either by the language itself or by the nature of the speaker. To justify Pope's creation of Clarissa as a prude, Trimble says:

> Through her he could dramatize prudery in action showing us, say, the prude's false piety, her native cunning, her primly self-righteous sermonizing, her artfully nuanced discourse with its lethal hints and exclamations. . . . Finally, if presently with her prudery discreetly veiled, she would enable him to sustain and enrich the already richly paradoxical mode of the poem.[13]

Clarissa, though a late addition to the poem, is central to the poem's development, certainly "open[ing] more clearly the MORAL of the poem." By complicating the original two-canto poem, Clarissa "opens" a fascinating and complex social sphere in which she plays a commanding role.

Recognizing Clarissa's importance and extending Trimble's argument, Pollak locates the chief opposition in *The Rape of the Lock* not between the Baron and Belinda, man versus woman, but between Clarissa and Belinda:

> But Clarissa's scissors are not her only two-edg'd Weapon. Her tongue, as the vehicle for her lecture to Belinda, is yet another instrument by which she attempts to ingratiate herself with the Baron while overshadowing her rival for his favors, the coquette. Seeming to befriend the failing belle at the beginning of Canto 5, she adopts a posture of superior "Merit" in order to deliver a sermon laced with invidious comparisons between women like herself who excel in moral virtue and women like Belinda who attend only to the virtues of the face.[14]

Trimble sees Clarissa's seemingly high-minded speech as rife with a self-righteousness that she intends to disguise as social pragmatism by employing such terms as "good humor," "virtue," and "Merit." But she coincidentally displays an opportunism that undermines any absolute moral value in these terms because she employs them exclusively for securing or preserving a socially advantageous position.[15] The deportment and carriage that Clarissa encourages perpetuate both women's marginal status and her superiority to Belinda within those margins. Thus she establishes herself as a corrupt collaborator in a hegemonic patriarchy.

Clarissa acts as a factor for the Baron and by extension for patriarchy, regardless of the degree of honesty of her speech. Belinda's coquetry encourages a flirtation with all men but a simultaneous rejection of every individual man: "Favours to none, to all she Smiles extends" (2.11). Clarissa apparently recognizes and envies the Baron's growing attraction to Belinda and perhaps intuits or fears that Belinda will reciprocate. Therefore she forces the issue, hoping that the Baron's premature assault will drive Belinda away from her developing sensibility and toward, instead, the extreme position of Belinda's defender, the termagant Thalestris. Clarissa's speech, which has traditionally been held up as a model of good sense, virtue, and morality, falls on the totally deaf ears of her poetic audience: "So spoke the Dame, but no Applause ensu'd" (5.35). Pope's satire of the *beau monde*'s sensibility is obvious here; as Parkin notes, "The lack of applause . . . makes it clear that virtue and useful skills are not an acceptable alternative for conquests of the heart."[16] But the silence of Clarissa's allies further evinces either the ineffectual nature of her speech or her already well-established prudery and the concomitant doubt that it casts upon the validity of her speech.

Yet Clarissa clearly exerts considerable social influence, bringing order to the social chaos following Belinda's assault with merely a "*grace*ful [wave of] her Fan" (emphasis added, 5.7). Clarissa demonstrates to Belinda that physical appearance, though formidable, is not woman's only power. Clarissa offers Belinda entry into what should be a very good and decent world, one which recognizes both physical beauty and its limitations, as well as the power of wit and of good humor—in effect a utopia. Yet at the same time Clarissa demonstrates the shortcomings of this world in practice, where an admirable trait like "grace" can legitimately claim the entire company's attention but can also be used to manipulate and tempt a man into performing an act of symbolic domination and humiliation. For Clarissa initiates the original assault rather than, as Weinbrot claims, "joins" it. By "drawing" her scissors "with tempting *Grace*" (3.127, emphasis added), she coincidentally draws the Baron into consummating the rape plot and demonstrates another instance of how Pope's word choice works to clarify and complicate simultaneously. And patriarchy consistently and ruthlessly employs domination and humiliation to maintain a status quo that Clarissa's policy of honesty and good humor can never hope to overcome, much less to shame into self-generated reform: her actions ultimately help to perpetuate the status quo. Women's greatest threat comes not from men but from other women; they can rely upon male treachery as endemic. Women are more unreliable and thus less trustworthy, as Belinda discovers in *The Rape of the Lock.*

Julia Kristeva's paradigm of oppositional female societies within a dominant patriarchy[17] parallels the situation of Pope's *The Rape of the Lock.* Kristeva argues in "Women's Time" that one group succeeds in gaining access to the power structure and is in turn absorbed by the dominant culture and employed as an instrument of its hegemony.[18] Thus Clarissa sanctions Belinda's entry into the established order of prudish matrimony. But clearly the tone of Clarissa's invitation, especially the last four lines of her speech, demonstrates an implicit hierarchy within second-class membership. By acknowledging Clarissa's superior status (domination) and accepting or acquiescing to her condescension (humiliation) as a type of initiation rite, Belinda recognizes and submits to two of the primary tools of patriarchy to gain the right to use them herself on future initiates. If Belinda refuses the terms of acceptance/initiation—both the general patriarchal system and Clarissa's superior status within the prudish subculture—Clarissa will exclude her entirely.

Opposing this assimilated group are what Kristeva calls more radical feminist currents who construct a countersociety by

> refusing homologation to any role of identification with existing power. . . . As with any society [including the dominant patriarchy], the countersociety is based on the expulsion of an excluded element . . . a purge which will finally exonerate the countersociety of any future criticism.[19]

Thus Thalestris offers both the carrot (inclusion) and the stick (expulsion) to Belinda at the end of canto 4 (ll. 95–120), prior to Clarissa's speech.

The characterization of Clarissa argued by Parkin, Trimble, and Pollak amply demonstrates that her rivalry with Belinda supersedes her willingness to welcome Belinda into the assimilated society. Belinda's frowning response proves Clarissa's actual though covert "success"; consequently, Belinda rejects her previous growing change of heart and willingly sides with Thalestris, whose militant antimale position has never wavered. Thus the opposition in the poem is neither between Belinda and the Baron nor between Belinda and Clarissa but, as Weinbrot says, between Thalestris and Clarissa: Clarissa claims to defend honor as virtue, but in practice she defends feudal submissiveness to male authority— woman as object of man's gaze and his desire and as the tool of his power. Thalestris, on the other hand, defends a world that patriarchal tradition calls hypocritical, one where virtuous reputation rather than true virtue equates with honor. Pope himself subtly cautions Teresa Blount about this world in his epistle to her, "On Her Leaving the Town, After the Coronation":

> As some fond virgin, whom her mother's care
> Drags from the town to wholsom country air,
> Just when she learns to roll a melting eye,
> And hear a spark, yet think no danger nigh;
> (*TE*, 6:124, ll. 1–4)

Restoration drama offers vivid representations of the dominant social patriarchy and ways that women can or must function within it. Etherege shows this world's threats and dangers in *The Man of Mode* and its experimenting Bellinda. Wycherley satirizes it in *The Country Wife* with Horner's "virtuous Gang" of assorted Fidgets and Squeamishes. Harold Weber, in "Horner and His 'Women of Honour': The Dinner Party in *The Country Wife*," presents a cogent analysis of how a Thalestrian type of Kristevan countersociety functions.[20] According to Weber, Horner and his virtuous gang

> achieve a harmony between social masks and natural desires denied to most of the other characters. . . . [This] dinner party, in presenting an image of a genuine community which the play's larger society moves to frustrate, displays the conception of human nature which the play assumes and the values which it celebrates.[21]

In contrast to the honor and good humor that Clarissa counsels— which act as little more than moral high ground that assuages the conscience of women who have allowed men to treat them badly— Horner and the women of honor (as reputation) are completely honest with one another, frankly declaring—rather than denying, as society demands—their essential sexual desires and needs.[22] The hypocrisy of women who equate honor with reputation, as Lady Fidget makes clear, mirrors a central feature of the patriarchal system: "Why should you not think, that we women make

use of our Reputation, as you men of yours, only to deceive the
world with less suspicion . . . to cheat those that trust us."[23]

The birth and success of this countersociety depend on these
women admitting their sexual nature to each other despite their
enormous reluctance. This policy of honesty clearly goes well beyond simple sexual rivalry, since their self-revelations immediately
break down all jealousy in favor of a sort of "time-share" arrangement with Horner's "china." The barrier to female desire or to
women's open and honest discussion of it has been patriarchy's
traditional centering and elevating of masculine desire to the exclusion of its female counterpart, or perhaps, adopting Pollak's
phrase, the constructing of the "myth of passive womanhood."
Nonetheless, this newly formed countersociety "demonstrates an
acceptance of their instinctual passions and an understanding of
how these desires animate their personalities."[24] However, the play
proves that the women of honor cannot succeed beyond the dimension of countersociety for the very reason that Clarissa's ideal
of an honest and straightforward world remains utopian: it is because "they are locked within the confines of the corrupt society
of which it is but a part."[25] At the play's conclusion, Sir Jasper
Fidget and Pinchwife, primary representatives of patriarchal control, are confronted with their obvious cuckoldry and, more important, are presented with the opportunity to reform themselves
and their society. But they "blink": they participate in a "Dance of
the Cuckolds," accepting horns and temporary humiliation rather
than risk a brave new world of social and sexual equality.

Yet Horner himself, the potential liberator and confidant, twice
subverts any audience hope for reform. First, throughout the dinner party he keeps Margery Pinchwife locked in an adjoining
room, never confessing this to his fellow honest revelers. Second,
and more ominously, he betrays his only friend, Harcourt, to protect his own sexual access to Margery, leaving the truly honest
Alithea open to public disgrace. Such overt and covert displays of
male hypocrisy reinforce the necessity for a female countersociety
that cannot trust men and, because of that very distrust, must
beware of other women, whether they are naively honest like Margery, stubbornly honest like Alithea (who has now formed her
own matrimonial countersociety with Harcourt), or treacherously
honest like Clarissa.

So what men call hypocrisy, women call self-preservation, for
only through deception and distance can women gain the physical
power and pleasure that men constantly seek at their expense.
Clarissa would have Belinda believe that women can attain plea-

sure and influence only by relinquishing power. Thalestris would have her exert her very real existing power by fighting to retain her pleasure, or at least her right to pleasure: the power to draw or attract every man's gaze and desire, recognize it, and then reject it.

As surely as Clarissa is a prude, Thalestris is a termagant. Samuel Johnson defines a termagant as "a scold; a brawling turbulent woman."[26] But "scold" seems too mild for this "fierce Virago," while "brawling" and "turbulent" are far more appropriate. In fact, once Belinda rejects Clarissa's position, Thalestris launches an all-out assault, rallying Belinda to the cause: "To Arms, to Arms! the fierce Virago cries, / And swift as Lightning to the Combate flies" (5.37–38). A contemporary reader is apt to misread Pope's use of "virago" here, picturing only the *OED*'s primary modern definition: "a bold, impudent woman; a termagent, a scold." But the *OED* also provides a "rare" definition of virago: "a man-like, vigourous and heroic woman; a female warrior, an amazon." This usage not only resembles Johnson's definition of amazon—"a female warriour, a woman with the qualities of a man" (441), but the *OED* cites Pope for his canto 5, line 38, example referring to Thalestris as a "fierce Virago."

In addition, commentators agree that Pope's use of "fierce Virago" echoes Dryden's description of "the Warriour Dame" Camilla in the *Aeneis,* his translation of Virgil. This "fierce Virago" initially demonstrates a startling likeness to Belinda; both produce a comparable effect on those who see them as they pass:

On Camilla,

> Men, Boys, and Women stupid with Surprise,
> Where e're she passes, fix their wond'ring Eyes:
> Longing they look, and gaping at the Sight,
> Devour her o're and o're with vast Delight.[27]

(7.1104–7)

While for Belinda,

> Fair Nymphs, and well-drest Youths around her shone,
> But ev'ry Eye was fix'd on her alone.
> On her white Breast a sparkling *Cross* she wore,
> Which *Jews* might kiss, and Infidels adore.

(*TE*, 2:158, 2.5–8)

Their final campaigns show a remarkable number of similarities as well. In the *Aeneid* 11 the opposing cavalries engage; the Latins, led by Camilla and her female companions (likened to "the Thracian Amazons of old"), sweep the Trojans from the field. Camilla's glorious man-slaying *aristeia* comes to an end when she singles out a particular warrior, Chlorus, for his elaborate display of gold armor:

> A Golden Helm his Front, and head surrounds;
> A gilded Quiver from his Shoulder sounds.
> Gold, weav'd with Linen, on his Thighs he wore:
> With Flowers of Needlework distinguish'd o're:
> With Golden Buckles bound, and gather'd up before.
> Him, the fierce Maid beheld with ardent Eyes;
> Fond and Ambitious of so Rich a Prize:
> Or that the Temple might his Trophies hold,
> Or else to shine her self in Trojan Gold:
> Blind in her haste, she chases him alone,
> And seeks his Life, regardless of her own.
>
> (11.1139–49)

With Camilla blinded by her single-minded pursuit of one man's gold, the treacherous Aruns, who has been stalking Camilla, sees his chance:

> He keeps aloof, but keeps her still in sight:
> He threats, he trembles, trying ev'ry Way
> Unseen to kill, and safely to betray.
> . . . .
> This lucky Moment the slye Traytor chose:
> Then, starting from his Ambush up he rose,
> And threw . . .
>
> (11.1128–30; 1150–52)

Although Aruns prays to Apollo for a successful spear cast and a successful return home, Apollo grants only the former. Diana, seeing "Her Vot'rys Death" (11.1227) at the hands of "the slye Traytor" (11.1150), pursues Aruns. When "Him, in refulgent Arms she soon espy'd, / Swoln with success" (11.1238–39), Diana slays him and guarantees that "his Name be abhorr'd. / But after Ages shall [Camilla's] Praise record" (11.1228–29). Like the cowardly slayer of Camilla, Pope's Baron, watching and admiring Belinda, makes a twofold prayer for success—"Soon to obtain, and long possess the Prize" (2.44). Likewise, "The Pow'rs gave Ear, and granted half his Pray'r" (2.45), again the first half, physical success.

These cowardly, overmatched male predators succeed only through fraud or trickery, rather than through manly force. For Pope, "manliness" goes well beyond physical strength or virility to include honorableness and integrity. After all, immediately following his attack upon the effeminate Sporus in *An Epistle to Dr. Arbuthnot*, Pope describes himself as "manly" (*TE*, 4:120, l. 337) without intentional irony. Weinbrot chronicles how classical sources commonly show Amazons succumbing to male antagonists in battle. With surprising regularity, their downfall is a traditional source of feminine beauty—the hair—which gives male combatants an unexpected handhold to immobilize their victims before dispatching them.[28] Despite the obvious mock-heroic connection to that tradition in *The Rape of the Lock*, the men's success in Virgil and Pope comes about only because their Amazonian rivals allow themselves to be distracted from the general melee in pursuit of a specific victim. Camilla kills every foe who crosses her murderous path; Belinda conquers every beau as long as she "Favours . . . none." When Camilla concentrates on the glittering Chlorus, Aruns sees his opportunity and seizes it. Similarly, when to Ariel's complete surprise, "Sudden he view'd, in spite of all [Belinda's] Art, / An Earthly Lover lurking at her Heart" (3.143–44), he must abandon his defense and helplessly watch the Baron's deceitful victory.

Unlike the Baron, Aruns's motive is selfless: he wants to prevent a Trojan rout. He seeks no immediate fame, knowing, on the contrary, that his victory is won "by stealth." In fact, he asks Apollo "to wash away / The Stains of this dishonourable Day / . . . . But with my future Actions trust my Fame" (11.1159–60; 1162). Instead, in an age when honor is paramount in war, his dishonorable actions "Branded the Wretch, and [made] his Name abhorr'd" (11.1228). This sharply contrasts with the Baron, who cares only for victory, whether he by "Fraud or Force attain'd his Ends" (2.34). Unlike Aruns, who "trembling . . . flies, / With beating Heart, and Fear confus'd with Joys" (11.1179–80), the Baron revels in his success, assured of his fame as long as scandal magazines are published and frivolity rules society. Of course, in both cases the victims achieve fame out of disgrace, while even the ravishers' infamy pales in comparison: Aruns's name becomes little more than a footnote to the *Aeneis*, and the Baron has no name at all but is only his title.

Taylor Corse devotes a chapter of *Dryden's Aeneid: The English Virgil*[29] to Camilla, "The Warrior Dame," in which he discusses the power of the image of the amazon in the age of Dryden and

Pope, a topic that Diane Dugaw's recent *Warrior Women and Popular Balladry 1650–1850*[30] further reinforces and develops. In *The Rape of the Lock* Pope attempts to diminish or disarm this power through his ridicule of both Thalestris and Belinda. Pope strategically selects the name Thalestris because of its apocryphal origins in Strabo and Plutarch, wherein the Amazon queen brazenly approaches Alexander the Great, seeking sexual gratification and impregnation. Thus, in eighteenth-century England, Amazonian matrimonial equality becomes linked with the frighteningly subversive demand for sexual equality. While such a demand generally meets with rejection, some writers try to avoid blatant hypocrisy by misdirecting their satire onto peripheral demands that are most often deemed outrageous. For example, in John Weston's farce *The Amazon Queen, or, The Amours of Thalestris to Alexander the Great* (1667), Alexander only rejects Thalestris's demand for yearlong chastity, not sex and conception, thereby implicitly accepting the naturalness of unbridled libidinal impulses in both sexes. Still, the moral imperative resides in the female; the request of Weston's Thalestris transgresses the "normal" male fear of patrilineal succession. Edward Young, in "Satire V. On Women" from *Love of Fame, The Universal Passion in Seven Characteristical Satires,*[31] finds "A shameless woman is the worst of men" (110) when she employs vulgar male language and attitude; but in such a case, her style, not her sense, is ill-chosen:

> Thalestris triumphs in a manly mien;
> Loud is her accent, and her phrase obscene.
> In fair and open dealing where's the shame?
> What nature dares to give, she dares to name.
>
> (110)

Nonetheless, Young underscores the real male fear of women as equals, and therefore, as potential superiors: "If thunder's awful, how much more our dread, / When Jove deputes a lady in his stead?" (110).

Patriarchy works hard to denaturalize transgressive females and thereby to deflect criticism of basically indefensible male actions. But underlying all the talk of the unnatural pursuits of these amazons in war and love rests a grudging admiration for female success: when Thalestris and Belinda display the aggressive self-confidence of Amazons, they sweep the field before them, demonstrated by the "enrag'd" Thalestris's effortless dispatch of "A Beau and Witling" in canto 5, Belinda's gloating triumph over the two male antagonists at Ombre, and her victory over the Baron's "manly Strength" with "A Charge of Snuff" and "a deadly Bodkin" in the final fray. Yet such female success, even if limited or temporary, celebrates masculinity. As long as the gendered domains remain predominantly separate, men can accept the occasional transgression or foray by Samuel Johnson's "woman with the qualities of a man" because her very difference from other women and likeness to men reestablish the "natural" dichotomy; even Belinda's "deadly Bodkin" is a debased symbol of patrilineal power, having once been her great-great-grandfather's seal rings (5.90–91).

Belinda remains self-confident and aggressive throughout the poem, except for her lament at the end of canto 4. Of course, this display of self-pity and longing for idyllic pastoral seclusion results from Umbriel's "Vial whence the Sorrows flow" (4.142), not from Belinda's natural emotions. Pope's own words, modeled on Achilles' lament for the slain Patroclus in the *Iliad* 18, further mitigate this show of weakness. Achilles' wrath, the subject of the *Iliad*, rises to new heights following this lament and sends him back into battle in a rage of murderous fury that ends only when he kills Hector. Likewise, Belinda recovers her composure and, along with Thalestris, leads the assault against the Baron's forces—"See Fierce Belinda on the Baron flies, / With more than usual Lightning in her Eyes" (5.75–76). The conquered Baron, like Hector, prophesies the victor's eventual fate: "Boast not my Fall (he cry'd) insulting Foe! / Thou by some other shalt be laid as low" (5.97–98).

To what end, then, does Pope fashion Belinda and Thalestris after classical warrior-heroes such as Camilla and Achilles, despite the period's seeming prejudice against Amazonian women? Pope must choose between two seemingly unattractive options; according to Taylor Corse, he does the "manly" thing and opts for tradition and honor. Corse sees Pope's choice as a reflection of his distaste for the debasing of the historical hierarchy of force over fraud.[32] In canto 2, the Baron begins his plot against Belinda:

> Th'Adventrous *Baron* the bright Locks admir'd,
> He saw, he wish'd, and to the Prize aspir'd:
> Resolv'd to win, he meditates the way,
> By Force to ravish, or by Fraud betray;
> For when Success a Lover's Toil attends,
> Few ask, if Fraud or Force attain'd his Ends.
>
> (2.29–34)

According to Corse:

> To a moral philosopher like Cicero, and to a theodicean poet like Dante or Milton, it would have mattered a great deal if a man chose fraud or force to attain his ends. Pope invokes the past to indict the present. Very few people have any sense of ethical discernment, and most are concerned only with "Success," the favorable outcome of an endeavor, and failure—the "Ends," not the means.[33]

The complexity of Pope's mock-heroic satire produces a double-bind: women are attacked for acting like men, but men are attacked for being lesser men than the women. This partially mirrors the neoclassical discomfort with the epic's barbaric glorification of violence. Unfortunately for the highly civilized men of the *beau monde,* their own miniaturization as epic heroes has enabled women—who are still crucial elements of the civilized world despite their unequal status—occasionally to contest the power men still wish to maintain but find ever harder literally and rhetorically to defend. Therefore, the Baron and his ally or cipher Clarissa, despite representing the traditional moral center of patriarchy, deserve readers' scorn for their hypocrisy because they employ fraud to attain their ends; Belinda and Thalestris, despite representing a position the patriarchy deems hypocritical, deserve readers' admiration for their aggressive use of manly force to assert and defend their honor as reputation.

Returning to Pollak's transformation of female subjectivity into the marginal objectivity of the male gaze and desire, one finds that this object of the gaze is in fact a carefully constructed illusion. When Belinda sits down to her daily toilet in canto 1, the "heav'nly Image" (1.125) that appears in the glass reflects not Belinda herself but the image that she will create with "the *Cosmetic* Pow'rs" (1.124). This objectivized female beauty is a construct—the mock-heroic warrior's armor. Belinda does not sacrifice her subjectivity; on the contrary, she exerts her subjectivity through the construct and does it so successfully that she subdues all male antagonists through the very act of drawing their gaze and desire. Clarissa calls on Belinda to abandon her armor and offer up her true subjectivity to the Baron's desire, thereby becoming absolutely objectivized and assimilated into the female society sanctioned by patriarchy. Conversely, Thalestris's speech to Belinda in canto 4 demands that she raise herself up to the defense of her illusion (her intentionally false objectivization) and thus take part in the countersociety:

> Was it for this you took such constant Care
> The *Bodkin, Comb,* and *Essence* to prepare;
> For this your Locks in Paper-Durance bound,
> For this with tort'ring Irons wreath'd around?
> For this with Fillets strain'd your tender Head,
> And bravely bore the double Loads of Lead?
> . . . .
> *Honour* forbid! at whose unrival'd Shrine
> Ease, Pleasure, Virtue, All, our Sex resign.
>
> (4.97–102; 105–6)

In fact, if Belinda refuses initiation, Thalestris threatens to make her the scapegoat for the Kristevan countersociety's purge:

> Methinks already I your Tears survey,
> Already hear the horrid things they say,
> Already see you a degraded Toast,
> And all your Honour in a Whisper lost!
> How shall I, then, your helpless Fame defend?
> 'Twill then be Infamy to seem your Friend!
>
> (4.107–12)

Indeed, the eighteenth-century man ridicules woman for exchanging reputation for honor and calls her hypocrite. Yet in marriage, when woman gives over the illusion, surrendering her falsely objectivized self, she in fact surrenders all claim to subjectivity. The common complaint of dramatic heroines is the loss of their husbands' interest and love soon after the nuptials. And husbands willingly admit their guilt and the complicity of patriarchy, as Rhodophil does in Dryden's *Marriage à la Mode:*

All that I know of her perfections now is only by memory. I remember, indeed, that about two years ago I loved her passionately; but those golden days are gone, Palamede. Yet I loved her a whole half year, double the natural term of any mistress, and think in my conscience I could have held out another quarter. But then the world began to laugh at me, and a certain shame of being out of fashion seized me. At last we arrived at that point that there was nothing left in us to make us new to one another.[34]

Rhodophil and Doralice, his neglected wife, finally arrive at a solution, with the aid of another honest and mutually attracted couple, by forming a countersociety that relies on the threat of intrasocietal cuckoldry as insurance against neglect. Of course, fashion and tradition alone do not estrange partners. Even with the radical shift in the economic culture of English society, the gendered hierarchy remains firmly in place. Newly dominant capitalism's most ardent proponents, like Wycherley's Sir Jasper Fidget, find the allure of the marketplace far superior to that of the bedchamber, even while recognizing the dangers of such a stance.

A more satisfactory arrangement occurs in Congreve's *The Way of the World,* a play with dark thematic implications despite its verbal and structural sparkle and elegance. Millimant successfully retains her subjectivity by refusing to relinquish her constructed objectivity: "I'll fly and be followed to the last moment. Though I am upon the very verge of matrimony . . . I'll be solicited to the very last, nay and afterwards."[35] But Pope seems far less sanguine about the institution of marriage than Millimant: Clarissa's sentiments echo Pope's own "Epistle to Miss Blount, With the Works of VOITURE," where marriage can at best be but endured, because "*Good Humour* only teaches Charms to last, / Still makes new Conquests, and maintains the past" (*TE,* 6:62, ll. 61–62). But preceding this bleak resignation, Pope warns against marriage (l. 45) with references to situations similar to those of Doralice (ll. 43–44) and Belinda (l. 47):

> Too much *your Sex* is by their Forms confin'd,
> Severe to all, but most to Womankind;
> Custom, grown blind with Age, must be your Guide
> Your Pleasure is a Vice, but not your Pride;
> By nature yielding, stubborn but for Fame;
> Made Slaves by Honour, and made Fools by Shame.
> Marriage may all those petty Tyrants chace,
> But sets up One, a greater, in their Place;
> Well might you wish for Change, by those accurst,
> But the last Tyrant ever proves the worst.
> Still in Constraint your suff'ring Sex remains,
> Or bound in formal, or in real Chains;
> Whole Years neglected for some Months ador'd,
> The fawning Servant turns a haughty Lord;
> Ah quit not the free Innocence of Life!
> For the dull Glory of a virtuous Wife!
> Nor let false Shows, or empty Titles please:
> Aim not at Joy, but rest content with Ease.
> (*TE,* 6:62, ll. 31–48)

Thus, in the competition for Belinda, Thalestris offers her the only dynamic alternative for attaining and maintaining selfhood. The heroic models or epitomes for such a stance may well be subjected to male mockery and satire, but only because an open confrontation with such opposition would expose the bankruptcy of the patriarchy that Clarissa defends.

Notes

1. John Trimble, "Clarissa's Role in 'The Rape of the Lock,'" *Texas Studies in Language and Literature* 15 (1974): 673–91.

2. Ellen Pollak, *The Poetics of Sexual Myth: Gender and Ideology in the Verse of Swift and Pope* (Chicago: University of Chicago Press, 1985).

3. Ibid., 79.

4. Howard D. Weinbrot, "'The Rape of the Lock' and the Contexts of Warfare," in *The Enduring Legacy: Alexander Pope Tercentenary Essays,* ed. G. S. Rousseau and Pat Rogers (Cambridge: Cambridge University Press, 1988), 41.

5. Ibid., 42–43.

6. Ibid., 40.

7. Ibid., 41.

8. *TE,* 2:119.

9. Rebecca Price Parkin, *The Poetic Workmanship of Alexander Pope* (Minneapolis: University of Minnesota Press, 1955), 127.

10. Weinbrot, "'The Rape of the Lock,'" 22.

11. *TE,* 2:95.

12. Trimble, "Clarissa's Role," 677.

13. Ibid., 678.

14. Pollak, *Poetics,* 81.

15. Trimble, "Clarissa's Role," 683–84.

16. Parkin, *Poetic Workmanship,* 127.

17. Julia Kristeva, "Women's Time," *Critical Theory Since 1965,* ed. Hazard Adams and Leroy Searle (Tallahassee: University of Florida Press, 1990), 471–84.

18. Ibid., 478–81.

19. Ibid., 479.

20. Harold Weber, "Horner and His 'Women of Honour': The Dinner Party in *The Country Wife,*" *Modern Language Quarterly* 43, no. 2 (1982): 107–20.

21. Ibid., 108.

22. Ibid., 110.

23. William Wycherley, *The Complete Plays of William Wycherley,* ed. Gerald Weales (New York: Norton, 1966), 351.

24. Weber, "Horner," 112.

25. Ibid., 116.

26. E. L. McAdam, Jr., and George Milne, *Johnson's Dictionary: A Modern Selection* (New York: Pantheon Books, 1963), 413.

27. John Dryden, *The Poems of John Dryden,* ed. James Kinsley, 4 vols. (Oxford: Clarendon Press, 1958), 3:1262. Further references to Dryden's poetry come from this source and are cited in the text.

28. Weinbrot; "'The Rape of the Lock,'" 39.

29. Taylor Corse, *Dryden's Aeneid:* The English Virgil (Newark: University of Delaware Press, 1991), 109–30.

30. Diane Dugaw, *Warrior Women and Popular Balladry, 1650–1850,* Cambridge Studies in Eighteenth-Century Literature and Thought 4 (Cambridge: Cambridge University Press, 1989).

31. Edward Young, *The Poetical Works of Edward Young,* 2 vols. (Westport,

Conn.: Greenwood Press, 1970), 2:59–140. Lines are not numbered in this volume, so I cite only page numbers.

32. Taylor Corse, "Force and Fraud in 'The Rape of the Lock,'" *Philological Quarterly* 87 (1966): 355–65.

33. Ibid., 364–65.

34. John Dryden, *Marriage à la Mode,* ed. Mark S. Auburn, Regents Restoration Drama Series (Lincoln: University of Nebraska Press, 1981), 17.

35. William Congreve, *The Way of the World,* 4.1.160–65, in *The Complete Plays of William Congreve,* ed. Herbert Davis (Chicago: University of Chicago Press, 1967), 449.

Finch, Pope, and Swift: The Bond of Displacement

Barbara McGovern

W HEN Anne Finch returned to London sometime around 1708, it had been exactly twenty years since the revolution had forced her and her husband to flee the capital, seeking refuge in the homes of various friends and relatives throughout the English countryside. There was little in her previous literary career to suggest that her poetry would soon enjoy prestigious publication and that she would be hailed by two leading literary figures as the foremost woman poet of her age. Since the time of her exile from London, Finch had been a displaced figure, politically, religiously, and aesthetically at odds with the mainstreams of early eighteenth-century culture. Yet this very displacement would soon become partially responsible for her entry into the world of English letters, largely through the efforts of Alexander Pope and Jonathan Swift.

As a maid of honor to Mary of Modena, future Queen Consort, Anne Finch had begun writing at age twenty-one in the literary environment of the Court Wits, though, as she was later to acknowledge, she kept her poetic occupation secret, fearing she might be ridiculed as a "Versifying Maid of Honour."[1] While at court she met and married Heneage Finch, who had begun a promising career as a member of Parliament and as a courtier and military officer in service to the future King James II. Following the 1688 revolution, however, the couple's steadfast commitment to the Jacobite cause and Heneage's refusal to take the oaths of allegiance to William and Mary dashed all their hopes of a return to public life. Only after the subsequent arrest of Heneage on charges of treason and a yearlong ordeal of court delays before his final acquittal did the hapless couple settle at the estate of his nephew in Kent, condemned to a quiet and often lonely retirement in the country.[2] It was then, after two decades of isolation, that

Anne Finch returned in her late forties to the intellectual and literary life of London.

In the spring of the following year, 1709, Jacob Tonson published the sixth of his *Poetical Miscellanies*. Three of Finch's poems—"A Pastoral Dialogue Between Two Shepherdesses," "Adam Pos'd," and "Alcidor"—were included, immediately preceded by Jonathan Swift's "Baucis and Philemon" and "To Mrs. Biddy Floyd" and immediately followed by Alexander Pope's "Pastorals." The significance of this miscellany was almost immediately recognized; Richard Steele acclaimed it in the 3 May issue of the *Tatler*, "a collection of the best pastorals that have hitherto appeared in England."[3] It was not only Finch's first venture into the world of publication since her return to London, but it was also the first evidence of Swift's efforts on her behalf. In addition, it marked Pope's first publication—which, along with the inclusion of Ambrose Philips's *Pastorals*, led to one of the most celebrated literary debates of the eighteenth century. In this collection, then, the careers of these three writers, Finch, Pope, and Swift, intersect in a symbolic way, their poems forming something of a literary triptych.

Finch's inclusion in such an important miscellany was most likely the result of her new friendship with Swift, who must have been the intermediary between her and Tonson. Swift was a friend of her husband's nephew Charles, third earl of Winchilsea and the Finches' host during their previous years of rural retirement, and Swift began a cordial relationship with her almost immediately after she moved London. By 29 December of that year he was, according to his account books, playing piquet with her, and two weeks later he reported to Robert Hunter, "I amuse myself sometimes with writing verses to Mrs. Finch."[4]

A result of his efforts is "*Apollo* Outwitted. *To the Honourable Mrs.* Finch, *under her Name* of Ardelia, Written, 1709," a sixty-four-line homage whose acknowledged intent is to convince Finch to allow her poetry to be published. Most of the poem is a humorous explanation for Finch's continued reluctance to appear in print.[5] Swift's narrative features the lovely Ardelia (the poetic name Finch took for herself), a young woman who attracts the attentions of Apollo, that lusty god noted for his amorous exploits. He attempts to seduce Ardelia, but she is not to be outwitted:

> HE in the old Celestial Cant,
>   Confest his Flame, and swore by *Styx*,
> What e'er she would desire, to Grant,

> But Wise *Ardelia* knew his Tricks.
> *Ovid* had warned her to beware
> Of stroking God's, whose usual Trade is,
> Under Pretence of Taking Air,
> To pick up Sublunary Ladies.
>
> (Swift, *Poems*, 1:120, 7–24)

In response to the god's offer to give her whatever she wishes, the poet coyly asks that all nine of the Muses be put at her disposal so that she may call upon them whenever she desires. Apollo obligingly grants her request, but before he can "Seize his due," Ardelia quickly calls up Thalia, the "Celestial *Prude*," to thwart his advances (37, 41). Unable to take back what he has already granted, the angry Apollo takes his revenge by inflicting upon Ardelia such modesty that she will be averse to making public her literary genius. "Deceitful Nymph," he cries:

> Let Stubborn Pride Possess thee long,
>   And be thou Negligent of Fame,
> With ev'ry Muse to Grace thy Song,
>   May'st thou despise a Poets Name.
>
> Of Modest Poets thou be first,
>   To silent Shades repeat thy Verse,
> Till *Fame* and *Eccho* almost burst,
>   Yet hardly dare one Line rehearse.
>
> (53–60)

Yet Apollo's vengeful curse contains an ironic twist. Ardelia is not doomed to remain forever in the shades of literary obscurity, but when she at last comes to know fame from publication, it will be only because she has finally yielded to the plea of one whose political leanings she detests, that Whig reprobate Jonathan Swift himself:

> May you Descend to take Renown,
> Prevail'd on by the Thing you hate,
> A [Whig], and one that wears a Gown.
>
> (62–64)[6]

The strong affection and praise in these lines must have had a powerful effect upon the hesitant Finch. (It was, incidentally, shortly after this poem was written that Swift, who was apparently twitted by her for his Whig propensities, became a Tory.) When Finch finally acquiesced to the publication of a small volume of her verse in 1713, her *Miscellany Poems, on Several Occasions* was printed by none other than Swift's own publisher and friend, John Barber.[7]

But Swift did more than simply urge Finch to publish. In addition to arranging for her inclusion in the important Tonson miscellany, he was also responsible for introducing her work to other influential writers. One of these writers was Delariviere Manley, who became a strong advocate for Finch, promoting her poetry in print on three separate occasions. Manley was a personal friend of Swift's and worked closely with him on the *Examiner*.[8] Around the time that he wrote "*Apollo* Outwitted" for Finch, he apparently gave a manuscript copy of some of her poems to Manley and most likely arranged for a meeting of the two writers. The first volume of Manley's *Secret Memoirs and Manners of Several Persons of Quality, of Both Sexes. From the New Atalantis, A Island in the Mediteranean*, which was brought out in May 1709, contains one of Finch's poems, along with some biographical information. The commendatory nature of the portrait of Finch suggests a personal acquaintance with her. The second volume of *The New Atalantis*, published five months later, and Manley's 1711 *Court Intrigues, in a Collection of Original Letters, from the Island of the New Atalantis* also each contain a poem by Finch. In all three instances these poems had not been published previously and appear in earlier versions than the ones printed in Finch's 1713 *Miscellany Poems*.[9]

Swift's regard for Anne Finch extended beyond her literary career. His concern for her personal welfare is evident in a letter to Stella in August 1712. Commenting on the sudden death of Charles, earl of Winchilsea, Swift laments: "what is yet worse, my old acquaintance, Mrs. Finch, is now Countess of Winchilsea, the title being fallen to her husband but without much estate" (Swift, *Corresp.*, 1:55). Swift had good cause for concern, for the Finches had very little income and the estate was involved in complicated litigation that would not be settled until eight years later, just a few months before Anne Finch's death. Furthermore, as Swift observed elsewhere, the previous earl, "Being very poor . . . complied too much with the party he hated" in order to receive public appointments (Swift, *Corresp.*, 1:138). The Finches, however, remained loyal to their Jacobite principles; consequently, after succeeding to the peerage Heneage again refused the oaths, causing him and his wife to remain ostracized from London's political and court circles.

Anne Finch was always to feel herself something of an outsider,

not only because of her gender, but also because of her political
ideology, her religious orientation, and her aesthetic sensibility—
all of which contributed to the special bond that she felt with
Swift. Further evidence of their friendship may be found in a
manuscript now owned by Wellesley College that contains poems
primarily from the last decade of her life.[10] This extraordinarily
rich collection has a curious poem entitled "The Misantrope," written probably around the time of Swift's exile to Dublin in May
1714. The poem is printed here in its entirety:

> Life at best
> Is but a jest
> A face a glass a fiddle
> A shew a noise
> Makes all its joys
> Till worn beyond the middle
>
> Age is worse
> The doatards curse
> Consumed in endless story
> In tales of tubs
> Intreagues and drubs
> Retold by Grandsires hoary
>
> Who wou'd then
> Converse with men
> More then his needs enforce him
> Since tedious fools
> Or boys from schools
> Are most that do discourse him
>
> These to fly
> Retired I lye
> Unknown and all unknowing
> And think't enough
> Not nonsense proof
> My own I am not shewing.[11]

The poem contains several apparent references to Swift's
involvement in recent political intrigues and to his subsequent
disappointments. His journalistic efforts on behalf of Tory causes
went unrewarded, and when he was passed over for the bishopric
he had hoped to receive and instead appointed dean of St. Patrick's
Cathedral in Dublin, Swift must indeed have felt as if he had been
dealt a cruel drubbing. There is also a reference to A Tale of a

Tub, the work that even more than his political journalism first earned him the reputation of being a misanthrope and a blasphemer.

The sentiments expressed in the first stanza are decidedly Swiftian, but apart from any possible references to Swift, of primary interest in the poem is the persona that Finch adopts. Speaking with the voice of a middle-aged man who is retiring from society, the poet recounts all the things that threaten aging men: becoming hoary grandsires whose conversational opportunities are limited to "tedious fools" and schoolboys—those "School-Boys [who] lag with Satchels in their Hands."[12] By withdrawing from society early, however (as Swift has with his forced retirement from the London cultural life he so loved), one can escape such a fate. Thus the persona is very like Swift, if not Swift himself, and by her sympathetic identification with him, Finch demonstrates the kinship that she felt with another writer who, like herself, was forced into exile for political reasons.

The most substantive literary relationship Anne Finch enjoyed during the last decade of her life was with the young Alexander Pope, yet until recently this relationship was misrepresented by virtually every critic who wrote about her.[13] The source of the misunderstanding was a key that Pope's enemies had published after the appearance in 1717 of *Three Hours After Marriage*, the play he wrote with John Gay and John Arbuthnot. That key falsely identified several of the satirical characters in the play with well-known friends of Pope, including Anne Finch, thereby giving the impression that Pope had maliciously attacked his friends. The truth, however, is that Pope admired her poetry, wrote verses in praise of it, and published her. Finch, in turn, wrote poems to him, defended him against the scurrilous charges of his detractors, and offered him strong reassurances of his genius. Both, moreover, sustained an intimate, personal friendship.

It is not known how Finch and Pope first became acquainted. No evidence exists that they knew each other when they both appeared in Tonson's *Poetical Miscellanies*. Swift's own acquaintance with Pope did not begin until early in 1713, which is the earliest verifiable date for the beginning of Finch's and Pope's friendship, so perhaps it was Swift who introduced them.[14] Another likely source for bringing these two poets together is the painter Charles Jervas.

Jervas was a close friend of Pope's, and his house was just around the corner from the Finches' Cleveland Row townhouse near St. James's Palace. By the spring of 1713 Pope had already been living for some months with Jervas, whose home became Pope's usual residence whenever he was in London.[15] Finch was certainly already acquainted with her neighbor by this time, for she praises one of his portraits in her poem "To Mr. Jervas, Occasion'd by the Sight of Mrs. Chetwind's Picture." In December of that year the poem appeared in Richard Steele's *Poetical Miscellanies*, along with another poem of hers, ascribed to "the Countess of W———." That miscellany included many of Pope's contributions, and since Finch does not appear to have been acquainted with anyone else connected with that miscellany, Pope is undoubtedly responsible for her inclusion. Moreover he did own a copy of "To Mr. Jervas" in an untitled earlier version of the poem, written in Heneage Finch's hand—further suggesting that Pope saw it before its revised published version and gave a copy to Steele.[16] (The few extant samples of Anne Finch's handwriting, incidentally, are nearly indecipherable, which is possibly why most of her poetry manuscripts are in her husband's hand.)

The same month that Steele's miscellany appeared, Pope was on cordial enough terms with Finch to dine with her and her husband—one of many such visits that would occur subsequently, for four years later he mentions the Finches in a letter to John Caryll as among the several friends he regularly visits, commenting that "All these have indispensable claims to me."[17]

An indication of the nature of the relationship between Finch and Pope in its early stages may be found in an exchange of poems they addressed to each other as the result of a friendly literary dispute. Implicit in both the tone and the subject matter of these verses is a mutual respect and trust. At some point when Pope was revising *The Rape of the Lock* for its first separate publication (4 March 1714), he showed the manuscript to Finch, apparently discussing his revisions with her and eliciting her opinions in such a manner that she felt comfortable jostling him about some antifeminist lines. The lines she took exception to are from the Cave of Spleen episode in canto 4, invoking the goddess Spleen:

> Parent of Vapors and of Female Wit,
> Who give th' *Hysteric* or *Poetic* Fit,
> On various Tempers act by various ways,
> Make some take Physick, others scribble Plays.
>
> (*TE*, 2:185, 4.59–62)

Being herself a sufferer of melancholy and noted for her poem "The Spleen," Finch must have bristled at the relationship between writing, female gender, and affected mental illness that this passage evokes.

To understand the extent of Finch's concern with a false representation of melancholy or a trivializing of female creativity, one needs briefly to consider "The Spleen." In this poem Finch carefully distinguishes between true melancholy and the feigned melancholic posturing that had become particularly fashionable among her female contemporaries. She also offers some poignant, personal lines on melancholy's destruction of her self-confidence and its debilitating effects upon her own writing:

> O'er me alas! thou dost too much prevail:
> I feel thy Force, whilst I against thee rail;
> I feel my Verse decay, and my crampt Numbers fail.
> Thro' thy black Jaundice I all Objects see,
>   As Dark, and Terrible as Thee,
> My Lines decry'd, and my Employment thought
> An useless Folly, or presumptuous Fault.[18]

Finch treats these melancholic attacks not with self-pity, but rather with a sense of moral responsibility to resist such neurotic and enervating thoughts. She links her devastating description of the crippling depression that the spleen brings upon her with the assertion that she will not submit to this malady without a battle.

Ironically Pope's own experience with melancholy was not unlike that of Finch's, for he also, like Swift, was afflicted with depression for much of his life.[19] In a letter to Swift he describes himself as being by nature "melancholy and thoughtful."[20] And elsewhere, in a letter to Judith Cowper, he comments on the splenic disposition of a mutual acquaintance, remarking on his own difficulties with this affliction and the danger of lapsing into melancholic posturing: "There is an Air of sadness about her which grieves me, and which I have learnt by experience, will increase upon an indolent (I won't say an affected) Resignation to it."[21]

Although what actually transpired during that amiable dispute between Finch and Pope can only be guessed at, we do have Pope's poetic response, which is here quoted in its entirety:

IMPROMPTU
To Lady WINCHILSEA.

Occasion'd by four Satyrical Verses
on Women-Wits, in the RAPE of the LOCK.

In vain you boast Poetick Dames of yore,
And cite those Sapphoes wee admire no more;
Fate doom'd the fall of ev'ry female Wit,
But doom'd it then when first Ardelia writ.
Of all examples by the world confest,
I knew Ardelia could not quote the best,
Who, like her Mistresse on Britannia's Throne,
Fights and subdues in quarrells not her own.
    To write their Praise you but in vain essay,
Ev'n while you write, you take that praise away,
Light to the Stars the Sun does thus restore,
But shines himselfe till they are seen no more.

                                                    (*TE*, 6:120)

It is evident from Pope's response that Finch took up the quarrel
on behalf of women writers in general, rather than arguing from
a personal position, and that the debate was conducted in good
humor. Citing women writers of the past, Finch had quarrelled
with Pope's trivializing of "Female Wit," but in the opening lines
of his "Impromptu" Pope subtly undermines her defense of female
poetic authority by dismissing these female authors as "Sapphoes
wee admire no more." He then continues in the next lines to
attribute "the fall of ev'ry female Wit" to Ardelia's having eclipsed
every other woman writer by the brilliance of her own talent. As
Valerie Rumbold correctly observes, here, as elsewhere, Pope
avoids the real issue of the legitimacy and worth of women's writing and resorts instead to what she terms "the method of gallantry."[22] Yet despite this evasiveness, his compliments to Finch
appear genuine.

Of particular interest in the "Impromptu" is the analogy he
draws between Finch and Queen Anne; in taking up the quarrel
on behalf of other women writers, she is, Pope asserts, like "her
Mistresse on Britannia's Throne," fighting and subduing "in quarrells not her own." Thus Finch's poetic accomplishments are likened to Queen Anne's military and political successes. In
analogously citing the female monarch's political authority and
prowess as a military leader, Pope thereby imbues Finch with
authority and power to write as a woman. In fact this particular
construction of the monarch as a figure of female authority on
women's behalf was used by a number of female writers during
the reign of Queen Anne.[23] Even though Pope was not willing to
take a stand on the value of women writers in general, it appears
that he was willing to assert the worth of this particular woman

poet and to back up his assertions with efforts to attain publication for her.

Finch responded with a poem of her own, "The Answer [to Pope's Impromptu]," which employs some of Pope's own strategies of evasion and extravagant compliment. The poem's opening lines both set the tone and the direction that her "answer" will take:

> Disarm'd with so genteel an airs
>   The contest I give o'er;
> Yet, Alexander, have a care,
>   And shock the sex no more.[24]

Finch puts aside the issue of literary authority for women by declaring at the outset that she concedes the contest. She does not, however, indicate any alteration in her views nor any capitulation to Pope's logic; indeed, it is not the force of his arguments that has caused her temporarily to turn from the issue, but his "genteel ... air," that very gallantry that he used in his "Impromptu" as a diversionary technique. Once that is established, Finch then chastises Pope for his antifeminist satire, recounting as a warning the tale of the mythical Orpheus and his fate. He, too, like Pope, was a poet who incensed women with his "scoffing rhimes," only to be torn to pieces by the avenging Thracian Maenads, his severed head left floating down the Hebrus toward the sea. But Finch reassures Pope that he will not share Orpheus's fate, humorously alluding to *The Rape of the Lock*:

> But you our follies gently treat,
>   And spin so fine the thread,
> You need not fear his aukward fate,
>   The lock wo'n't cost the head.[25]

After some commendatory lines Finch admonishes Pope within the remainder of the poem to take more care not to offend female egos. "Sooth[e] the Ladies," he is advised, for even she herself, Finch admits, has her share of pride. Thus the poem remains throughout, from its opening affectionate address to him as "Alexander" to its concluding confession and mild reproof, a testament to the confident, if gently bantering, nature of their friendship.

It appears that this was not the only poetic dispute over gender issues that Finch and Pope were involved in during this period, nor the only time that they took to verse to argue their positions.

Each wrote an epilogue to Nicholas Rowe's *The Tragedy of Jane Shore*, which was first performed at Drury Lane Theatre on 2 February 1714. Though Rowe was an acquaintance of both poets, neither epilogue was ever published with the play nor spoken in the theater.

Why Pope's epilogue was not included in the publication and the performance of this play has long puzzled scholars, particularly since Rowe requested the epilogue and Pope thought enough of it to include it in the 1717 edition of his *Works*. Norman Ault offers the most feasible explanation. Arguing that if Rowe himself were responsible for the rejection of the epilogue he would hardly have been able to retain the friendship of the easily offended Pope, Ault concludes that the actress Mrs. Oldfield is the most likely source for the poem's rejection.[26] Anne Oldfield, who portrayed Jane Shore in Rowe's play, was as widely noted for her beauty as for her numerous love affairs. When she had starred in Joseph Addison's *The Tragedy of Cato* the previous year, her pregnancy from a recent amorous entanglement was so far advanced that as a precautionary measure a midwife was kept in attendance at the theater.[27] It was at the time of those performances, while Oldfield was playing the part of Cato's naive, young daughter, that Pope first offended her by writing and circulating a satirical epigram pointing out some obvious differences between the actress and the character she was portraying.[28] Therefore she would certainly have been alert to any derisive nuances in Pope's most recent epigram. Moreover, as Ault observes, the wording of Pope's subtitle, "Design'd for Mrs. Oldfield," which deviates in phrasing from any other epilogue titles of the time, suggests in its peculiarly ambiguous wording that the lines were designed not to be spoken by Mrs. Oldfield, but, rather, designed with her in mind.[29]

The first fourteen lines of Pope's epilogue are addressed to women and recall the final words Rowe offers to his audience in his own epilogue to his play: "Be kind at last, and pity poor Jane Shore."[30] Pope's opening lines, in contrast, sarcastically express amazement that Jane Shore should expect to find any mercy from her own sex:

> Prodigious this! the Frail one of our Play
> From her own sex should mercy find to day!
> You might have held the pretty head aside,
> Peep'd in your fans, been serious, thus, and cry'd,
> The Play may pass—but that strange creature, *Shore*,
> I can't—indeed now—I so hate a whore—

Just as a blockhead rubs his thoughtless skull,
And thanks his stars he was not born a fool;
So from a sister sinner you shall hear,
"How strangely you expose your self, my dear!"

(*TE*, 6:113, 1–10)

Pope's epilogue is condescending to women, implying that they are frivolous, hypocritical creatures who, like the blockhead who smugly rejoices that "he was not born a fool," self-righteously condemn Shore though they themselves are equally guilty of sin. But when Pope deflects his words onto the actress who portrays the whore on the stage, he heightens the incongruity between the real-life situation and the theatrical representation, thereby creating a devastating tension. This is particularly evident when Oldfield is made to comment: "So from a sister sinner you shall hear, / 'How strangely you expose your self, my dear!'"—as Oldfield, too, is exposing herself. Small wonder if the actress balked at reciting Pope's epilogue from the stage.

The poem continues its commentary on "virtuous ladies" who express indignation at the wicked ways of Shore, suggesting that they may themselves have their own "reserve" of such vices as wrath and gluttony. From this examination of women's probable responses to the moral character of Shore, the epilogue then moves to the responses of men. Directly addressing the males in the audience, the actress/persona advises them that if their own preferred vices are both culinary and sexual, they should choose their female companions accordingly: "Wou'd you enjoy soft nights and solid dinners? / Faith, gallants, board with saints, and bed with sinners" (114, ll. 23–24).

The poem turns next to Jane Shore's husband, who in the play displays remarkable charity and forgives his wife her transgressions. He is, Pope writes, a "kind cuckold" who "might instruct the City" (l. 42), implying sardonically that most contemporary wives are unfaithful and have made cuckolds of their husbands. And the concluding six lines of the poem are again addressed to women:

If, after all, you think it a disgrace,
That *Edward*'s Miss thus perks it in your face,
To see a piece of failing flesh and blood,
In all the rest so impudently good:
Faith, let the modest matrons of the town,
Come here in crowds, and stare the strumpet down.

(45–50)

In other words, the poet, speaking through the persona of the actress, has tried to convince the females in the audience that Jane Shore is no more immoral than most contemporary British women. But if he has failed, he writes, then these "modest matrons" should come to the theater in crowds to "stare the strumpet down." And again, this final admonition, spoken by Oldfield, increases the tension that the poem has created in the dichotomy between the theatrical world and the real world, between the dramatic presentation of a strumpet and the real-life strumpet who portrays her.

Anne Finch's poem "An Epilogue to the Tragedy of Jane Shore," bearing the subtitle "To be spoken by Mrs. Oldfield the night before the Poet's Day," is in several ways uncharacteristic of Finch. It is, for example, more strongly feminist in a modern-day sense than any other poem of hers.[31] It is also the only epilogue that she ever wrote for another author's play.[32] Moreover, the tone of this poem creates the effect of a polemical offensive, as if it were part of an ongoing dialogue and a response to something beyond the play itself. This reaction is also suggested by the fact that it was not written prior to opening night nor intended for all performances, but only for one particular night. Furthermore, the type of moralistic stance frequently adopted by the respectable, aristocratic Finch, noted for her piety, is absent here. Unlike "The Prodigy" or "Ardelia's Answer to Ephelia," poems in which Finch excoriates women as well as men for their abandonment of the traditional values of chastity and marital fidelity, this epilogue sets up a male/female dichotomy and quarrels with a distinctly patriarchal view of women, even to the point of defending an acknowledged adultress. The most probable explanation for this poem's polemical peculiarities is that Finch had read Pope's epilogue for *Jane Shore*, had discussed with him its subsequent rejection by Anne Oldfield, and then had written her own epilogue as part of a continuing dialogue.

Unlike Pope, Finch objects not so much to Jane Shore's appeal for pity, but rather to the playwright's characterization of her as a whining, simpering woman. Her poem's persona is not at all satiric about Anne Oldfield and actually assumes much of the actress's character, even to the point of having her declare that had she known more fully what the play was like before promising to act the part, she would "have staid at home, and drank my tea."[33] The epilogue's persona also complains that in the play Shore's husband is brought in "To hear her own and aggravate her fault" and asserts that the playwright "must be mad" to have Shore confess her affair.[34]

In putting these lines in the mouth of an actress widely noted for her promiscuous behavior, Finch, like Pope, plays off the audience's awareness of the dichotomy between the world of the stage and the world of reality, except that here the two momentarily overlap. Unlike Pope's epilogue, Finch's identifies sympathetically with the actress. Finch here criticizes the difference between moral values for women and those for men—the very double standard Pope employs to make Oldfield condemn herself. And Finch turns the tables, allowing this woman of questionable character to speak in defense of both Jane Shore and herself.

Although both poets respond to Jane Shore's repentant mode in the play, and specifically to her plea for the audience's pity, Finch's reactions differ from Pope's. Finch takes offense at Rowe's patronizing tone toward Shore, particularly in his epilogue, and her satiric jabs are never aimed at Oldfield nor at women in general. Finch has Oldfield define how she would have preferred Jane Shore to be portrayed in the play: Shore should be able to continue "lavish, careless, gay and fine," not to grovel and whine in repentance.[35] Oldfield, in the lines Finch has written for her, would not have the audience come to stare down the "strumpet," as Pope would have it, nor would she have the audience condescend to Shore with their pity, as Rowe would have it.

In Finch's epilogue, Oldfield becomes a spokesperson for women's equality and for abandoning the discrepancies in standards of gender-specific behavior. She berates the playwright for showing Shore only in her time of disgrace, after she has lost her youthful beauty, rather than "In the first triumphs of her blooming age."[36] Through a progression of epithets worthy of being quoted at length, the epilogue satirically contrasts the fate of aging women with the fate of men:

> There is a season, which too fast approaches,
> And every list'ning beauty nearly touches;
> When handsome Ladies, falling to decay,
> Pass thro' new epithets to smooth the way:
> From *fair* and *young* transportedly confess'd,
> Dwindle to *fine, well fashion'd,* and *well dress'd.*
> Thence as their fortitude's extremest proof,
> To *well as yet;* from *well* to *well enough;*
> Till having on such weak foundation stood,
> Deplorably at last they sink to *good.*
> Abandon'd then, 'tis time to be retir'd,

And seen no more, when not alas! admir'd.
By men indeed a better fate is known.
The pretty fellow that has youth outgrown,
Who nothing knew, but how his cloaths did sit,
Transforms to a *Free-thinker* and a *Wit*;
At Operas becomes a skill'd Musician;
Ends in a partyman and politician;
Maintains some figure, while he keeps his breath,
And is a fop of consequence till death.[37]

Both Jane Shore and Anne Oldfield are given the opportunity by Finch to exonerate themselves. Moreover, Finch corrects whatever harmful images of women she thinks the playwright perpetuates through his characterization of Jane Shore. In the final words that Oldfield speaks in Finch's epilogue, she indicates that she would have preferred to show the pleasant, joyful, attractive Jane Shore, but if the audience prefers to see her sorrowful, they should come the following day for the Poet's Day performance. For if the playwright has a full house, he will certainly not be convinced to "fast and pray" about his negative portrayal of women, about what he "makes us women do or say." Pope concludes his epilogue with a suggestion that crowds of women attend the following day to "stare the strumpet down," as a way of making a statement regarding their disapproval of Shore's (and Oldfield's) character. Finch, however, suggests that filling the theater the next day would *not* be the way to convince the playwright to correct his erroneous portrayal of women; instead, what she calls for, at least by implication, is a general female boycott of Rowe's play.

Finch wrote two additional poems to Pope. In one of them, titled simply "To Mr. Pope," she takes a stance that suggests an older, worldly-wise aunt who is both protective and supportive in offering advice to the brilliant protégé who has recently embarked on a literary career. Its reference to *Windsor Forest,* which was published in 1713, would also help date it to some time early in their friendship. Cast in heroic couplets, most likely as a tribute to Pope, the poem offers generous praise and some rather sententious advice on how to deal with the envy and malicious criticism that fame can bring. Even though the poem is not particularly noteworthy, Pope thought enough of it to include it as one of the customary commendatory poems in the first collected edition of his works.

Of far more interest is "The Mastif and Curs, A Fable inscribed to Mr Pope," which Pope included in the 1717 miscellany he edited, along with a very generous selection of Finch's poems, all bearing proper attribution.[38] Strongly evident in this fable is the mutual affection between this aging poet, now in her midfifties, and the widely acknowledged young star of the literary scene, still in his twenties. Finch depicts Pope as the strong English "masty" who must bear the spiteful, petty attacks of sneaky lapdogs:

> The little dogs by ladies kept
> Who snarl or flatter for reward.[39]

Though they throw their "dirt and scandal" on him, none, she writes, dare "fasten on his skin," for they all recognize his "greater strength." When someone questions the mastif about why he endures these attacks, he replies:

> Tis fit that some account I yield,
> Why I'm so slow to take the field;
> Or to employ my well known pow'r,
> Such carping vermin to devour.
> But whilst I keep them all in awe,
> From their assaults this good I draw;
> To make you men the diff'rence see,
> Between this bawling troop, and me.
> Comparison your observation stirs,
> I were no masty if there were no curs.[40]

Finch's "The Mastif and Curs" presents Pope as a highly principled man, one in whom "Candor with resolution join'd."[41] While its date of composition is not known, internal evidence suggests that it was written later than the other poems that Finch provided him, and most likely shortly before Pope published it. That period was marked by so many vituperous attacks on him, ranging from charges of indecency to ingratitude and treachery, that George Sherburn calls 1716 a "lamentable year" in Pope's life.[42] Finch's strong defense of him in this poem is therefore understandable. The voice behind these verses is that of a tried, steadfast friend, and the sympathy expressed for the falsely maligned poet is intimate, not detached. It is the sort of poem that could never have been written by a casual acquaintance.

Finch recognized in Pope, as she did in Swift, a writer who, like herself, was in many ways a displaced figure. Aware that her gender excluded her from much of London's intellectual society, she felt a natural empathy with the physically deformed Pope and once reminded him fondly in verse that though "short of beauty of [his] own," he was a literary giant.[43] Both, in addition, were afflicted for much of their lives with a chronic nervous disorder and probably identified with aspects of each other's temperament.

Finch and Pope shared other similarities in their personal lives. Though accepted into some aristocratic circles, they were both nevertheless marginalized people, alienated from the mainstream of society and at odds with the dominant values of the time. In their poetry, as in their lives, discourses on politics were closely intertwined with discussions of religion. And because of their political and religious ideologies, both were denied many of their civil rights.

The oaths of allegiance and supremacy imposed under William III had given rise to the Nonjuring movement within the Church of England, which had political as well as theological implications. Anne Finch and her husband were both very active Nonjurors who had much to fear from the government, particularly with the new Jacobite uprisings that followed the death of Queen Anne and the collapse of the Tory government.[44] Because of his continued refusal to take the oaths following his accession to the peerage in 1712, Heneage Finch, now Lord Winchilsea, was not even permitted to take his seat in the House of Lords.

While Finch suffered for her religious principles, Pope's persecution for his faith was even greater. As a Roman Catholic he also refused the oaths of allegiance, and, like Finch's husband, could not hold public office, but Pope also could not vote, attend a public school or university, pursue a career in law, or live within ten miles of London. Moreover, the severity of anti-Catholic laws increased following the death of Queen Anne.[45]

One final poetic tribute to the supportive and nurturing relationship that Pope and Finch enjoyed comes from John Gay. In 1720, shortly before Finch's death, Pope completed the arduous task that he had been working on for years—his translation of the *Iliad*. To celebrate his completion, Gay wrote "Mr. Pope's Welcome from Greece," a poem that describes the friends who appear to welcome Pope back from his lengthy metaphoric journey to Greece. And there, waiting on the quay, Gay writes, is "Winchilsea, still meditating song."[46]

In both Pope and Swift Finch found enlightened men who did not dismiss her poetry simply because it was, as she bitterly noted in her poem "The Introduction," "by a Woman writt."[47] And she, in turn, felt a bond with these two writers whom she recognized as similarly displaced figures. They helped ease her admittance into the masculine world of eighteenth-century English letters.

They nurtured her talent, they wrote poems celebrating her verse, and they offered her their friendship. And she reciprocated.

Notes

1. Anne Finch, countess of Winchilsea, *The Poems of Anne Countess of Winchilsea*, ed. Myra Reynolds (Chicago: University of Chicago Press, 1903), 8. The remark is from the prose preface Finch affixed to the privately circulated folio manuscript of her poems, first published in 1903 in the still-standard though incomplete edition of her works.

2. For biographical information on Finch see Barbara McGovern, *Anne Finch and Her Poetry: A Critical Biography* (Athens: University of Georgia Press, 1992).

3. Richard Steele, *The Tatler* (London: Dent, 1953), No. 10.

4. Jonathan Swift, *The Account Books of Jonathan Swift,* transcribed and intro. by Paul Thompson and Dorothy Jay Thompson (Newark: University of Delaware Press, 1984), 60; Swift, *Corresp.,* 1:121.

5. Finch had had some poems, primarily songs and religious verse, published in scattered miscellanies, but these were all anonymous.

6. The Williams edition, which uses the 1713 printing of this poem with "A——" beginning the final line, indicates that "A Whig" occurs in the 1727 edition. Swift, who had already become a Tory by the time this poem was first published, understandably deleted the reference to his recent Whig affiliation.

7. Barber was a royal printer to Queen Anne during the last four years of her reign. For additional information on Barber's friendship with Swift see the following: J. Alan Downie, *Jonathan Swift: Political Writer* (London: Routledge and Kegan Paul, 1984), 175; and Ehrenpreis, 2:610, 633–35.

8. Ehrenpreis, 2:471, 644, and 680; Fidelis Morgan, *A Woman of No Character: An Autobiography of Mrs. Manley* (London: Faber and Faber, 1986), 18 and 174.

9. The poem in vol. 1 of *New Atalantis* is "Progress of Life." Vol. 2 contains "The Hymn," and "The Sigh" appears in *Court Intrigues*. See my *Anne Finch and Her Poetry,* 120–21, for a discussion of the Finch-Manley relationship.

10. I am currently editing this manuscript for the University of Georgia Press. Selections from this manuscript, hereafter referred to as the Wellesley Manuscript, are quoted by permission of Wellesley College, Margaret Clapp Library, from its English Poetry Collection.

11. Wellesley Manuscript, 96.

12. The quotation is from one of Swift's best-known poems, "A Description of the Morning," written during the same year as "*Apollo* Outwitted." See *Poems,* 1:125, l. 18.

13. For a detailed account of their relationship that corrects the conventional and misleading view, see my *Anne Finch and Her Poetry,* 102–7.

14. For a discussion of the early friendship between Swift and Pope see Mack, 195–99.

15. Ibid., 226–27.

16. BL Add. MSS 4807. Finch's poem appears on the back of Pope's transcription of part of the eleventh book of *The Iliad*. Pope, ever the paper-saver, frequently used the backs of letters and other manuscripts for writing drafts of his poems.

17. Pope's letter to John Caryll dated 15 December [1713] recounts an evening

of dining with Finch (Pope, *Corresp.*, 1:203–4. The later letter, acknowledging his frequent visits to the Winchilsea household, is also to Caryll and is dated 6 August 1717 (*Corresp.*, 1:417–18).

18. Finch, *Poems*, 248, ll. 74–80.

19. References to Swift's bouts of melancholy are scattered throughout his letters: for example, *Corresp.*, 2: 360–61, 392, 429–30; 3:382.

20. Ibid., 2:480.

21. Ibid., 2:202.

22. Valerie Rumbold, *Women's Place in Pope's World* (Cambridge: Cambridge University Press, 1989), 151–52.

23. This theme is explored in Carol Barash's "'The Native Liberty . . . of the Subject': Configurations of Gender and Authority in the Works of Chudleigh, Egerton, and Astell," in *Women, Writing, History 1640–1740*, ed. Isobel Grundy and Susan Wiseman (Athens: University of Georgia Press, 1992), 55–69.

24. Finch, *Poems*, 102, ll. 1–4.

25. Ibid., 103, ll. 25–28.

26. Norman Ault, *New Light on Pope: With Some Additions to His Poetry Hitherto Unknown* (1949; reprint, Archon Books, 1967), 133–38.

27. Mack, 235.

28. George Sherburn, *The Early Career of Alexander Pope* (New York: 1934; reprint, Russell, 1963), 124; Mack, 234–35 and 859n. Though the epigram, titled "On Cato," is included in the Twickenham edition under the section of poems of doubtful authority, both Sherburn and Mack argue strongly for its authenticity.

29. Ault, *New Light on Pope*, 136.

30. Nicholas Rowe, *The Tragedy of Jane Shore*, ed. Harry William Pedicord (Lincoln: University of Nebraska Press, 1974), 75.

31. The only possible exception is "The Unequal Fetters," which is a response to the *carpe diem* convention and particularly to Robert Herrick's "To the Virgins, to Make Much of Time." A discussion of this poem may be found in my *Anne Finch and Her Poetry*, 48–50.

32. Finch's own play, *Aristomenes: Or, The Royal Shepherd*, contains an epilogue.

33. Finch, *Poems*, 100, ll. 15–17.

34. Ibid., ll. 19, 26.

35. Ibid., l. 13.

36. Ibid., l. 6.

37. Ibid., 101, ll. 27–46.

38. This poem is not included in the Reynolds edition of Finch's collected poems.

39. *Pope's Own Miscellany, Being a Reprint of Poems on Several Occasions, 1717, Containing New Poems by Alexander Pope and Others*, ed. Norman Ault (London: Nonesuch Press, 1935), 131, ll. 10–11.

40. Ibid., 132–33, ll. 45–54.

41. Ibid., 131, l. 8.

42. Sherburn, *Early Career of Pope*, 183. For an account of the numerous attacks upon Pope during that year, see pp. 149–85.

43. "To Mr. Pope," *Poems*, 105, l. 38.

44. Though the term *nonjuror* was not necessarily synonymous with *Jacobite*, for all practical purposes there was little distinction between the two. As Paul Kléber Monod observes, "In an age that took oaths very seriously, Nonjuring was

a very strong political statement" (*Jacobitism and the English People, 1688–1788* [Cambridge: Cambridge University Press, 1989], 139).

45. For a discussion of anti-Catholicism in Pope's time see John M. Aden, *Pope's Once and Future Kings: Satire and Politics in the Early Career* (Knoxville: University of Tennessee Press, 1978), 3–20. Patricia Bruckmann offers an account of Catholics in England during the reign of William and Mary in "Catholicism in England," in *The Age of William III & Mary II: Power, Politics and Patronage, 1688–1702*, ed. Robert P. Maccubbin and Martha Hamilton-Phillips (Williamsburg: College of William and Mary, 1988), 82–88. Monod offers another account that includes subsequent years as well (Ibid., 132–38).

46. John Gay, *Poems of John Gay*, ed. John Underhill, 2 vols. (London: Routledge, 1983), 1:210, st. 6.

47. *Poems*, 4, l. 8.

The Manl(e)y Style: Delariviere Manley and Jonathan Swift

MELINDA ALLIKER RABB

DURING the first decade of the eighteenth century, Delariviere Manley and Jonathan Swift independently published their first important prose satires: Manley's *Secret History of Queen Zarah and the Zarazians* (1705) and *New Atalantis* (1709), and Swift's *Tale of a Tub* and *Battle of the Books* (1704). Manley's *New Atalantis* was one of the period's most popular narratives, although modern critics, until very recently, have hesitated to confront its interpretive possibilities or its distinctive ironic style.[1]

What critical or theoretical approach will confer significance upon the amorous escapades of now-forgotten Whigs and obscure nobility made even more obscure by the apparatus of the *roman à clef*? Feminist efforts at recovering and rereading texts by women have included Manley to a degree. Most of the commentary on her work, however, has been biographical or has been based on theories about the early novel and its origins such as for example, the relationship between romance, *roman à clef,* scandal chronicle, and epistolary narrative. The overriding question has been about her role in the rise of the novel. Ros Ballaster's *Seductive Fictions,* a study of Behn, Haywood, and Manley, takes this point of departure. The perspective of this essay is not on Manley primarily as a writer of amatory fiction, but as a political satirist. Gwendolyn Needham's prescient article of 1949 establishes a beginning, as does Ballaster's recent article on the female satirist. Manley's association with Swift is not her claim to fame but a means of seeing her accomplishments more clearly and of correcting some old misconceptions in Swift studies. This critical discussion also will propose a way of reading Manley as a satirist, using as illustrative texts the *New Atalantis*, the *Examiner* (1711), and *A True Narrative of what pass'd at the Examination of the Marquis De Guiscard* (1711).

Like Swift, Manley was concerned with abuses of power. She

too became a Tory propagandist, and in fact she preceded Swift in this allegiance. But ultimately partisan politics give way in much of her work (as in Swift's) to more inclusive criticism of human nature. The *New Atalantis*'s success is well known.[2] Belinda's immortal lock remains "as long as *Atalantis* shall be read," according to Pope's *Rape of the Lock*.[3] Her first satire on Sarah Churchill, duchess of Marlborough (1704) is subtitled "a Looking-Glass for ――― in the Kingdom of Albigion [England]." This figure—the "Glass" of satire, "wherein Beholders do generally discover every body's Face but their Own" (Swift's famous definition in the *Battle of the Books*[4])—is a suggestive rhetorical coincidence and exemplifies the metaphorical slippage from specific to general satire that characterizes both writers' works. Broadly significant conventions, such as the naively dangerous gaze of Narcissus and Eve at their own reflections, become occasions for more complicated irony. The ambiguous cipher of the mirror, the blank that can be filled infinitely, that conflates contradictions like truth and distortion or self-knowledge and blind vanity, suggests a more extensive congeniality between the two authors.

Swift scholars have not been eager to see this relationship. Unlike the Scriblerian associations, Swift's involvement with the woman who wrote the century's most popular scandal chronicle has been minimally recognized. Yet a relationship undoubtedly exists. They jointly edited and wrote the Tory *Examiner*.[5] They were propagandists but not hacks who put themselves at risk for political causes. Both experienced the efficacy and liability of satiric attacks during Queen Anne's reign. Both created compelling satiric fictions whose sometimes reckless energies could subsume particular historical people and specific corruptions of power. Both committed a variety of fictive indulgences and excesses not strictly justified by their ostensible subjects. Both wrote provocatively of physicality, so that the biological demands of the body become a satiric vehicle. They also shared the real consequences of the fate of the Tory ministry in the form of personal losses both material and idealistic. Sufficient trust and respect must have existed between them to permit Manley's reliance on Swift in her legal will. This document requests "my much honoured friend the Dean of St. Patrick's Jonathan Swift . . . as he was privy to this promise" to "aid and assist" her sisters in obtaining the income never paid to her.[6]

Manley's claims as a satirist are significant, although her portrayal of "love" has dominated critical memory. In *The Rise of the Woman Novelist*, for example, Jane Spencer argues that Aphra

Behn "widened the woman writer's scope," whereas Manley "declared that love was the only subject for a woman."[7] She has a reputation for frankness about female sexuality that may distract readers from her irony: Elizabeth Barry, the actress who played the lead in *The Royal Mischief* (1696) and who "had an unrivalled reputation in smouldering tragic parts," thought certain lines from the play too "warm" to say on stage and at first refused the role.[8] And Manley's autobiographical fiction, *The Adventures of Rivella*, in which male readers confuse the body of the text with the body of its author, contributes to the writer-as-seducer pose.

But the steamy scenes of sex and seduction should not cloud our critical judgment. Five years before Swift had the price of three hundred pounds put on his head for publishing *The Public Spirit of the Whigs* (1714), Manley had already been arrested for seditious libel and incarcerated in the Tower for publishing the first volume of the *New Atalantis*.[9] She defended herself wryly at her examination by insisting that the work was all a romantic fiction. She was released, although few readers could have missed the irony of love in Atalantis. The narrator Intelligence exclaims: "O let me ease my Spleen! I shall burst with Laughter; these are prosperous Times for Vice."[10] When volume 2 of the *New Atalantis* appeared, a verse on the frontispiece asserts Manley's purpose: "O Sacred Truth inspire and rule my Rage, / So may reforming Satir mend a vicious Age." In the *New Atalantis*, the countess who steals Charlot's lover says that "Love shou'd only be a handle towards . . . Interest, and Establishment in the World" (1:345). Desire and power (the desire for power/the power of desire) have persistent political resonance in Manley's eroticism.

Romance plots could serve the ends of political satire, as Manley's contemporaries seem to have understood. She was imprisoned not because the *New Atalantis* was considered lewd but because it criticized the Whig ministry so effectively. Lady Mary Wortley Montagu remarks:

> I am very glad you have the second part of the *New Atalantis;* if you have read it, will you be so good as to send it me? I promise to get you the Key to it. I know I can. But do you know what has happened to the unfortunate authoress? People are offended at the liberty she uses in her memoirs, and she is taken into custody. Miserable is the fate of writers: if they are agreeable, they are offensive; and if dull, they starve. I lament the loss of the other parts which we should have had; . . . after this, who will dare to give the history of *Angela* [London]? . . . [N]ow she [Manley] will serve as a scarecrow to frighten people from attempting anything but heavy panegyric.[11]

Arthur Mainwaring, the Whig M.P. who read the *New Atalantis* for the duchess of Marlborough (she was afraid to read the attacks on herself that her friends were gossiping about), attacks the "nauseous" book but is forced to admit its satirical efficacy: "Yet I am afraid it will be very difficult to cure the mischief," he concludes, even if they take (and they did) legal action.[12]

Thus exclamatory passages, like this one from the *New Atalantis*—"Glorious Destiny, cry'd he, with a transported Tone, by what means, Fortune, hast thou made me thy happy Darling?" (1:307)—were understood by readers like Montagu and the Marlboroughs as political in purpose and clearly antithetical to earnest panegyrics about the delights of love. Swift called Manley's *Memoirs of Europe* "noble." When he criticized the florid style ("It seems to me, as if she had about two thousand epithets and fine words packed up in a bag; and that she pulled them out by handfuls, and strewed them on her paper") he was consoling Addison, whose satiric portrait as Maro they both recognized.[13]

Manley could and did switch at will to a lean style, what she calls "the short and the long on't, in plain, downright Terms" (1:423). The country-woman's narrative in the *New Atalantis*, like certain dialogue in her heroic plays and elsewhere, is designed to reduce the inflated pretensions of love. Her contemporaries may have indulged her stylistic excesses as part of her fictional claim to be merely translating from Italian—a "warmer" language than English. The repetitive plots of desire, seduction, and betrayal have clear political analogues to power-mongering in high places. Characters, identified in the famous "Keys," almost always have "real-life" counterparts among well-known political, social, or literary figures of her day. Yet the men and women who enact the amours hardly seem "real." The artificiality of her characters is intended to make them seem what she ironically implies they are—not fully human.

Curiosity about Manley's life has far exceeded criticism of her work, as if her bigamous marriage, pregnancy, abandonment, and later affairs could "explain" her work sufficiently. Various attempts have been made to downplay Swift's collaboration and friendship. His biographers and editors, if they deal with Manley, typically confuse the work with the woman and the woman with her sexuality. An example of this confusion informs Irvin Ehrenpreis's *Swift: The Man, His Works, and The Age.*[14] Ehrenpreis, who must frequently acknowledge Manley during the years 1710–14, is unable to mention her without a reference either to her body or to her sex life.

Ehrenpreis claims that "it was part of Swift's worldly good manners, among gentlemen [sic] of fashion" to tolerate "a kept mistress like Mrs. Manley" (2:45–46). She is, at different points, called "the plump Mary Manley (2:680),"[15] "Barber's mistress," "the scandal-writer" (2:644), and "inelegant" author (2:527). He endorses Swift's remark to Stella (a remark that we may read as motivated by a desire to placate Stella, see below) that Manley is "very homely and very fat," but dismisses Swift's praise of her "very generous principles" (*Journal to Stella*) as "Pickwickian." He also claims that "before John Barber installed the plump Mary Manley as his mistress, she had obliged Captain [Sir Richard] Steele with her choicest favours." None of Manley's biographers, who are certainly interested in her affairs, finds any basis for this gratuitous slur.[16] Rather, Ehrenpreis has misconstrued a comment by Steele about his literary disputes with Manley.[17] Perhaps the most interesting way in which Ehrenpreis maneuvers history to marginalize the woman is his celebration of John Barber, printer, financial agent, and alderman of the City of London:

> Although Swift often visited Barber, dined with him, and employed him as a financial agent, he usually suppresses his name, and calls him "a friend in the City," because it would have been ruinous for them if anyone could prove that Swift wrote the libellous pamphlets that Barber printed. Their friendship and mutual trust grew, I think, far deeper than anyone has realized; and Swift extended this trust to include Barber's mistress, the scandal-writer Mary de la Rivière Manley, who, in her editorship of the *Examiner* and other propaganda for the ministry, would often take her orders from Swift himself. (2:644)

Ehrenpreis implies that Swift became attached to Barber and then tolerated his "mistress." But Manley's biographers have shown that it was she who introduced Swift to Barber.[18] And further, the evidence about Manley's life suggests that she may not have been Barber's mistress, although she and her sister did live with him and have business dealings with him.[19] Perhaps *she* is the "friend in the City" with whom Swift frequently dined. In Ehrenpreis's construction, a passive Manley is "installed" for the convenience of superior men, sexually serving Barber and "taking her orders" from "Swift himself."

Ehrenpreis argues that Swift did not want Esther Vanhomrigh (Vanessa) to follow him to Letcombe by traveling with John Barber (Swift, *Corresp.*, 2:96–97) because "[t]he notion of a respectable gentlewoman's making such a trip with Mrs. Manley's keeper shocked Swift" (2:749). Such insinuating squeamishness is unfounded, either in the letter cited by Ehrenpreis or elsewhere. Manley is never mentioned by Swift in this context; he simply does not want Vanessa to bother him in Berkshire. We know from the correspondence that in London Vanessa visited Barber (and thus Manley) without compunction[20] and that Manley had dined at the Vanhomrighs with Swift.[21] Vanessa and Barber exchanged letters, and Barber held her jewels in pawn until after her death (Swift, *Corresp.*, 2:360).

The modern editor of the *Examiner*, Herbert Davis, is also uncomfortable with Manley. In the *Journal to Stella* Swift refers to *Examiner* papers "written by a woman" and to other political essays "by the same woman."[22] This reference has been misconstrued as derogatory. Davis dismisses Manley's contribution with this quotation from the *Journal*: "No, I don't like anything in the Examiner after the 45th, except the first part of the 46th; all the rest is trash; and if *you* like them . . . your judgment is spoiled by ill company and want of reading" (*JS*, 1:315, emphasis added). Swift is mostly annoyed that Stella has not noticed the change of authorship and irked that she likes some essays that are not his. More recent critical assessment of Manley's work in the *Examiner* and in numerous other Tory pamphlets has been slight. Davis finds it "strange . . . that [Manley's *Examiners*] were allowed to be included in the fifth volume of the collected works, printed by Faulkner in 1738," (Swift, *Prose*, 3:xxvii). Swift tells Stella that Manley wrote *A Learned Comment upon Dr. Hare's Excellent Sermon*, a pro-peace pamphlet, "only hints sent to the printer from Presto, to give her" (Swift, *Prose*, 3:xxxiii). From this remark Davis creates an imaginary and condescending rationalization for her authorship:

> [Swift] *may well have* sent to the printer a copy of the original sermon with his own comments in the margin; and this material *would have been* used by Mrs Manley. . . . The passages from Hare's sermon which are quoted and answered were *probably* those marked by Swift. . . . For instance, all that Swift *probably* wrote opposite the first passage he comments on, was "is this sense or truth?" And opposite the words, "if we be content to wait His Leisure" he *may have* written the query "God's or Marlborough's?" *Perhaps* a sentence like this was suggested by Swift: "But if he means the present Ministry, it is certain they could find their own Interest in continuing the War as well as other People; their Capacities are no less, nor their Fortunes so great, neither need they be at a loss how to follow in a path so well-beaten." (Swift, *Prose*, 3:xxxiii–xxxiv; emphasis added)

But what Swift "may well have" done or "probably" did or "perhaps" suggested is an editorial musing that has no critical weight. The extent of Davis's attempt to deny Manley's authorship may be a backhanded tribute to the quality of the essays in question. If they are good, he implies, surely a woman could not have written them alone. Why should "hints" among the Scriblerians be creative interchange and possible hints to a woman be grounds to undermine her authority?

There really is no basis for believing that Manley was not given license to write as she pleased, to cook things up in her own style, as Swift says elsewhere. Manley is a deliberate writer; even her excesses in the erotic works cannot be construed as the involuntary outpourings of an amorous woman. She has her own style of irony. Robert Adams Day describes Manley as "a woman who writes with an unusually masculine ironic style, and knows it."[23] Patricia Koster reports a computer study revealing "that under all the exclamation points [Manley's style] has some quantitative resemblance to that of Swift" (1:xxii).

The view of Manley implied by Swift's *Journal to Stella* (the text most often cited with reference to their relationship) needs reinterpretation.[24] Although readers have valued the journal as a record of the rise and fall of the Tory ministry under Queen Anne, it also is an interesting record of Swift's private manipulation of Stella. We know that there are many things he does not tell her, such as his important involvement with Vanessa. And it would not be surprising if Swift wished to downplay his relationship with a woman of so famous and so tarnished a reputation as the author of the *New Atalantis*. "I dined with people you never heard of, nor is it worth your while to know; an authoress and a printer." Silence and evasion can be telling. Swift elsewhere mentions dining at John Barber's (the "friend in the City" whom Ehrenpreis assumes must be Barber and not Manley), but often omits the fact that Manley (who lived with Barber) would have been there. After passages in which Manley's work is acknowledged (like the one quoted by Davis), Swift subtly reminds Stella of more "proper" womanly roles: waiting at home, accepting childish treatment or the infantilization of babytalk, and being grateful for presents like a new apron and a pound of chocolate:

> I have sent the set of Examiners; the first thirteen were written by several hands, some good, some bad; the next three-and-thirty were all by one hand, that makes forty-six: then that author, whoever he was, laid it down on purpose to confound guessers; and the last six

were written by a woman. Then there is an account of Guiscard by
the same woman, but the facts sent by Presto. . . . Vindication of the
Duke of Marlborough entirely by the same woman; Comment on
Hare's sermon by the same woman, only hints sent to the printer from
Presto to give her. Then there's the Miscellany, an apron for Stella,
[and] a pound of chocolate . . . for Stella. (*JS*, 2:402–3)

Stella is removed from the political journalism in which Manley
was so involved: "Have you seen Toland's Invitation to Dismal?,"
he asks Stella, ". . . But it is an Imitation of Horace, and perhaps
you don't understand Horace" (2:544). If he praises Manley, "She
has very generous principles . . . and a great deal of good sense
and invention" (2:474), he reassures Stella that "she is about forty,
very homely, and very fat." Swift clearly relied on her and could
accept the contradictions between the sensationalist and the articulate advocate of monarchy, peace, and economic stability, between "one of her sort" and "Mrs. Manley the author."

Delariviere Manley was aware of the contradictions she represented. Ironic wordplay on her own name is suggestive. From
"Delariviere," she derives Delia and Rivella, the contrasting heroines of her two explicitly autobiographical narratives. Delia is all
innocence; Rivella, an experienced sensualist. They rework the
same crucial events: Manley's seduction by her cousin, her bigamous marriage, her pregnancy, confinement, abandonment, and
literary career. The double names, of course, also refer to the
cultural constructions of the "nature" of woman, both the good
victim and the bad tempter. Manley also finds irony in puns on
her surname; married or single, innocent or ruined, she is always
"Manl(e)y" and she succeeds in a man's profession. She creates
female characters who are strong in "Manl(e)y" ways. The heroine
of the *Royal Mischief* (1696) also suffers a confinement by her
husband. A bundle of pent-up energy, she defies all the rules of
feminine conduct. Manley, who was fluent in French, seems to
have named her with a self-reflexive pun, Homais (*homme*-ly).
The members of the all-female society, the Cabal, in the *New
Atalantis*, "do not in reality love men, but dote of the representation of men in women" (2:206). To an extent, Manley encouraged
the representation of herself as the purveyor of verbal aphrodisiac
because it was one obvious way a woman writer could claim power.
Later, in the role of Examiner, she defends her own originality as
follows: "I am so far from being obliged to others for my matter,
as to be forced to father my own upon those who will please to
accept it" (*Examiner* 48).

In various permutations, powerful women, as aggressors or as victims of seduction, are the essential ingredients in many of Manley's works. *Queen Zarah* and the *New Atalantis* rework these ingredients repeatedly. Their extraordinary popularity may be due to a general love of scandal, but more specific reasons explain the effectiveness of these works a political documents. The seduction scenario, played out so relentlessly in various combinations of male and female pawns and power seekers, refers to the central nexus of power surrounding Queen Anne and the women who politically "seduce" her: the duchess of Marlborough, and later Abigail Masham and the duchess of Somerset. The *New Atalantis* begins when William III, "the King of this island," is "just dead." No weeping women follow his hearse; instead, they celebrate their new authority. "[T]he new Empress" [Anne] "condole[s] with her the Favorite over some Flasks of sparkling Champaign" (1:291). Playing on the motifs of women, power, and seduction, Manley struck a chord with many reverberations among her readers. In *Memoirs of Europe,* she transforms Queen Anne into the male figure Constantine, vulnerable to the wiles of crafty women. Manley may sensationalize, but she is not alone in understanding the politics of Queen Anne's reign according to this model.

The "Letter to the Examiner" (a preface to the collected essays by Henry St. John, Lord Bolingbroke) constructs an overview of recent political events out of a similar conflation of women, power, and seduction. Whig corruption is framed in the contrast between Queen Anne and Sarah Churchill, "the best" and "the worst" of [their] Sex." Honest Englishmen are caught between the benevolence of the perfect mother and the manipulations of a dangerous seducer:

[A] Queen possess'd of all the virtues requisite to bless a Nation and to make a private Family happy, sits on the throne. . . . Instead of the Mild Influences of a gracious Queen Governing by Law, we soon felt the miserable consequences of Subjection to the will [of an Arbitrary Junto] and to the caprice of an Indolent woman. Unhappy Nation, which expecting to be govern'd by the best, fell under the tyranny of the Worst of her Sex! . . . [who would] pursue [the Queen] even into her Bed-Chamber. (Swift, *Prose,* 3:225.)

Does Swift think in these terms? His *Examiner* papers often depict male assemblies and suppress the figure of woman. However, the *Journal to Stella* is instructive. The Tory leaders Bolingbroke and Harley have a kind of innocence, if not ineffectuality about them: "I cannot but think they have mighty difficulties upon them; yet I always find them as easy and disengaged as schoolboys on a holiday," he writes (*JS*, 1:162–63). Powerful women surrounding the Queen are more inscrutable and dangerous. They are like Manley's Zarah, "the pipe that conveyed the royal bounty to the subject." Lady Oglethorpe is a "cunning . . . devil." Mrs. Masham [who replaced the duchess of Marlborough] was with [Harley] when I came . . . 'tis well she is not very handsome; they sit alone together settling the nation. . . . she gave me some lights to suspect the Queen is changed." "[The] Duchess of Somerset, who now has the key [to the queen's closet], is a most insinuating woman . . . and I believe will endeavour to play the same game that has been played against [her]" (1:206). "Parliament should be dissolved before Christmas . . . this is all your d——d Duchess of Somerset's doings. Those scoundrel, starving lords would never have dared to vote against the court, if Somerset had not assured them that it would please the Queen" (2:434–39). Even "the Queen is false . . . sooner than turn out the Duchess of Somerset, she will dissolve Parliament and get a Whiggish one, which may be done by managing elections." What are schoolboy politicians and starving lords to do in the face of these strong, manipulative women? Unauthorized by the title of "minister" or "secretary," they wield considerable power.[25]

The visibility of women at the center of power does seem to have influenced Manley and other women writers. Queen Anne had many reasons to depend on women friends: her unhappy girlhood, unsatisfying husband, perpetual sequence of illness, pregnancy, miscarriage, and stillbirth or infant death, her quarreling ministers and licentious court—these and other factors kept her often closeted with her women. A recent article on the abundance of women playwrights during Queen Anne's reign notes that expressions of love and friendship between women are considered an acceptable aspect of female sexuality.[26] There is no doubt that the women Anne loved had great influence over her and often served as the means by which male politicians won or lost their suits. How does this old-girl network affect Manley, aside from simply knowing about it? Manley, whose father had been a governor and who had given her a close look at the exercise of authority, was better educated than the duchess of Marlborough. As a girl, Sarah Jenyns "had little if any advantage from education." She "never read any Book as she used to say but the World." She claimed to "hate writing of all things" and when she did put pen to paper it looked "as if a child had scrabbled over the paper."[27] Manley's attacks on her have the confidence of a woman who does not consider herself inferior. Sarah's replacement in Anne's affection was Abigail Masham, Manley's social equal (before the bigamous marriage). It is likely that Abigail Masham knew Manley and encouraged Harley's correspondence with her.[28] There are "broad hints in the book itself [the *New Atalantis*] that Mrs. Manley had been encouraged and rewarded by the queen's bedchamber woman and favorite Abigail Masham."[29] Harley and Masham are, one should recall, idealized extravagantly in the *New Atalantis*. Harley included Manley in his propaganda campaign soon after her acquittal and release from seditious libel charges by the Whigs and before he engaged Swift to work for the Tory cause.[30]

In order to describe some of the ways in which Manley responds to the political struggles of her time, I wish to look first at some examples from her fiction. Swift had written, "Oh, I could tell you ten thousand things of our mad politics, upon what small circumstances great affairs have turned" (*JS*, 2:448). Manley's narratives are built precisely upon this principle: episodic "small circumstances" accumulate into greater matters. I here touch on several significant concepts: sexual promiscuity as Manley's satiric counterpart to madness, the motif of knaves and fools, representations of the mob and of the body, parody of the conventions of heroism and love, ironic and contradictory definitions of happiness, and the withholding of a clearly articulated ideal.

In Manley's fiction humanity is driven by promiscuous desires. In *Queen Zarah,* her earliest and least complex satire, this principle is central to the kingdom of Albigion [England]: "[I]t is the Custom of the Grandees of that Country, when they have not a particular Inclination for any Woman, to take this to Day, and another to Morrow: And having lost the Taste of Love, to Search for Pleasure in Change and Variety" (1:15–16). The subtitle, with its fill-in-the-blank metaphor of the satiric mirror, "a Looking-glass for ———," suggests that the reflected face may change, as it does in Swift's "glass." Like King David's "promiscuous use of concubine and bride" in Dryden's *Absalom and Achitophel,* or like the characters who "promiscuously . . . swive" in Rochester's "Ramble through St. James Park," such behavior indicates a lack of coherence that endangers political stability and ultimately undermines the meaning of being human. Promiscuity threatens social/civic constraint, confusing and isolating individuals driven by pride and hunger for power. The lawlessness of desire leads Manley's characters into adultery, rape, incest, bigamy, disease, and death. "What Man of Quality in Atalantis is faithful to his

Wife?" asks Intelligence (1:776–77). In one example, a twice-married baron begins an adulterous affair with a "military's wife," but "at a Midnight Debauch, from one Excess to another (Women being introduced) got a Present which he imparted to" his mistress, wife, and presumably the wronged husband. Venereal disease quickly traverses the social hierarchy with no promise of abatement: The narrator is bluntly judgmental: "She wept! she complain'd! but Tears cure nothing!" Lovers' bodies parallel the vulnerable body of the state. Manley's characters cannot resist passion. No education in virtue withstands the pressure of temptation. No successful plot brings content. The restlessness of desire is the thread that connects the seemingly random episodes of Manley's fiction.

Promiscuity is the satiric counterpart to madness in Manley's vision of society. If rising vapors in the brain explain everything in Swift's *Tale of a Tub,* aroused lust is the crucial motivator in the *New Atalantis.* Swift satirizes Jack's mad Scottish Calvinism through his violent alteration of his coat. Manley satirizes Scottish politics through the anarchic propensities of "Utopia": "They change parties, they change monarchs, with the same ease that they shift their linen. . . . No obligation, no interest can fix them . . . so fond are they of change, that they . . . call out loudly for revolution, though 'tis odd, but they are ruined by what they require" (2:116). The refusal to abide within the "common forms" also can be fascinating. All of history—its sequence of powerful figures and ideas rising and failing—is reduced to these two "disturbances" of body and mind. Lack of control, disregard for law and custom, overweening egotism, the desire to subdue others, preoccupation with the body and physical need, the mechanization of emotion, the force of the irrational—all of these qualities pertain to both promiscuity and madness. Tickling and tinsel in the *Tale,* kisses and jessamine flowers in the *New Atalantis* are details that both attract and repel us. Lack of "government," in bed or in Bedlam, leads both authors to darkly reductive observations.

Rhetorical flights and metaphorical excesses in both cases suggest that language itself is unstable in a world ruled by mad desire. Sincerity, if attempted, becomes ineffectual, almost comical. The narrator of the *Tale* is ludicrously sincere: "I profess . . . in the integrity of my heart, that what I am going to say is literally true this Minute I am writing" (Swift, *Tale,* 36). Manley's "young and artless" Elonora says, "I told him indeed, 'twas true" (1:599). But the truth she tells is momentary. Neither character succeeds in fixing meaning in an enduring way. Sexual and rational disorder are more conducive to the shiftiness of irony. In the *New Ata-lantis,* the narrative is divided among three speakers: Astrea, Virtue, and Intelligence. Astrea and Virtue are unironic narrators, sincere, prone to panegyric, and sometimes too simple. Manley suggests that we are to view them, especially Astrea, from an ironic perspective. Near the end of the narrative, after witnessing relentless scenes of human treachery, Astrea comments obtusely: "I don't find Lady *Intelligence,* that in this *World* of yours, *Vice* is an *Obstacle* to *Advancement*" (1:771). The dominant voice belongs to Intelligence, a highly ironic reporter whose remarks often undercut the sincere exclamations of her companions. Intelligence speaks with almost Stendhalian detachment of "Tears! Complaints! Horrors! *and what not*" (1:783, emphasis added).

Manley's tales of "love" often lack pathos because they do not depict struggles between good and evil, but between fools and knaves. Manley, echoing Swift, alludes to the poetry of Rochester. Her characters know "the perfect joy of being well-deceived." "'Tis one great Property of humane kind, upon the simplest Movement to impose first upon their own Beliefs, so self-deceiv'd are better fitted to deceive others" (1:701), says Intelligence. They live fantasies in which they believe they manipulate others, but are manipulated in turn. The good Chariot is self-destructively naive, a "pauvre fille trompez." The clever and wicked countess gets the duke, but he is not worth having. Don Antonio (1:596) "has a Manner so *sincere* and open in *Appearance,* that the most wary are deceiv'd by him." Accomplished deceivers easily find dupes, and then prey upon one another. The "Germanicus episode" is the most familiar example.[31] Manley, like Swift in the *Tale,* adapts Rochester's distinction between fools and knaves to her satiric fictions. Allusions to "A Letter from Artemisia in the Country to Chloe in the City" and *A Satyr Against Reason and Mankind* support this idea.[32] Love in "Artemisia to Chloe" is "grown . . . an arrant trade." "How is love governed, love that rules the state?" asks the fine lady. The Corinna story, like so many of Manley's, is a "knaves and fools" story: seduction, betrayal, and revenge occur without heroism or justice.[33] Rochester's cynical categories accommodate the economic and political implications of scandalous sex. These categories suit Manley's fiction much more adequately than conventional romance categories. Innocent maidens wooed by clever seducers differ qualitatively from Manley's deceivers, whose culpability is often ambiguously presented. The struggle in Manley is not between evil aristocratic libertine and good bourgeois virgin: the struggle occurs within the upper classes over political allegiance and personal greed.[34] Fools and knaves vie for power, and few characters are consistently attractive.

Difficult choices are demanded of the reader of both Swift and Manley. If individual desire is liable to the self-sabotage of madness and lust, the idea of community would seem to offer a safer alternative. However, this ideal receives problematic representation. Manley's New Cabal or, later, Swift's Houyhnhnmland are disturbing utopias. The Houyhnhnms' ignorance of the conventions of heterosexual love has been one the most difficult details in the fourth voyage for readers to tolerate. The New Cabal's lesbian society similarly rejects fundamental cultural myths abut the relations between men and women. In place of community, family, or friendship, readers more often encounter a "filthy crowd" like the "rabble" who press and stifle one another in Leicester fields (Swift, *Tale*, 46). As a political observer, Manley also shares Swift's distaste for "the mob." In the *New Atalantis*, "Crowds [of characters] justle together," losing their integrity in "a Congress of coaches . . . a swarm of populate of both sexes, a ridiculous medley of Humankind," or "a miscellany of company." Like vultures, "numerous crowds of guards and attendants" [finish with the dead king and] "flock about the New Empress" (1:357). Mobs are capable of bestiality and violent destruction: "The people . . . rush'd unanimously upon the two Usurpers, with as much ease and fierceness, as a hungry Lyon, the devouring Woolf, or Tyger, falls upon the harmless Flock; and, with the same expedition . . . rends 'em piecemeal! scatters their Body small as Dust thrown into the Air!" (1:319). A trustworthy consensual body is hard to find.

The body itself figures significantly in Manley's fiction, as readers might expect in "amatory" stories. But the pleasures of the body are really much less vivid in a work like the *New Atalantis* than are its pains. Lovemaking usually is signified by hackneyed metaphors and hyperbolic euphemism. Characters "lavishly sacrific'd to Love" (1:307); they are grasped to ravished bosoms: "he held me in his eager Arms, wand'ring o're my Face and Neck, with ten thousand ardent Breathings" (1:598). "[E]ndearments, Embraces, Kisses, perpetual Claspings" (1:552) and "Amorous, incessant *Sighs* and *Graspings*" (1:598) occur predictably, one might say dismissively, every few pages. However, physical realities do find their way into the narrative. Manley's lovers are fastidious, frequently bathing and perfuming themselves to counteract the unsavory effects of the "heat." The concern with physical cleanliness in circumstances of moral impurity has an ironic edge.

Manley's lovers wear lace, but are far from delicate. Their primitive, aggressive impulses unclothe the Yahoo within.

In memorable instances Manley is determined to portray the disgusting explicitly. She often emphasizes the pains of the body and of sex: danger, violence, sensory disgust, and abuse threaten various characters.

The *New Atalantis* explores numerous sexual perils. "A Lady of most *agreeable* Merit, *young, ingaging, and tender*," is married for her dowry to a madman. "[E]very Night in going to Bed, she did not know but she was stepping into her Grave; his unaccountable Sallies being of a Nature to alarm any one" (1:801). Manley describes the effects on characters who take "soporific" drugs and emetics. She describes physical cruelty in marriage. Barsinia's mother torments her sickly husband:

> This inhuman Wife, scarce allow'd him any part of the coarsest cheapest Food. Endeavouring one Day to turn himself in his Bed, when he had none to assist him . . . he broke his Leg . . . he roar'd out with the very Anguish, his Wife came to him, he told her his Misfortune, that he was ready to die with Pain and intreated her to send for a *Surgeon*. She bid him hold his Tongue for a *cowardly Sot*. . . . Thus abruptly she left him, not to Languish, but to roar out in Torture for three whole Days and Nights, without ever ceasing. At length she found herself so disturb'd by his Noise, that she got a Surgeon to him, who actually show'd her, that his Leg was broke short off at the Ankle. . . . [T]he Anguish had inflam'd his Blood, and put him into a Fever, of which in a very few Days he dy'd" (1:781–82).

While Manley recounts stories of seduction among the rich and famous, she insists on the natural consequences of bodily functions and needs: sex leads to pregnancy, childbirth, and sometimes death. A suggestive specter is the "Person of Condition, dress'd in white, with the Veil of white Taffaty over her Face," who is no bride at the altar but a "woman nail'd dead to the Gibbet" (1:420).[35] Another woman's "Body was found down the River, where the Stream had carry'd it" (1:515). They suffer the fate of lovers. Pregnancy is represented as a time of discomfort and fear. Scenes of childbirth, usually illegitimate, are described as lonely and painful. Women in labor "drink their tears," convulse, and tear their flesh (1:567). The infants rarely live. Manley comments that this is not melodrama, but "common to all the female kind." Among the *New Atalantis*'s many disturbing moments is a series of images of women with covered faces, whose bodies have become their only identity. These faceless women are seen in lovemaking, childbirth, and death. Ianthe's "lovers say [she is] one of the handsomest Women in *Atalantis*, from the Chin downwards." "A *Gauze Handkerchief* of *Turkish Embroidery*, she has suffer'd, by her *nice well-contriving Lovers*, to be cast over her *Visage*, lest something *less* charming than her Body, shou'd *pall* their Ardors" (1:738). Women bear illegitimate children while covered with a scarf so that the midwives who attend their labor can say, "I did such a sort of Lady . . . the good office, but can't for my Life imagine who she is" (1:545). The hanged woman in her white taffaty veil has already been mentioned. The inescapable physical facts of female sexuality become, for Manley, an ironic commentary on the aspirations of "love," "according to that celebrated poet [Rochester]" : "That cordial drop, heaven in our cup has thrown, / To make the nauseous draught of life go down!" ["Letter from Artemisia . . . to Chloe," 11. 44–45] (1.654–55).

In some ways, the unpleasantness of the body may remind us of Swift's irony about the inevitability of defecation and of other biological realities that become part of his satiric fictions. The body becomes the ultimate text of the human condition. It cannot be rewritten and its physicality cannot be "reformed." Both Manley and Swift carry this essential insight to extremes, sometimes embarrassing or offending readers. Manley, however, avoids scatology and misogyny, and this is an important difference. She uses the female body's objectification to satirize society rather than to satirize women or women's sexuality per se. There is more to fear and loathe about the body than its need to excrete waste, such as its suffering during childbirth and its vulnerability to rape.

A final observation about the *New Atalantis* shifts attention from the body to human emotions. One of the most striking features of the narrative is its obsessive preoccupation with "happiness." The word "happy" occurs with unusual frequency and with constantly shifting significance. Often "happiness" is the state of self-deception, of being, however briefly, the delirious fool. New lovers are "happy," no matter if they are adulterous, incestuous, polygamous, or mistaken in the identity of their partners. While happiness may mean the gratification of erotic desire (sexual union is euphemized as being made "happy"), it also describes the acquisition of wealth. Rich and powerful characters are "happy" in their possessions. The term is morally ambiguous, referring to love-struck innocents as well as jaded seducers. It becomes increasingly ironic as examples pile up during the progress of the narrative. When Charlot yields to the Duke's seduction, the narrator Intelligence exclaims, "that happy Week sublim'd him almost to an Immortal. *Charlot* was form'd to give and take all those Raptures necessary to accomplish the Lover's happiness . . . none were ever more Happy!" (1:344). Within a few pages, the "happy" couple are moving toward betrayal and death. The narrator's exultation takes on a bitter tone: a happy week is hardly long enough to celebrate, suggesting that felicity does not endure. If "none were ever more happy" than this self-destructive pair, what hope is there for everyone else? Astrea says that the poet Anne Finch (whose "Progress of Life" is interpolated into the *New Atalantis*) is "one of the happy few that write out of pleasure and not necessity." Yet even this compliment is compromised within the context of the narrative's ironic use of "happy." Finch's good fortune seems a reminder that Manley wrote for bread.

In each case, happiness does not follow from admirable achievements or inner worth, but from sex, money, self-delusion, and luck. Swift's definition of happiness in the "Digression concerning . . . Madness" as "a perpetual Possession of being well Deceived" applies to many of Manley's scenarios of temporary bliss. The amatory rhetoric serves as so much "Varnish and Tinsel" to assist "the Felicity and Enjoyments of Mortal Men." But for Manley's satirized lovers, the "sublime and refined point of felicity [is] the possession of being well deceived; the serene and peaceful state of being a fool among knaves" (Swift, *Tale*, 174).

Manley's reworking of the conventions of love and heroism suggests deep cynicism as well as anger at the failure of ideals. Her motives, although not her precise manner, bear comparison with Swift. Frequent gender reversal functions subversively. The Germanicus episode in the *New Atalantis* inverts conventions by portraying the male body as the object of a desiring female gaze. Germanicus is feminized, but not like Sir Charles Grandison or Lord Orville. He emerges damp and fragrant from the bath and arranges himself on the bed, "Limbs . . . exactly form'd, his skin shiningly white . . . diffus'd Joy and Desire throughout all his Form; his lovely Eyes seem'd to be closed, his Face turn'd on one side . . . obscur'd by the Lace depending from the *Pillows* on which he rested; the Duchess . . . giving her Eyes, time to wander over Beauties so inviting, and which encreased her Flame; with an amorous Sigh . . . threw her self on the Bed" (1:306) The episode, involving Barbara Villers and John Churchill, quickly proves sordid in the extreme.

In contrast, Manley's *Examiners* (like Swift's) are relatively moderate and are less distinctive stylistically. Her five *Examiners*

do have examples of typical "Manl(e)y" irony. Her first contribution alludes covertly to her satiric success in the *New Atalantis:*
"I have sometimes had it in my Head, to write a particular History
of Abuses and Corruptions." Like the satiric fiction, the political
essays contain some striking images of women. They extol the
queen as mother and female warrior. Public credit is personified as
a languishing woman, "still alive, but subsisting only upon strong
Cordials, in utter ignorance of her approaching Dissolution" (*Examiner* 46, 5:312). *Examiner* 49 frames an attack on the duchess
of Marlborough by "translating" the story of Fulvia's visit to the
House of Pride. The Goddess Pride is an antimonarch: ruling in
total self-absorption, "she fixt her Eyes upwards, unless when by
Intervals they were cast upon a Mirror she held in her Hand."
Fulvia/Sarah is a "bold and enterprising woman" who makes a
terrifying appearance:

> On one side marched Envy, lashing her with Whips and Snakes; giv-
> ing her to drink by intervals from a Cup of Wine mingled with Gall and
> Wormwood: Her other supporter was Wrath, who continually tossed a
> flaming Brand, directing her sight to a Dagger which he held; his
> Looks ghastly, his Limbs trembling, his Body half exposed, the rest
> cloathed with a Robe stained with Blood, and torn by his own Fury,
> which was so fierce he could not restrain it from sometimes falling
> upon himself. His Breath was incessantly applyed to the Lady's Spleen
> and Brain, from whence violent Agonies and raging Phrenzies suc-
> ceeded, as was evident by a Toss and Motion. (*Examiner* 49,
> 5:330–31.)

The passage, in the context of the *Examiner*'s relatively bland
prose, recalls the metaphorical power of sex and physical pain in
the *New Atalantis*. Fulvia's "Beauty" is corrupted. Two male figures threaten her. Envy's whips and snakes, Wrath's flaming
brand, his half-exposed body and heavy breathing, the "violent
agonies" and "raging Phrenzies" that seize them seem part of the
violent allegorical world of her other work.

Manley's advocacy of peace and her fear of moneyed interest
controlled by an ambitious few are expressed in metaphors of
contaminated bodies and crumbling buildings. Avarice is a disease
that undermines the body: "Public Credit" is sick; the former ministry to "put a good face upon a decaying Constitution" but could
not survive. Pride weakens the foundations of civilization. The
"House of Pride" resembles the spider's mansion in the *Battle of
the Books* and the modern projects satirized in *Gulliver's Travels*.
"The Architect seemed to consider how to be most profuse," but

the edifice is built upon sand and air: "A Number of Chambers, but none convenient; fine Gardens without Water; the whole Building raised upon a sandy Foundation; every Breath from Court, every Blast puffed away some Grains of that huge fleeting Hill, upon which this Palace was erected" (*Examiner* 49, 5:330). Metaphors of pollution and architecture also are used to describe the satirist/ journalist's position. In an uncomfortable and dirty world, the author tries not "to rake into . . . particular Absurdities" of writers whose "excessive Dulness" circulates "weekly Poisons." The *Examiner* looks to the country, "where Truth arrives late," but where it may abide in a solid English country house. In her final *Examiner*, Manley writes: "I have waded through Seas of Scurrility, without being polluted by any of that Filth they have incessantly cast at me."

She discusses irony, its use and importance, in *Examiners* 45, 48, and 50. *Examiner* 50 takes "leave of the Town" by casting a last aspersion at the Medley's failure to use or to comprehend irony.[36] She witheringly thanks him "for so constantly explaining what he thought my Meaning in any dark Allusions, or Allegories." She describes the vicissitudes of reading and writing when identity and meaning succumb to the change that afflicts other aspects of society, especially the politics of an unstable ministry. Anonymity is both the author's defense and undoing because readers are "so often and so wretchedly mistaken":

> This Pamphlet is certainly from such a Hand; they know his Manner perfectly: That Paper of Verses is infallibly of such a Poet, no Man in England could write it but he; and this sometimes even upon the first Essay of an Author. I, among the rest, used to determine formerly at the same Rate; but shall be more cautious for the future; having seen the World and my self so often and so wretchedly mistaken. (*Examiner* 50, 5:335.)

She ironically cites "knowing" readers who are ignorant of her gender: "How many Fathers has this Paper of mine been attributed to? Among all the Men of Wit, who are in the Interest of the present Ministry, I know not one who has escaped some Report or Suspicion of being the Author." The instability of governments, identity, and language as represented by Manley's *Examiners* recall the reckless world of her satiric fiction. She urges support for Harley's ministry specifically ("the advantageous Change that hath been made"), but she has established a general need for stability of meaning and form: "[S]ince all changes are not good, let us Change no more."

A final perspective on Manley's involvement in the *Examiner* further justifies her direct (as opposed to indirectly through Swift) claims as editor and author. Her role went far beyond merely "taking . . . orders from Swift himself." The Tory *Examiner* engaged in direct verbal combat with the Whig periodical *The Medley*, written and edited primarily by Arthur Mainwaring. Manley had a great personal grievance to settle with Mainwaring. Her imprisonment in 1709 had been instigated by the duchess of Marlborough and her son-in-law, Secretary of State Sunderland, who issued the warrant for the arrest.[37] But neither of them had read the *New Atalantis*. They based their plan to arrest Manley and "push it as far as [we] can by law" on the account of the book given by Mainwaring in a fulminating letter to the duchess. After the arrest, Sunderland wrote to her:

> if this affair does not at last end well, not withstanding all this disagreeable proceeding, it will settle us, and keep every thing quiet, and I am sure every honest man, must always acknowledge the doing of it to you. . . . I believe Mr. Maynwaring had given you an account of the lady I have in custody for the New Atalantis, and of the noble worthy persons she corresponds with.

He promises to "spoil their writing, at least for some time for I promise them I will push it as far as I can by law."[38]

When the *Examiner* began its attacks on the Marlboroughs, the duke urged discretion and wished to leave England, but Sarah characteristically wished to counterattack. She supported and encouraged Mainwaring's *Medley*.[39] It is not surprising that Manley, again facing the publishing conspiracy of the duchess and Mainwaring, would wish to avail herself of the opportunity to do battle with her former enemies. This time she wrote from a position of greater strength. She had survived the legal attempts to silence her over the *New Atalantis* and now was collaborating with Tories of considerable stature and public respect.

Finally, a discussion of Manley's and Swift's accounts of the attempted assassination of Harley by the Marquis de Guiscard further shows the strength of their relationship. Swift's agitated reaction ("violent pain of mind . . . greater than ever I felt in my life"—*Corresp.*, 1:213–14) to this event is recorded in his letters and in the *Journal to Stella*: "Pray pardon my distraction. . . . The poor creature [Harley] now lies stabbed in his bed by a desperate French popish villain." "Pity me . . . Pity Presto," he entreats Stella (1:212), and admits it may be "foolish in me to be so much in

pain as I am" (1:214). His mood fluctuates with Harley's recovery:
"Mr. Harley is better tonight, that makes me so pert." The event
held enough personal importance for him that he kept the handle
of the broken penknife and the first plaster removed from Harley's
wound until his death. Swift also recognized the political importance of Guiscard's treason. For a government suffering from internal dissension, the episode could serve as circumstantial glue,
uniting Tories and Whigs in support of their leader. But Swift's
efforts in this direction did not go well. His main concern was to
reconcile Harley and St. John, whose mutual distrust and competition was a growing problem, now exacerbated by all the public
attention being lavished on Harley. Swift devoted *Examiner* 32 to
the assassination attempt. Hoping to spread the glory around and
appease St. John, he claimed that Guiscard had intended to stab
both St. John and the queen, and failing in that design, tried to
"murder the Person whom he thought *St. John* loved best" (109).
He implied a larger Whig conspiracy shadily connected to the
stabbing. As David Nokes comments, "this is pretty unconvincing
stuff."[40] Swift's account of Guiscard only made things worse, and
he turned to Manley to write the official account, *A True Narrative
of what pass'd at the Examination of the Marquis de Guiscard at
the Cock-Pit, the 8th of March, 1710/11.*[41]

The importance of this episode for Swift should indicate to us
the degree of trust and confidence that motivated him to ask Manley to take over the publicity of Harley's stabbing. The rationalization to Stella that he "had not time to do it" is transparent. "I was
afraid of disobliging Mr. Harley or Mr. St John . . . and so would
not do it myself" is more to the point (*JS*, 1:244, 245). His remark
that Manley "cook'd it into a six-penny pamphlet, in her own style"
(*JS*, 1:244–45) has been taken as dismissive by critics. But what
does Swift mean by "her own style" and why is it suited to the
tricky business of handling ministerial egos? He seems to have
been thinking of her satirical fiction and plays and their brief but
vividly realized scenes of lawless passion. Harley's stabbing was
an event in which life rivaled invention. All of the ingredients of
an adventure story were there to be "cook'd up": a handsome
French spy, wronged women, knife wounds, intercepted letters,
clattering swords, and heroic utterances. The frame for Manley's
propaganda is scandal. While *A True Narrative* may be only a six-
penny propaganda pamphlet, it is considerably more entertaining
than Swift's *Examiner* 32.

Manley's retelling of the events of 8 March 1711 begins much
earlier. She postpones the actual attack on Harley until halfway

through the forty-three-page pamphlet. This central episode is preceded by a long section developing the character of Guiscard and followed by another part extoling Queen Anne and national unity. This plan accomplishes several purposes. Attention is deflected away from the sensitive issue of whether Harley or St. John was the greater hero. It also allows her to create a quasi-allegory in which evil grows powerful, engages in a mighty conflict, and then is replaced by the light of goodness and hope. Facts that might deflate such pretensions—the smallness of the penknife, the petty jealousy between ministers, Harley's speedy recovery—are glossed over by the pamphlet's drama.

First, she develops the character of Guiscard. The first page or so (which may be by Swift) states emphatically that Guiscard was of "a vicious and profligate nature," though of a "noble family." The following pages elaborately describe his profligacy, but have no direct bearing on the assassination attempt. His crimes are sexual and economic. He seduced a nun, ran off with his brother's sweetheart, ruined and poisoned her, and went on to keep several mistresses at once. He disgraced his French hometown, attempted insurrections in Switzerland, fled abroad (where he tricked two governments into supporting him with pensions), and finally betrayed England to France.

Manley might have left her villain flat, but instead she affords him some stature. To be hurt by an imbecile is not as heroic as contending with a formidable embodiment of evil. Thus Manley gives Guiscard some qualities reminiscent of Milton's Satan and Dryden's Achitophel:

> [He is] brutish, bold, desperate, an Engine fit for the blackest Mischief, revengeful, busy to Design, though full of inconsistencies, and preposterous in his Management: his schemes impracticable to any less rash and inconsiderate, as may be seen at large in those his ill-formed Projects of Rebellion against his Prince. (13)

Driven by vicious impulses, Guiscard moves frenetically between France, Switzerland, Holland, and England. He becomes a less simple villain as the details accumulate. The pamphlet becomes less episodic and more dramatic as Manley reaches the climactic scene of the examination. Here she stages an heroic scene in which Guiscard's restlessness becomes a dominant feature. When questioned by the ministers, "the posture of his feet [is] restless and unassured, his hands [are] in perpetual motion, fumbling in his pocket" (18). His facial expressions shift constantly, puzzling his interrogators: "[His] colour came and went. Earl Poulet, before he was brought in, had desired Mr. St John to change places with Mr. Harley, that Guiscard's Face might be full in the Light, and its countenance better perceived, in any alterations that might happen"(17). The psychological signs of guilt—fumbling in the pockets, shifting feet, telltale blushes—absorb much of the reader's attention.

While distracting the reader with the behavior of the trapped but cunning villain, Manley attempts to smooth over the problem created by Swift's *Examiner* as to which minister was Guiscard's real target. During the dramatic scene of interrogation, a trapped and frantic Guiscard spontaneously abandons his original plan of betraying the queen and "form'd to himself the destruction of those two dreadful enemies to France, Mr. HARLEY and Mr. St. John" (20). Thus both men equally are given heroic roles:

> If . . . [Guiscard] could get Mr. St. John to withdraw, Mr. Harley might possibly be of the party, and he have a chance to murder them both before they could be assisted.[When this plan fails, he desperately] stab'd Mr. HARLEY, redoubling the stroke, the penknife broke, which he was not sensible of; but running on towards Mr. St. John, overthrew the clerks table that stood between. Mr. St. John saw Mr. Harley fall, and cry'd out, The villain has killed Mr. Harley: Then he gave him a wound . . . [and] was resolved to kill him. (20)

The scene is action-packed. The scuffle and sword fight highlight the heroism of St. John, whose eloquent interrogation and speedy revenge lead to Guiscard's capture. Once Guiscard is secure, the heroic spotlight shifts to Harley: "Let us turn our eyes from so detestable an object, to another . . . of a quite different kind" (23–24). Harley is "the man that may truly be said to know himself, whom even assassination can't surprise." Each minister is given several memorable lines, appropriate to the differing characters of soldier- and philosopher-hero. Harley and St. John are gentlemen whose composure is not easily shaken. Faced with a raving murderer, they are able to control their feelings and even to coin *bon mots*.

By devoting so much of the pamphlet to the character of Guiscard (and relatively little to the rival ministers), Manley focuses on a point of agreement, a common villain to scorn. Scandal and suspense also have a popular appeal. The final panegyric on the queen again insists on a point of agreement. Anne is described as "all-merciful and Saint-like" in allowing Guiscard to be attended by physicians and ultimately "privately interred." This is offered as a sign of English superiority, "a Mercy no Nation but ours would have conferred upon a Spy, a Traytor, and an Assassin." Swift sends Stella a different account of Guiscard's fate: "We have let Guiscard be buried at last, after showing him pickled in a trough this fortnight for twopence apiece" (*Corresp.*, 1:224). Manley, however egregiously she distorts matters to make her uplifting appeal to English nationalism ("Parties break their Force against one another, do the Work of our Foes"), moves unabashedly from "libertine" to "liberty." She shares Swift's sardonic awareness that in "true accounts" and "histories," as well as in fiction and irony, language has the power to change things. Both were capable of six-penny pamphlets full of purposeful distortion, of being wrangling spiders as well as ironists.

It must have been with considerable irony that Manley responded to the charge "of my being a contemptible hireling and a little mercenary fellow" in her final *Examiner*: "I do not wonder to have a wrong interpretation put upon my labors, and my self, tho entirely otherwise, [to be] accused . . . of the desire of making my fortune, by application to the prevailing party. But let such who are my accusers remember that the Paper was begun whilst yet the late Ministry were at the helm" (*Examiner* 50, 5:334). As the only woman Tory pamphleteer, she could not hope for a place, could not be driven by a desire for personal power; she had already been prosecuted for writing satire and had been paid only half the one hundred pounds promised her by Harley "to quiet uneasy creditors." The reckless desire for power is central to her satiric fictions. But in reality, her considerable influence over public opinion against the Whigs still left her soliciting Harley and St. John, now Lords Oxford and Bolingbroke, for support. The "modesty and silence" recommended to Charlot in the *New Atalantis* bring no lasting reward, but neither do the immodesty and outspokenness of its author. In the end this contradiction is as disturbing as the contradiction between "good" and "fallen" woman that has marginalized Manley as a writer about love.

Rather than seeing Manley merely as a convenient ally of Swift, we should now be able to propose a deeper affinity between them as writers. Neither fits comfortably into the satiric models—Horatian or Juvenalian—proposed by Dryden in his *Discourse Concerning Satire*.[42] Both are more aptly described as Varronian or Menippean satirists, and, in fact, both described themselves in that way. Their work exhibits characteristics of the carnavalesque as described by Bakhtin and Castle. Swift's relation to Rabelais, for example, has been extensively considered. If Manley and Swift share a "kindred spirit" as satirists, it is the spirit of the *menippea*. Almost every Menippean characteristic may be identified in Manley's work.[43] Her adaptations of romance conventions increase their comic potential. Her plots are loosely constructed and are free of legend and "realism." Her heroines and heroes in the *New Atalantis* (and *Memoirs of Europe*) "wander through unknown and fantastic lands" as a "mode for searching after truth." She indulges in the "slum naturalism" that admits erotic excesses and physical unpleasantness into her fictions. Scandal is recurrent. The world is represented in "stripped down *pro* and *contra*," usually Tory and Whig, but sometimes female and male. Like Swift, the *pro* and *contra* options can become a source of irony, as in the frustrating choice between fools and knaves. Sharp contrasts, abrupt transitions, and shifts are typical of her writing. The *menippea* often includes "elements of social utopia which are incorporated in the form of . . . journeys into unknown lands," such as Astrea's visit to the Cabal. Manley's multitoned style (the high-flown rhetoric of lovers, the plain talk of common folk, the ironic commentary of Intelligence, for example) combine with another Menippean characteristic, the concern with topical and current issues. The general effect of these traits is to destroy "the epic and tragic wholeness of a man and his fate," or more aptly, of man and woman and their ill-fated desires.

Finally, and according to Menippean precedent, Manley establishes an unusual point of view from which to observe events. That point of view is partly achieved by fictional frames, such as the use of figures like Astrea, Justice, and Intelligence, who, in addition to becoming invisible at will, descend as "foreigners" into the restless and promiscuous world of the satire. Like Gulliver, or other of Swift's "*personae*," they enable revealing perspectives. Critics of Swift have often remarked that there is a profoundly distinctive positioning of the satirist in Swift's work. Various writers, among others, have coined phrases like "satire of the second person" (Sams), "self-satire" (Carnochan and Ehrenpreis), satiric "over-plus" (Rawson), to describe this quality. Most agree that Swift could not simply assume a "Horatian" or "Juvenalian" stance in relation to his subject matter. Surely Manley also achieves a unique satirical position as well, in the face of some different and perhaps greater obstacles to herself as a writer. As a woman participating in the male tradition of political satire, she must reject much (such as its misogynistic conventions) and must adapt the generic opportunities more congenial to her (such as French *romans à clef*). Like Swift, she was connected to but not secure in the inner circles of government and social advancement. By developing her own style of satire, she finds a way for a woman's irony and indignation to influence the power-mongering world that tries to exclude her.

Notes

1. Little extensive work has been done on Manley and Swift. Some fine discussions of Manley exist, however, and interest is growing. Gwendolyn Needham's "Mary de la Rivière Manley, Tory Defender," *Huntington Library Quarterly* 12 (1948–49): 255–89, is a pioneering study. John J. Richetti devotes a chapter to Manley in *Popular Fiction Before Richardson: Narrative Patterns, 1700–1739* (Oxford: Clarendon Press, 1969), 119–67. Although Richetti finds Manley's popularity "embarrassing" and believes that the *New Atalantis* possesses "none of the unity of theme or characterization that makes a narrative meaningful to us" (121), his purpose is to construct a literary history that leads to Richardson. The chapter on Manley contains an interesting discussion of the political significance of struggles over power and sex in the scandal chronicle. Fidelis Morgan has written a biography of Manley, interweaving contextualizing facts with the texts of Manley's autobiographical self-representations. See *A Woman of No Character: An Autobiography of Mrs. Manley* (London: Faber and Faber, 1986). An excellent recent study of Manley's fiction is chapter 4 of Ros Ballaster's *Seductive Forms: Women's Amatory Fiction, 1684 to 1740* (Oxford: Clarendon Press, 1992), 114–52. Ballaster's discussion appeared while this essay was nearing completion. She argues persuasively for the innovative uses of French romance conventions in England, specifically as exemplified by the works of Madame D'Aulnoy, and skillfully explores some of the ironic possibilities in Manley's work. Ballaster also includes Aphra Behn and Eliza Haywood in her study. Her recent article on Manley as satirist discusses the advantages of the liminal position of the female satirist in relation to politics. See Ros Ballaster, "Manl(e)y Forms: Sex and the Female Satirist" in *Women, Texts, and Histories, 1575–1760*, ed. Clare Brant and Diane Purkiss (London and New York: Routledge, 1992), 217–41. Because most of my own work on this topic was completed before the publication of Brant and Purkiss's collection, I must merely cite the article with respect.

2. The success of the *New Atalantis* is more familiar than that of *Queen Zarah*, perhaps because of Pope's allusion to it in *The Rape of the Lock* and references to it by Swift, Montagu, and others. The wide popularity of *Queen Zarah* is suggested by the frequency of editions: 1705, 1707, 1709, 1711, 1712, and French translations in 1708 and 1711.

3. It is possible that Pope's allusion, in the context of the mock-heroics of *The Rape of the Lock*, (*TE*, 2:178, 3.165) is an ironic diminution of his heroine's fame. That is, he may be implying that neither the *New Atalantis* nor Belinda are truly immortal. Pope himself, however, wrote satire in which topical references required "keys." In any case, the reference indicates the popularity of Manley's narrative.

4. Swift, *Tale*, 215.

5. The *Examiner* had been started by St. John in August 1710 after Queen Anne had dismissed Godolphin and the Whig ministry. Its purpose was to justify the new ministry to the public, especially to its readership of country squires

living far from London. Swift took over most of the writing by the end of October, and numbers 14 through 44 (2 November 1710 to 14 June 1711) are attributed to him. Manley edited the journal with him. When Swift's "style being soon discovered and having contracted a great Number of Enemies, [he] let it fall into other Hands" (*Memoirs relating to that Change in the Queen's Ministry in 1710*), Manley took over, writing numbers 45 through 50. Quotation from Swift's *Examiner* essays are to vol. 3 of Swift, *Prose*, entitled *The Examiner and Other Pieces Written in 1710–11*, ed. Herbert Davis (Oxford: Basil Blackwell, 1966). Quotations from Manley's *Examiner* essays (they are not included in Davis's edition) are taken from volume 5 of *The Works of Jonathan Swift*, ed. George Faulkner (Dublin, 1738) and cited parenthetically in text.

6. See "Mrs. Manley's Will," *Notes and Queries* 8, 7th ser. (1889): 156–57. Manley died in 1724. Few of her requests were realized.

7. Jane Spencer, *The Rise of the Woman Novelist, from Aphra Behn to Jane Austen* (London: Basil Blackwell, 1986), 53.

8. Fidelis Morgan, *The Female Wits: Women Playwrights of the Restoration* (London: Virago Press, 1981), 210.

9. David Nokes, *Jonathan Swift, a Hypocrite Reversed: A Critical Biography* (Oxford: Oxford University Press, 1985), 127. Nokes describes the relatively benign and unconsummated threats of legal repercussions to Swift for publishing satire.

10. Patricia Koster, ed., *The Novels of Mary Delariviere Manley, Including The Secret History of Queen Zarah, 1705, Parts I and II. The New Atalantis, 1709, Volumes I and II, Memoirs of Europe, 1710, Volumes I and II, The Adventures of Rivella, 1714*, 2 vols. (Gainesville, Fla: Scholars' Facsimiles and Reprints, 1971), 1:459. All references to the novels are to this edition and are cited parenthetically in the text.

11. To Frances Hewet, October 1709, in *The Complete Letters of Lady Mary Wortley Montagu*, ed. Robert Halsband, 4 vols. (Oxford: Oxford University Press, 1966), 2:17.

12. BL Add. MSS 61460, fol. 85: Mainwaring to SM, 15 October 1709.

13. Swift, *Corresp.*, 1:170.

14. References to Manley (erroneously cited as Mary de la Rivière Manley) occur in volume 2, *Dr. Swift* (1967), of Ehrenpreis.

15. Patricia Koster cleared up the confusion over Manley's first name in "Delariviere Manley in the DNB," *Eighteenth-Century Life* 3 (1977): 106–11. An entry of the birth of a "Mary Manly" (Sloane MS 1708, fol. 117) had been mistaken for Manley's birth record. "Mary Manly," whoever she was, was not the writer who knew Swift. Manley's many signatures and references to herself never use "Mary," nor does she ever add an "e" to her real name, Delarivier. Ehrenpreis accepts the mistaken nomenclature of the DNB, although his skills as a biographer might have led him to question its accuracy had he consulted Manley's works themselves.

16. See Morgan, *A Woman of No Character*, 114–19, and Gwendolyn Needham, "Mrs. Manley: An Eighteenth-Century Wife of Bath," *Huntington Library Quarterly* 14 (1948–49): 259–85.

17. See Ehrenpreis, 2:681.

18. See Morgan, *A Woman of No Character*, 153–54.

19. See the discussion of Manley's relations with Barber in ibid., 153. It is also suggestive that Manley acknowledges her love affairs with John Manley and John Tilly in her autobiographical writing, yet does not specify Barber. Further,

Barber is mentioned without remorse and with continued friendship in her will (Barber had married another woman): "notwithstanding the Dean's [Swift's] letter and Alderman Barber's solicitations from whom I acknowledge to have received so many favours that I cannot with any assurance make any claims from him of the half of this fifty pound a year from the patent [the printing patent they shared] only begging he may out of his usual goodness assist my executors in their lawful claims upon Mr. Benjamin Took's share. . . ."

20. Ehrenpreis notes that on 27 February, Swift's "accounts show that he gave Hessy fourpence that day. Since he also dined in the City with Barber, it is probable that she turned up there, for he could not possibly have met her at the other places" (2:643).

21. "Near the end of the month Mrs. Manley . . . dined with Swift at Mrs. Vanhomrigh's" (Ehrenpreis, 2:644).

22. Davis, The Examiner, xxxiii–xxxiv, emphasis added.

23. Robert Adams Day, Told in Letters (Ann Arbor: University of Michigan Press, 1966), 141. To be precise, Day's discussion of Manley's style includes comments about the New Atalantis like "particularized and pointed" (156) and conducive to representing "characters" feelings and motivations analyzed more or less in the modern manner" (122). He does, however, refer as well to the play Love upon Tick, whose attribution to Manley is questionable.

24. Williams's notes on Manley share the problematic language of Davis and Ehrenpreis. For example, he places the burden of sexual misconduct on her by describing her "marriage" to John Manley as a consciously illicit action: "She early contracted a bigamous relationship with John Manley" (JS, 1:123).

25. A recent book on the Augustan court briefly considers the relationship between the queen and the women around her. "Anne's poor health, shyness, and strict morality . . . ensured that, apart from her husband, her chief ministers, and medical staff, she would be surrounded, even guarded by other women" (117). Bedchamber service "led to significant financial and social advancement. It also conferred real political significance upon those who regulated access to the Queen, whether that access was face to face or through verbal or written messages." See R. O. Bucholz, The Augustan Court: Queen Anne and the Decline of Court Culture (Stanford: Stanford University Press, 1993).

26. Kendall, "Finding the Good Parts: Sexuality in Women's Tragedies in the Time of Queen Anne" in Curtain Calls: British and American Women and the Theater, 1660–1820, ed. Mary Ann Schofield and Cecelia Macheski (Athens: Ohio University Press, 1991), 165–76.

27. BL Add. MSS 61422, fol. 194: narrative by SM; BL Add. MSS 61458, fol. 98: Mrs. Bumet's character of SM. Cited in Frances Harris, A Passion for Government: The Life of Sarah, Duchess of Marlborough (Oxford: Clarendon Press, 1991), 13, 354.

28. Letters by Manley, Masham, and Harley suggest rather than prove this claim, and more historical reconstruction needs to be done. Masham and Harley are secretive and coded correspondents in many instances.

29. Factotum, No. 21, December 1985, 23.

30. Harley's involvement with "party writers" is described in J. A. Downie, Robert Harley and the Press: Propaganda and Public Opinion in the Age of Swift and Defoe (Cambridge: Cambridge University Press, 1979).

31. In order to detach himself from his mistress, the Duchess (Barbara Palmer), and marry Jeanitin (Sarah Jennings), the Count Fortunatus (John Churchill, duke of Marlborough) arranges a "bed trick." His friend Germanicus

(Henry Jermyn) takes his place in the Duchess's boudoir, and the pair are compromisingly "discovered." The scene is especially interesting for its gender reversals, in which Germanicus is feminized and the "male gaze" is given to the woman. Manley here imitates/parodies Marie D'Aulnoy's *Travels into Spain* (1692), 55–56.

32. See *The Complete Poems of John Wilmot, Earl of Rochester*, ed. David M. Vieth (New Haven: Yale University Press, 1968), 94–101; 104–12.

33. Rochester's "Letter from Artemisia . . . to Chloe" may have appealed to Manley because it is framed as a conversation between women. Its multiple seduction stories portray victims who are not particularly worthy of sympathy, although the poem does not condone the seducers, either. The idea of illicit sex as a metaphor for power and as a means of self-definition in his poetry may explain Manley's interest in his work.

34. Richetti argues, "That myth, the destruction of female innocence by a representative of an aristocratic world of male corruption, is a well-known eighteenth-century preoccupation, from its prominence in the drama and the prose fiction which begins with Richardson and expands all over Europe" (*Popular Fiction Before Richardson*, 125). Ballaster urges the limitations of this view (*Seductive Forms*, 16–19).

35. The white dress did not signify a wedding gown to Manley's contemporaries, but it does provoke that association for modern readers. The more general connotations of "white"—unspotted, as in Dryden's milk-white hind—are appropriate to the irony of the image.

36. *The Medley*, the Whig journalistic mouthpiece, engaged in weekly verbal sparring with the *Examiner*.

37. PRO, SP 44, 78. Warrants also name Morphew, Woodward and Barber (bookseller, publisher, and printer), but these men were released. The warrant ordering Manley's arrest has her name handwritten in the margin. She was not released.

38. BL Add. MSS 61443, fol. 35: Sunderland to SM, 9 November 1709.

39. For a description of Sarah Churchill's role in the *Medley*, see Harris, *A Passion for Government*, 177–84.

40. Nokes, *Jonathan Swift, a Hypocrite Reversed*, 131.

41. *A True Narrative of what pass'd at the Examination of the Marquis De Guiscard at the Cock-Pit, the 8th of March, 1710/11. His stabbing Mr. Harley, and Other precedent and subsequent Facts, relating to the Life of the said Guiscard* (London: Printed for John Morphew, 1711).

42. Manley's departure from and awareness of Dryden's privileging of Juvenal in the *Discourse Concerning Satire* is noted in Ros Ballaster's "Manl(e)y Forms: Sex and Female Satirist" in *Women, Texts, and Histories 1575–1760*, ed. Clare Brant and Diane Purkiss (London and New York: Routledge, 1992), 223–24.

43. Mikhail Bakhtin, *Problems of Dostoevsky's Poetics*, ed. and trans. Caryl Emerson (Minneapolis: University of Minnesota Press, 1984). See especially Bakhtin's analysis of the essential characteristics of Menippean satire in chap. 4, 101–22. See also Eugene P. Kirk, *Menippean Satire: An Annotated Catalogue of Texts and Criticism* (New York: Garland, 1980), ix–xxxiii.

The Shared Worlds of Manley and Swift

CAROLE FABRICANT

CRITICAL reactions to Delariviere Manley, both in her own life-time and in later generations, point to deep-seated anxieties over the threat of contamination and promiscuous commingling: of male with female (as her very name ironically suggests), of aristocracy with lower class, of neoclassical standards with those of the marketplace. For recent critics as well as for her conservative male contemporaries, Manley has presented the possibility of blurred boundaries, intensifying their fear of being unable to discriminate between great art and hack writing, between elite and popular culture. Typically characterized by such critics as "the scandal-writer" and "the hack who also served as mistress to the printer John Barber,"[1] Manley was, and continues to be, transformed into the contemptible Other that serves by contrast to shore up a culturally sanctioned Augustan identity and to define the "true" Augustan moral and literary values.

The fact that these same critics have found it impossible, in certain instances, to clearly differentiate between her and Swift's contributions to the *Examiner* or to ascertain the precise extent of each one's role in the authorship of other political tracts seems only to have increased the shrillness of the insistence upon keeping them in separate categories at all costs, and regularly produces comments like the following: "[Richard Steele] explicitly added insult to injury in dealing with the new Dean of St. Patrick's in the same manner in which he would deal with scribblers of the kidney of Delariviere Manley, the author of *The New Atalantis*."[2] Quite apart from the fact that the latter work—here presumably cited as an example of the inconsequential hack writing of a mere "scribbler"—was in its day a highly influential political satire, helping to undermine public confidence in the Whig government and create a climate favorable to a Tory takeover, it should be noted that Swift himself was far less dismissive of Manley's abilities and not nearly as eager to deny his own links to the kind of writing she produced, even if he chose to characterize these links in sometimes contradictory ways.

Appearing in Swift's textual references now as an "understrapper" working under his direction and producing only pieces "ordered to be written" (JS, 2:421, 1:254), now as a writer fully responsible for her own compositions, Manley highlights the ambiguities surrounding questions of authority and authorial control when they involve the kind of political propaganda both of them produced at the behest of others. At times Swift's comments suggest a hybrid text that bears the signature of both: "I had not time to do it myself: so I sent my hints [about the circumstances surrounding Harley's stabbing] to the author of the *Atalantis*, and she has cook'd it into a six-penny pamphlet, in her own style, only the first page is left as I was beginning it" (JS, 1:244–45). Swift's enumeration, in the *Journal to Stella*, of the two writers' contributions to the Tory cause simultaneously clarifies and complicates the relationship between their respective works:

> I have sent to Leigh the set of *Examiners*, the first thirteen were written by several hands, some good, some bad; the next three and thirty were all by one hand, that makes forty six: then that author, whoever he was, laid it down on purpose to confound guessers; and the last six were written by a woman. Then there is an account of Guiscard by the same woman, but the facts sent by Presto. Then *An Answer to the Letter to the lords about Greg*, by Presto; Prior's *journey*, by Presto; *Vindication of the duke of Marlborough*, entirely by the same woman. *Comment on Hare's Sermon*, by the same woman, only hints sent to the printer from Presto to give her. (JS, 2:402)

In the very act of seeming to establish clear lines of authorial demarcation and responsibility, Swift here in effect dramatizes the impossibility of such a task, given the collaborative and public (not to mention anonymous) nature of the writing in question. The exact connections between providing "facts" or "hints" for a tract and actually writing it remain ambiguous enough in Swift's formulation to allow later critics to reclaim the "best" parts of these tracts for Swift while giving Manley credit (such as it is) for the rest. Herbert Davis, for example, interprets Swift's wording to mean that Manley's *A Learned Comment upon Dr. Hare's Sermon* was "a work prompted and partly written by him" and goes on to observe that "it is not difficult to pick out certain phrases which sound as though they had been first written down by [Swift] as marginal comments" (Swift, *Prose*, 3:xxxiii–xxxiv). While treating the work as a whole, and particularly its subject, condescendingly ("Swift was not in a mood to bother much with such an antagonist as Dr. Hare"), Davis appears desirous of salvaging its wittiest and most incisive passages for Swift. A similar impulse is evident in Davis's remarks about Manley's *A Modest Enquiry into the Reasons of the Joy Expressed ... upon the Spreading of a Report of Her Majesty's Death,* in which he points to passages that "perhaps ... may be regarded as indications of Swift's part in the paper" and declares on one occasion that "One would like to think that Swift was responsible for the [following] sentence" (Swift, *Prose,* 8:xvi).

These remarks, ranging in tone from confident assertion to wishful speculation, represent at the same time a determined (or at least hopeful) denial and a tacit confirmation of Swift's inextricable ties to the world of scandal-mongering, political propaganda, and journalistic "hackdom" associated with Manley. If Swift's own attitude toward these links can reveal similar contradictions, it also includes an acknowledgment of them that belies critical efforts at disassociation. Peter Stallybrass and Allon White have used Swift, interchangeably with Dryden and Pope, as an example of how the "grotesque physical body" (of low-class culture, vulgarity, linguistic messiness, the feminine, and so forth) was treated during this period as "a phobic set of representations associated with avoidance and with others [never the self]."[3] However, Swift's attitude toward Manley (like other aspects of his life and writings) suggests that his relationship with the anti-Augustan "grotesque body" differed in important ways from Dryden's and Pope's, reflecting on the one hand a deeper ambivalence and, on the other, a greater willingness to embrace its subversive energies and violations of Augustan decorum.

His poem *Corinna,* commonly interpreted as a satiric attack on Manley,[4] in fact underscores Swift's complicated view of her and what she represented, a view by no means uniformly negative or dismissive. Presenting her with a genealogy reminiscent of the one Cadenus gives to Vanessa—

> This Day (the Year I Dare not tell,)
> *Apollo* play'd the Midwife's part;
> Into the World *Corinna* fell,
> And he endow'd her with his Art
>
> (ll. 1–4)

—Swift portrays the infant Corinna as part-victim, part-beneficiary of the joint ministrations of Cupid and a satyr, who "stroke her Hands, and rub her Gums" (7) while she lies in the cradle. Predictably enough growing into a precocious child—"She seem'd to laugh and squawl in Rhimes, / And all her Gestures were Lampoons" (15–16)—Corinna winds up producing a commonplace book filled with scandal: "She pours it out in an *Atlantis,* / Or *Memoirs* of the *New Utopia*" (31–32). Although there are several cutting jibes at Manley's personal life, including a censorious glance at her connections with Edmund Curll ("Turns Auth'ress, and is *Curll's* for Life" [28]), the poem also slyly points to the common ground Manley and Swift share, as fellow satirists and recorders of intimate scenes others might well think obscene. Thus the satyr pronounces that "The World shall feel her scratch and bite" (12), and Corinna subsequently learns to turn whatever she sees into poetic farce, at times provoking comparison with the scatological voyeur of *The Lady's Dressing Room* and *Strephon and Chloe:*

> She made a Song, how little Miss,
> Was kiss'd and slobber'd by a Lad:
> And how, when Master went to p——,
> Miss came and peep'd at all he had.
>
> (ll. 21–24)

Hardly a "vitriolic satire" on Manley, then, *Corinna* is a typically Swiftian piece—not unlike his mocking trifles and epistles directed at close friends such as Thomas Sheridan and Patrick Delany—that embodies coexisting levels of satiric distancing and ironic self-recognition and that combines alienating censure with implied intimacy or partial identification.

Although there are instances where Swift chooses to gloss over or veil his connections with Manley, he shows little inclination to deny them phobically, and there are times when he openly recognizes both her being and her worth in ways that declare affinity rather than otherness. Thus he can tell Stella at one point, "I dined with people that you never heard of, nor is it worth your while to know; an authoress and a printer [Manley and John Barber]," but then declare in a later journal entry, "Poor Mrs. Manley the author is very ill of a dropsy and sore leg; the printer tells me he is afraid she cannot live long. I am heartily sorry for her; she has very generous principles for one of her sort; and a great deal of good sense and invention" (*JS*, 1:154; 2:474). While the reference to "her sort" seems to qualify as a distancing technique and a form of projection consonant with the exclusionary procedures discussed by Stallybrass and White, the simultaneous expressions of heartfelt sympathy and praise of Manley's mental attributes point to a very different attitude, one likewise apparent in the *Journal* passage where Swift refers to "a set of *Examiners*, and five pamphlets, which I have either written or contributed to, except the best, which is the *Vindication of the duke of Marlborough;* and is entirely of the author of the *Atalantis*" (*JS*, 2:390–91).

Swift's sense of connection with Manley was shaped not only by what she wrote, but also by the world she inhabited, which simultaneously supported and hindered her role as writer, offering an abundance of material for her keen satiric eye but posing significant dangers to her physical and economic well-being once her writings were in print. Swift alludes to these discouragements and dangers—as relevant to his own situation as to hers—in a *Journal* entry describing a visit to Lord Peterborough's, during which he found Manley "soliciting [Peterborough] to get some pension or reward for her service in the cause, by writing her *Atalantis*, and prosecution, &c. upon it. I seconded her, and hope they will do something for the poor woman" (*JS*, 1:306). Manley's plight as a neglected underling of the powerful, subjected to judicial harassment and prosecution for expressing her views in print, would have been only too familiar to Swift, bringing to mind his own dependency and vulnerability. If Manley was a "kept" woman, after all, her status was not all that different from Swift's, who was likewise a hireling of "my lord keeper," Robert Harley (*JS*, 1:244), and maintained as part of the Tory ministry's stable of journalists. The need for a patron of one sort or another was as much class- as gender-based: a necessary part of the politics of survival for a low-ranked Irish cleric without preferment as well as for an abandoned woman without independent resources. Given that economic anxieties and basic material concerns as well as political interests formed an important link between them, it is apt that Manley, in her will, should have turned to "my much honored friend the Dean of St. Patrick, Dr. Swift" for assistance in helping her executors gain access to money promised her from patents granted by Queen Anne.

It would have been difficult for Swift to have rejected what Manley represented even had he been inclined to do so, for such rejection would have constituted nothing less than a profound self-denial of even greater proportions than his periodic attempts to disassociate himself from his Irish birthright. Far more than either Dryden or Pope, Swift participated in the kind of literary world associated with Manley, one marked by libel, scurrility, and anonymously published "underground" satire. His preference for popular to classical satiric forms places many of his writings alongside Manley's as examples of stylistic and generic innovation. Even in his exalted role as confidant to Bolingbroke and Harley and chief defender of the Tory ministry, Swift frequently showed his affinities for a "low" style: "Lord treasurer was hinting as if he wished a ballad was made on [Lord Nottingham], and I will get up one against to-morrow. . . . I was this morning making the ballad, two degrees above Grubstreet. . . . The printer came before we parted, and brought the ballad, which made them laugh very heartily a dozen times" (*JS*, 2:430–31). A work like the *Journal to Stella* (among many others) not only contains evidence of these affinities, it is itself an embodiment and testimonial to them, with its adaptation· of popular subgenres connected with private memoirs and familiar epistolary writing. Snippets of gossip, hints of scandal, satiric commentary, minute details of social and domestic activities, personal letters, a blend of factual and fictive self-dramatizing techniques: features such as these typify both Swift's and Manley's characteristic modes of expression.

Parallels between the two writers are suggested as well by Manley's brand of marginality, which consisted in the frequent testing of the boundaries between the licit and the illicit, the respectable and the scandalous, the high and the low. Her problematic relationship to the law was epitomized by her long-term romantic involvement with John Tilly, a prison warden who himself on occasion fell afoul of the law, as well as by her own paradoxical position as a writer in defense of a traditional order and in opposition to acts of social disruption (see, for example, *A True Relation of the Several facts and Circumstances of the Intended Riot and Tumult on Queen Elizabeth's Birth-day*) who was herself briefly imprisoned for allegedly violating the law through her writing and who later turned these circumstances into a quasi-fictionalized representation of persecuted innocence in her autobiographical novella, *Adventures of Rivella:*

> I ask'd her how she would like going to *Newgate*? She answer'd me very well; since it was to discharge her Conscience. . . . this poor Lady was close shut up in the *Messenger*'s Hands from seeing or speaking to any Person, without being allow'd Pen, Ink and Paper; where she was most tyranically, and barbarously insulted by the Fellow and his Wife who had her in keeping. . . .[5]

Manley's life and activities underscored the fine, often arbitrary line that separated those "on the outside" of prison walls from

those "inside": more broadly speaking, of sanctioned (hence rewarded) behavior from behavior deemed transgressive (and therefore punishable). This was something Swift himself would learn
from firsthand experience through his continuing battles with the
authorities—first in England, later in Ireland—over his publications. Although he managed to avoid prison (his printers, of
course, were not so fortunate), his encounters with governmental
harassment and threats of prosecution impressed upon him the
"outlaw" status of (political and satiric) writers, along with those
deemed their accomplices, in a society increasingly subject to cen-
sorship and bureaucratic control, symbolized by "diligent enquir-
ies into remote and problematical guilt, with a new power of
enforcing them by chains and dungeons to every person whose
face a Minister thinks fit to dislike" (Swift, *Prose*, 9:33).

Manley's description of hardships she has incurred as a dissi-
dent writer targeted for political persecution finds an echo in
Swift's lament that he "dare not venture to publish" his views on
public affairs: "For however orthodox they may be while I am now
writing, they may become criminal enough to bring me into trou-
ble before midsummer" (9:33). Like Manley, Swift enjoyed a paradoxical relationship to the law, fulminating against the forces of
disorder in England, when speaking for the Tory establishment,
while later, in Ireland, urging organized resistance to established
authority and exuberantly promoting the spirit of misrule by
(among other actions) proposing a charivari in which William
Wood is to be "executed" (hung in effigy) in accordance with the
workings of popular street justice. The arbitrariness of the bound-
ary separating the licit from the illicit, the respectable from the
deviant or corrupt, is attested to in Swift's metaphoric use of the
madhouse to represent governmental institutions (such as *A
Character, Panegyric, and Description of the Legion Club*) and
his use of prisons and courts to portray suffering innocence and
unpunished—indeed, officially sanctioned—guilt, as in his satiric
attacks on Chief Justice Whitshed.

Yet despite these similarities, the respective fates of Swift and
Manley, both as writers in their own lifetimes and as authors
judged by a later critical establishment, differed significantly, for
reasons that cannot be reduced to a single factor but that serve
to highlight the effects of gender differences. Manley, like Aphra
Behn before her, was acutely aware of how these differences func-
tioned to hinder her literary and social aspirations. She attributed
the failure of her first play, *The Lost Lover*, to the fact that "the
bare name of being a woman's play damned it beyond its own

want of merit" and the condemnation of her second play, *The Royal Mischief*, to "the prejudice against our sex."[6] Moreover, she protested the existence of a sexual double standard through the words of the male narrator of *Adventures of Rivella*, who observes that *"If she [Rivella/Manley] had been a Man, she had been without Fault:* But the Charter of that Sex being much more confin'd than ours, what is not a Crime in Men is scandalous and unpardonable in Woman, as she her self has very well observ'd in divers Places, throughout her own Writings" (7–8).

But even apart from the crippling effects of overt prejudice and misogyny, Manley's gender worked against her ambitions in subtler, more insidious ways. Take, for example, her abiding interest in history, undoubtedly nourished early on by the influence of her father, Sir Roger Manley, whose family were direct descendants of William the Conqueror and who published several historical accounts, including *The History of the Late Warres in Denmark* and *The History of the Rebellion*. His daughter eagerly tackled contemporary historical issues in her Tory tracts and (like Swift) expressed interest in writing a history of the Tory ministry and the period just before Queen Anne's death.[7] It is not surprising, however, that Manley never realized this ambition, for reasons related to why it would have been virtually unthinkable for Manley to have fulfilled a role similar to Gibbon's as England's great chronicler of the rise and fall of empires. Instead, Manley's passion for history had to express itself in a variety of sublimated or indirect forms: in commentary about the nature of historical writing in relation to the genres of romance and the novel,[8] and in fictionalized, satirically or romantically transformed, representations of history (such as *The New Atalantis* and *Lucius*). In addition, at the outset of *The Memoirs of Europe* she strikes a defiantly bold tone, promising her readers a fearless treatment of her elevated subject matter and triumphantly consigning to oblivion the bulk of histories written before her: "Of all those numerous *Histories* which in all Ages have been wrote, how few, very few, have remain'd with Applause to Posterity? ... How many more (like *Mushrooms* of a Night, or *Abortives* under the Mother-Pangs) have left their unhappy Parent the *Mortification* of seeing 'em *expire* as soon as they began to *Be*?"[9]

Nevertheless, Manley never became the kind of historian she at one point envisioned. This fact, along with the common denigration of her most historically resonant writings as mere scandal sheets or Grub Street productions written only to make money, cannot be understood apart from prevailing assumptions about the nature and shape of a career, since they applied very differently to men and to women in the eighteenth century. Exalted conceptions of "philosophical history," of the historian's need for an imperial command of the past, and of both the Augustan and the Enlightenment project meant that historians (and historical narratives) were necessarily defined in masculine terms—as embodiments of a specifically male authority. The "feminine" in this arena was reserved for historical sources that could be made to passively yield up their treasures to the historian's probing eye; Gibbon, in one telling example, referred to his voluminous library as his "seraglio," catering to his unfettered choice and keen appetite.[10] While it is a misleading stereotype that women during this period were universally forced into domestic roles and denied access to all professional pursuits, their ability to engage in such pursuits was often severely circumscribed, by ideological paradigms of public and private identity as well as by concrete sociopolitical constraints.

The definition of a career was intimately connected with modes of self-fashioning and self-invention that are by now familiar to students of recent Renaissance and eighteenth-century scholarship—activities that were profoundly affected by matters of gender. Manley indicates her realization of this fact in her own best-known example of self-fashioning, *Adventures of Rivella,* which shows what was permitted a woman (and, by implication, what was denied) in the way of constructing a coherent narrative of her life and representing a female career acceptable for public consumption.

While there is truth in the claim that Manley was "particularly adept at "'managing the media'" and cleverly used the autobiographical format to "control her own image,"[11] she could exert such managerial skills only within (and against) the limits set down by a society as concerned with defining the parameters of possibility for a woman's image as it was with regulating institutional practices affecting women's material lives. Thus, on the most overt level her account presents, through the mediation of a male narrator pointedly named Sir Charles Lovemore, the story of a woman whose life and career have revolved around the fine art and exquisite sensibilities of love: one whose reputation in this regard fans the young chevalier D'Aumont's desire to become acquainted with her as "the only Person of her Sex that knows how to *Live,* and of whom we may say, in relation to Love, since she has so peculiar a Genius for, and has made such noble Discoveries in that Passion, that it would have been a *Fault in her, not to have been Faulty*" (120).

Errancy and excess can be openly acknowledged, even flaunted—"She has carried the Passion [of love] farther than could be readily conceiv'd" (4)—as long as they occur within the safely "feminine" arena of romance. Other types of transgressive behavior (such as trespasses into largely male domains of public activity) are duly noted—indeed, in the case of Manley's clash with the authorities over the publication of *The New Atalantis*, they are treated at some length so as to emphasize her courage and firmness of conviction (109–15)—but symbolically repudiated through the intercession of the narrator, who assures us that Rivella "now agrees with me, that Politicks is not the Business of a Woman, especially of one that can so well delight and entertain her Readers with more gentle pleasing Theams, and has accordingly set her self to write a Tragedy for the Stage" (117). This recantation can hardly be read without irony, since the work in which it appears is itself in places a political *roman à clef,* and since the promised "Tragedy" results in a play (*Lucius*) with a significant political dimension. Nevertheless, the recantation does point to Manley's awareness of what a woman had to do to create a representation of the female writer that would be acceptable to her contemporaries. There are a number of subordinate threads running through the work, each of which could have been expanded to produce a very different narrative of the female writer, focusing not on her romantic or erotic aspects but on her political, intellectual, or artistic development. But the time had not yet arrived when a woman could register her claim to fame by writing a "history of [her] own mind" or by charting "the growth of [her] intellectual stature."[12] Hence these threads remain in the background, a testament both to the limits placed on women's powers of self-definition and to the ways in which these limits could be indirectly pointed out, and thus subtly protested.

Manley's memoir presents a distinctively "female" narrative, not only in content but in form as well. Marked by discontinuous episodes and sudden disruptions in her life, *Adventures of Rivella* lacks the sense of linear progression and teleological denouement that characterize the published self-reflections of male contemporaries who viewed their formative years as a careful preparation for, and movement toward, the moment when they would don the mantle of greatness and become their country's poet or historian or statesman. We might consider this difference in light of a recent critic's comment that Manley and others comprising "the first generation of modern London hacks . . . [were] a sorry lot not so much because [they] lacked talent as because they lacked focus and a clear sense of where, besides winding back alleys and steep-staired garrets, novelty and innovation might lead."[13] Whatever the descriptive merits of this statement, its evaluative implications need to be questioned, for the conscious planning and teleological imperative that the statement seems to be invoking as criteria of excellence had on the whole little relevance at this time to the lives of women (or the poor), whose confused windings along the back alleys—of both Grub Street and life in general—were the result of circumstances beyond their control, and whose daily struggle for survival took precedence over long-range projections for the course of their lives, let alone grand schemes for shaping their culture's future. Such projections (however problematically realized in actual life) were reserved for those with the gender and class identification of a Hume, who could complacently declare, "I went over to France, with a View of prosecuting my Studies in a Country Retreat; and I there [?then] laid that Plan of Life, which I have steddily and successfully pursued."[14]

It is quite possible, of course, that the coherence and closure we commonly ascribe to the lives and careers of canonized male writers are more the ex post facto constructions of later critics than patterns that actually existed. Nevertheless, the lives and careers of these writers, in comparison to their female counterparts, are far more apt to have followed a course amenable to such constructions, ones that included a series of social or political advancements and that helped foster a sense of themselves as representatives and/or shapers of their nations and cultures—as individuals connected to the linear progression of public as well as private history. Even Jerome Christensen, whose poststructuralist study of Hume's career questions a preexistent unified identity reflected in writing, acknowledges his subject's plausible and at least partly successful attempts to convey this more traditional representation of self: "'Hume' is a considerably less global abstraction than 'Enlightenment.' But focus on Hume is justified at least in part by his endeavor to compose a career that would convincingly impersonate the Enlightenment, that would take advantage of the machine."[15] What needs to be stressed here is that only a man could hope to carry off such an impersonation. For women, on the contrary (most obviously middle- or working-class women attempting to earn their own livelihoods), forms of isolation, instability, and disruption tended to be the governing principles of life, and these were impervious to the recuperative patterns, to the "global abstraction[s]," through which men characterized their age and recreated themselves in its image.

Even Manley, who was neither lowborn nor poor, fell victim to a specifically "female script" that derailed her youthful aspirations and placed continual roadblocks in her path. Her seduction and deception by her older cousin, John Manley, which landed her in a bigamous marriage, and the pregnancy and childbirth that followed, were among the many gender-specific catastrophes that marked Manley's life. While Swift lived a far-from-privileged existence, one subject to many of the same uncertainties and disruptions that his female contemporaries faced—evidenced, for example, in his autobiographical memoir *The Family of Swift* (Swift, *Prose,* 5:187–95), with its fragmentary form and its characterization of a *non*-career, a life made up of thwarted expectations and ruined prospects rather than steady advancement—he did have access to sources of income, power, and status generally unavailable to women, as his various public roles (Anglican churchman, Irish patriot, and so on) attest. It is this fact, among others, that enabled Swift to represent himself as a man with a specific calling and mission in works such as the *Verses on the Death of Dr. Swift* and that has allowed us to see in Swift's life a defined purpose, a sense of accomplishment, and an integrity of outlook that seem to be absent from Manley's.

Manley, I believe, was well aware of this problem—indeed, she attempts to address it in the beginning of *Adventures of Rivella,* through Lovemore's account of her early years growing up in her father's house:

> There was then such a Foundation laid, that tho' Youth, Misfortunes, and Love, for several Years have interrupted so fair a Building, yet some Time since, she is returned with the greatest Application to repair that Loss and Defect; if not with relation to this World (where Women have found it impossible to be reinstated) yet of the next, which has mercifully told us, *Mankind can commit no Crimes but what upon Conversion may be forgiven.* (12)

Here Manley not only exposes the sexual double standard as it functions empirically, to permanently stigmatize a "fallen" woman and prevent her return to society's good graces even after appropriate atonement, but she also points to the way in which this double standard affects the kind of life history a woman can construct out of her experiences, impeding her ability to build a sturdy autobiographical edifice no matter how firm the "Foundation," and making it impossible to recuperate her "losses" through a narrative

that subsumes all interruptions and gaps into a larger scheme
defined by single-minded ambition and ultimate achievement.
Prospects for worldly "reinstatement" are reserved for men, just
as the conventional tropes symbolizing such reinstatement—the
Fortunate Fall, the Prodigal Son, and others—offer structural and
allegorical resources for specifically male life histories.

Yet Manley does not let her readers off the hook easily. She
challenges them with a portrait of a woman whose steadfast moral
and political convictions significantly qualify the memoir's overall
picture of a woman associated with the volatile images of sexual
passion, and in so doing counteracts societal stereotypes of
women's inconstant and frivolous "nature"—stereotypes given notable expression in Pope's *Epistle to a Lady,* which posits that
"'Most Women have no Characters at all'" (*TE,* 3.2:l. 2), portraying
them as "variegated Tulips" and "Chameleons" (ll. 41 and 156).
Rivella's convictions are rooted in her birthright as the daughter
of "the Second Son of an Ancient Family" who "left the University
at Sixteen Years of Age, to follow the fortunes of K. *Charles* the
First," later suffering for his fidelity to the royal family during the
Civil War (14). We are made to understand her indebtedness to
"a Liberal Education, and those early Precepts of Vertue taught
her and practised in her Father's House" (12), which have been
so deeply ingrained that they survive all of Lovemore's strenuous
efforts to tear Rivella away from her championship of Tory causes:
"I brought her to be asham'd of her Writings, saving that Part
by which she pretended to save her Country, and the ancient
Constitution; (there she is a perfect *Bigot* from a long untainted
Descent of Loyal Ancestors, and consequently immoveable)" (116).

This stress upon her constancy, her uncompromising adher-
ence to principle, not only belies misogynistic assumptions about
women's fickle nature, but it also serves to disassociate Rivella
from the feminized world of the newly emergent capitalist system
as portrayed in Augustan political journalism, where "Credit is
symbolized as a goddess having the attributes of the Renaissance
goddess Fortune. . . . stand[ing] for that future which can only
be sought passionately and inconstantly, and for the hysterical
fluctuations of the urge towards it."[16] In this sense Rivella's stead-
fastness functions no less as a pointed political statement than as
an assertion of personal integrity. Manley's characterization of the
capricious and mercurial behavior of the Whig leaders and their
sycophants—the fawningly covetous courtiers who "know no Principles of their own, but shift as often as do their Patrons, and only
wear *appearing Vertues* . . . as they are fashionable Habits!"[17]—

lends indirect support to the view that the new capitalist order "has endowed society with an excessively hysterical nervous system."[18] But Manley at the same time rejects the metaphor's misogynistic implications by imputing such "hysteria" largely to male figures, and by suggesting that the ailment's antidote can most readily be found in the female constitution (as exemplified by Queen Anne and Rivella herself).

Manley's Tory allegiance, which Gwendolyn B. Needham suggests was even more exemplary than Swift's, since "Unlike the Dean, she never changed parties, but remained first, last, and always a loyal Tory,"[19] provoked often virulent criticism in her own day, replaced in more recent times by a certain perplexity and consternation over the fact that someone often viewed as an early feminist should have identified herself (in no uncertain terms, to boot) with a political ideology generally deemed antiprogressive, even reactionary. The result has been an attempt to "save" Manley from a contaminating association with Tory, especially aristocratic, values—in many ways an ironic counterpart to the attempts, noted earlier, to "save" Swift from the contaminating association with Manley herself (though in each case a very different set of ideological credentials is being defended). Thus, for example, in speaking of the emergence of a middle-class readership in the early eighteenth century with particular reference to Behn, Manley, and Eliza Haywood, Dale Spender argues: "So a change [in writing] begins to take place. Far from supplying the heroes for fiction, the aristocracy becomes the recruiting ground for 'villains.' And I suspect that this version of class politics could only have originated in a woman's view of the world."[20] The fact is, however, that the "class politics" Spender here speaks of is precisely that— meaning a politics of class, not gender—and cannot automatically be equated with "a woman's view of the world," especially since so many of Manley's male contemporaries were similarly engaged in a critique of aristocratic society and values. Apart from the fact that there was no monolithic "woman's view" in the eighteenth century—no more than there is today—the identification of Manley with an antiaristocratic outlook is particularly misleading given her frequent privileging of ancient birth and "natural breeding" (her own as well as others) and her attacks on common-born upstarts who, by cultivating high connections, acquire ill-deserved titles and status. We may recall, for example, her scornful depictions of Lord Fortunatus (John Churchill, later duke of Marlborough), who was "rais'd by the concurrent Favour of two Monarchs, his own, and his Sisters Charms, from a meer Gentleman to that

Dignity he is posting now."[21] Manley's self-composed epitaph reveals a class consciousness equally inimical to that of the lower orders and the *nouveaux riches*: "Here / Lyeth the Body of / Mrs Delarivier Manley / Daughter of Sr Roger Manley Knight / Who suitable to her Birth & Education / was acquainted with several parts of knowledge / And with the most polite writers / Both in the French and English Tongue. . . . [22]

Current critical discomfort in this regard is perhaps understandable, given that the Tory model of kingship, rooted in an assumed immutability of hierarchic order authorized by Divine Right and supported by such rigidly gendered theories as Sir Robert Filmer's, in his *Patriarcha*, would seem fundamentally inimical to a feminist perspective. The Tory model contrasts with the seemingly more congenial Whig one growing out of the Glorious Revolution and based on a constitutional relationship between the monarch and his subjects. In its most radical interpretation, it presupposes the idea of a contractual agreement along with its counterpart, the possibility of contractual dissolution. We may recall one such "feminist" appropriation of Whig ideology in the scene from Vanbrugh's *The Provoked Wife* in which Lady Bute, contemplating the prospect of breaking with her husband and having an affair with her lover, makes the following rationalization:

> What opposes? My matrimonial vow? Why, what did I vow? I think I promised to be true to my husband. Well; and he promised to be kind to me. But he han't kept his word. Why then I'm absolved from mine. Aye, that seems clear to me. The argument's good between the king and the people, why not between the husband and the wife?[23]

Lady Bute's analogy—and common critical assumptions—notwithstanding, there is no necessary correlation between sympathy for the plight of women in a male-dominated society and identification with the interests of an upwardly mobile middle class rather than with royal privilege. In their zeal to bring as many female writers as possible into the "subversive" fold, certain feminist critics too often wind up glossing over necessary distinctions and emptying the term of all meaning. This has equally deleterious consequences for both literary criticism and political analysis—as well as, one might add, for a commitment to genuinely revolutionary modes of thought and action, which are apt to become hopelessly diluted or trivialized by such absence of analytic rigor. Throughout the eighteenth century (as in earlier and later periods) many largely conservative writers, both male and female, produced texts that were subversive of certain aspects of the status quo while supportive of other aspects of it. Not only Manley, but Behn as well, found ways (for example, through the mediation of the romance genre) to incorporate aspects of Tory ideology into their respective visions of female empowerment. The ideological asymmetries and contradictions in Behn's treatment of gender, class, and race in *Oroonoko* point to the ways in which "progressive" and "conservative," even "reactionary" elements can coexist in the same text. We thus need to use a model of ideology that does not flatten out these contradictions in a misguided attempt to produce a seamless whole, in this case a coherently "subversive" outlook.

Another reason to forego such attempts at ideological consistency in this particular case is that early-eighteenth-century Toryism was itself a rather schizophrenic ideology, one characterized by contradictory impulses and serving as a political umbrella for highly disparate groups in society. While there is a tendency to identify Tories with "high-flyers," the landed gentry, and aristocrats clinging to a politics of nostalgia, the urban poor were no less ardent supporters of the party; indeed, it has been argued that "the most enthusiastic anti-Whigs were the London populace . . . and the lower orders in general."[24] This motley association of high and low, propertied and propertyless, country and city elements, brought together by their common opposition to the wealthy commercial and urban monied interests, created a curious brand of populism, part elitist and part preproletarian, whose internal contradictions have been well captured in the term *Tory radicalism*.[25] What this means in Manley's case is that she could embrace aristocratic values and traditions while at the same time identifying herself with the oppressed and the exploited. Thus her self-portrait in *Adventures of Rivella* presents a woman of distinguished birth, given to wearing "[fashionable] Garb" (11), who "understands good Breeding to a Punctuality" (12–13), yet no less a woman "always inclin'd to assist the Wretched" (65), who insists upon risking imprisonment by assuming full responsibility for *The New Atalantis* because "she could not bear to live and reproach her self with the Misery that might happen to those unfortunate People [the poor *Printer*, and . . . the *Publishers*]" if she chose to remain silent (112). No doubt her awareness of having been victimized as a woman in a society controlled by men strengthened her sense of empathy with the "three innocent Persons" who, unjustly detained, stood to be "ruin'd with their Families" (109) through the arbitrary workings of a corrupt system.

Along with these expressions of sympathy for tradesmen threatened with loss of livelihood, strains of the hybrid populism infusing Tory ideology run throughout Manley's political tracts, especially those that condemn the war policy of the Whigs by exposing its disastrous consequences both at home and abroad. In these tracts the will of "the people" is set against the selfish interests of a small but powerful faction who stand to profit from the war's continuation: "Could there be a poll made, and voices collected from house to house, we should quickly see how unanimous our people are for a peace; those excepted, who either gain by the war, or, concealing their hoards, pay but small proportions toward it."[26] Prominent among these exceptions are the duke of Marlborough and his chaplain, Dr. Francis Hare, whose sermon occasioned by the former's victory at Bouchain unwittingly betrays the belief that "nothing in *Nature,* is *so Eligible* as Self-Interest, tho' purchased at the Price of a lasting War, the Blood and Treasure of his Fellow-Subjects, and the Weal of his Native Country."[27] The scope of Manley's sympathetic concern here expands beyond a few individuals she knows personally (such as her printer and publishers) to include a large and diverse segment of the English population, linked to her only through common bonds of victimization: "Let us consider how long we shall be able to pay such a price for so small a conquest [the surrender of Bouchain]! I speak only of our money; having learnt by good example not to value the blood of those poor wretches that are yearly sacrificed in vast numbers, in trenches, and at the foot of walled towns."[28] In chronicling "our personal sufferings at home," Manley underscores the shared interests of those groups who were, or were in the process of becoming, strange bedfellows in the Tory camp—the London poor and the backwoods gentry:

> Let us look into our Gazettes, for the number of bankrupts: along the streets of our metropolis, and observe but the decay of trade, the several shops shut up, and more in daily apprehension of failing. Let us remove ourselves into the country, and see the penury of country gentlemen, with small estates and numerous families, that pay in such large proportions to the war; and there let us inquire how acceptable, nay, how indispensable, peace is to their farther subsisting.[29]

In their forceful denunciations of the Whig war policy, their incisive analyses of the self-serving motives of its promoters (in particular the duke of Marlborough, along with the newly emer-

gent capitalist class centered in London), and their blistering exposure of the war's devastating consequences through graphic
details underscoring the swelling numbers of corpses abroad and
beggars at home, Manley's tracts call to mind the similarly impassioned and eloquent antiwar (and later, anticolonialist) pamphlets
of Swift:

> We must become not only Poor, for the present, but reduced by further
> Mortgages to a state of Beggary, for endless Years to come. . . . We
> have been fighting for the Ruin of the Publick Interest, and the Ad-
> vancement of a Private. We have been fighting to raise the Wealth and
> Grandeur of a particular Family; to enrich Usurers and Stock-jobbers;
> and to cultivate the pernicious Designs of a Faction; by destroying the
> Landed Interest. . . . And this is what we charge [those in power] with
> as answerable to God, their Country, and Posterity, that the bleeding
> Condition of their Fellow-Subjects, was a Feather in the Balance with
> their private Ends. (Swift, *Prose*, 6:52, 59)

Both writers insist upon focusing their readers' attention on the
concrete, material conditions of their existence, stressing the
changes these have undergone throughout the war's duration, and
both eschew abstract arguments for empirical evidence, as well
as appeals to common sense and common decency. If none of
Manley's tracts exerted the immediate and dramatic impact of
Swift's *Conduct of the Allies* on the course of the war (and we
should, of course, keep in mind that neither did anyone else's),
their cogency and persuasiveness would suggest that the reason
had less to do with any rhetorical deficiencies in her writing than
with the lack of opportunity she was given, because of her sex, to
produce a major document urging the war's cessation. However
happy Harley and his associates were to avail themselves of Manley's skillful polemics, in moments of political crisis or decision it
was not to a woman they would ever think to turn. The reason is
obvious: at a time when even poetry was considered a largely male
domain where a woman practitioner risked being viewed as "an
intruder on the rights of men,"[30] military adventures and matters
of foreign policy were deemed clearly out of bounds for women—
subjects presumably beyond their comprehension and of little im-
port to their domestic sphere of activity.

Manley, as might be expected, was determined to refute this
perception by showing that war is an issue of immediate concern
to women, affecting their lives in very direct and profound ways.
Her method of demonstration seems peculiarly appropriate to
those Manleyian personae whose main preoccupations revolve

around bodily activities: "If we continue thus prodigal of our Blood and Treasure, in a few Years we shall have as little of the one as the other left; and our Women, if they intend to multiply, must be reduc'd, like the *Amazons,* to go out of the Land, or take them Husbands at home of those wretched Strangers, whom our Piety and Charity relieved."[31] If this threatening scenario derives its force partly from the xenophobia and implicitly racist nationalism that was one of the more reactionary elements of Tory ideology ("Of the Natives there will be scarce a Remnant preserved; and thus the *British* Name may be endangered once more to be lost in the *German*"), it also conveys a more radical message: if men persist in inflicting senseless carnage on one another ("Let us have War, what have we to do with Peace? we have beaten our Enemy, let us beat him again")—and ultimately on themselves, in an act of cultural suicide—women will have to take matters into their hands and assume responsibility for the nation's future. Of course, what is presented here is not as radical a statement about the relationship between woman and war as we find in later feminist writings—in, say, Virginia Woolf's *Three Guineas*—but it does represent one important way in which Manley feminizes Tory ideology, demonstrating its adaptability to the specific interests of women.

Another aspect of this feminization may be seen in Manley's celebration of specifically female monarchs as the great models of peace-making and peace-keeping. Whereas Anne Bradstreet exalted Queen Elizabeth as a warrior ("Our Amazon in th' Camp of Tilbury") whose forceful actions ensured England's dominance around the world—"Her victories in foreign coasts resound; / Ships more invincible than Spain's, her foe, / She wracked, she sacked, she sunk his Armado"[32]—Manley eulogizes her as "a true friend to Peace, it being her constant Maxim, *That it was more glorious to prevent a War by Wisdom, than to finish it by Victories.*"[33] Following in her great predecessor's footsteps, Queen Anne "hath no Enemies but such as are Enemies to Peace" (194), her unflagging energies having been devoted to ending England's involvement in a bloody conflict that could only bring ruin to her subjects:

She thought fit to stop the Vital Streams of the Blood and Treasure of Her People, and to put a Period to a War, that now serv'd only to gratify the Covetousness or Ambition of those She was Confederated with, as well as the vast Designs of a Faction at Home; and with Peace to endeavour to settle such a Commerce as might in some measure reimburse Her Subjects of the vast Treasure they had expended. (186)

Eschewing the masculine, aggressive imagery associated with an Amazonian leader (or even the more muted allusions to Queen Anne as a hunter "protect[ing] the Sylvan Reign" in *Windsor Forest*), Manley portrays Anne as a maternal figure whose loving nurture of her offspring has met with ingratitude: "She may truly complain, *She has nourish'd and brought up Children, but they have Rebelled against Her....* Monsters sure are they, that can rejoice for the Loss of a Life worn out in their own Service" (187, 186). The queen's behavior is characterized in terms of the stereotypically feminine qualities of self-denial and self-sacrifice, but these qualities function here as signs of inner strength and nobility, not of "womanly" weakness or subservience. There is room for legitimate debate as to whether this type of portrayal is more "radical" or more "reactionary" than depictions of women "in breeches" appropriating traditionally masculine roles, but such debate only underscores the fact that feminist criticism, like feminist ideology in general, is not a monolithic set of values or perspectives.

Perhaps the most interesting and suggestive instance of what I have been calling Manley's feminization of Tory ideology occurs at the conclusion of *Adventures of Rivella*, where Lovemore, after recounting the protagonist's many trials and tribulations, suggests an alternative, more agreeably entertaining, narrative that he might have told his listeners:

> I should have brought to you her Table well furnish'd and well serv'd; have shown you her sparkling Wit and easy Gaiety, when at Meat with Persons of Conversation and Humour: From then carried you ... within the Nymphs Alcove, to a Bed nicely sheeted and strow'd with *Roses, Jessamins* or *Orange-Flowers* ... and there have given you leave to fancy your self the happy Man, with whom she chose to repose her self, during the Heat of the Day, in a State of Sweetness and Tranquility: From thence conducted you towards the cool of the Evening, either upon the *Water,* or to the *Park* for Air, with a Conversation always new, and which never cloys. ... (119–20)

At first blush this passage seems to represent a conventional male fantasy of sensual indulgence and gratification, complete with an Epicurean-oriented Eve eager to service her Adam in an Edenic bower fully equipped for pleasure. But the repeated mention of Rivella's art of "Conversation"—a word, here as elsewhere in the work, that punningly brings together several different kinds of skills—alerts the reader to the existence of a more multidimensional picture. What initially might strike us as the depiction of a female sex object—and Rivella is technically the object of a male narration (not to mention the object of titillation for a male listener) within the fiction's framework—turns out to be that of a sexual subject who chooses her own amorous companions and who possesses exceptional qualities of mind as well as body. Indeed, the ultimate effect of the memoir is to underscore the interconnectedness of the two by (re)defining sensuality in nonphallic, nonejaculatory terms, as a mental and physical continuum that takes place in public as well as private settings and that has a serious social as well as personal dimension. This is suggested early on, when the Chevalier D'Aumont admits to having been "softned by the Charms of Madam *Dacier*'s Conversation; a Woman without either Youth or Beauty, yet who makes a Thousand Conquests, and preserves them too" (2). When Lovemore objects that "Talking to Her is conversing with an admirable Scholar, a judicious Critick, but what has That to do with the Heart?," D'Aumont counters that "there is no being pleas'd in [Women's] Conversation without a Mixture of the Sex which will still be mingling it self in all we say" (3).

The argument set forth here, that a woman's mental abilities, eloquence, and social interactions—her "conversation" understood in the broadest sense—can be as desirable, as sexually stimulating to a man as her physical attractiveness or other specifically "feminine" attributes, serves to undermine central aspects of the period's dominant gender ideology, with its emphasis on female beauty, passivity, and intellectual inferiority to, and therefore necessary dependence on men. Hence there is a need to substantially qualify a common view of Manley's contributions as a writer, as exemplified in the following remark: "Where Behn widened the woman writer's scope, Manley declared that love was the only subject for a woman. In moving from Behn to Manley we move from a declaration of independence to an attempt to found the woman writer's authority on her femininity, conceived of as eroticism."[34] For as the preceding discussion shows, however much femininity and eroticism dominate Manley's writings, they are reconceptualized in such a way that they transcend their conventional meanings and comprehend a broad range of physical, emotional, and intellectual elements. In this way Manley, no less than (though differently from) Behn, "widened the woman writer's scope" and presented her own special kind of "declaration of independence" from the rigidities and constraints of male-determined

gender ideology. Unlike later feminists such as Mary Wollstonecraft, Manley affirmed women's rational faculties while steadfastly
refusing to deny the importance of their passion. Her vision contrasted as well with later male memoirists such as Gibbon, who
posited a connection between private and public spheres, but only
to the extent that the "private" was narrowly circumscribed and
drained of all intimate bodily realities. As Gibbon put it, "I may
expatiate, without reproach, on my private studies; since they
have produced the public writings, which can alone entitle me to
the esteem and friendship of my readers. . . . [But] the pains and
pleasures of the body, how important soever to ourselves, are an
indelicate topic of conversation."[35] For Manley, on the contrary,
the body's sometimes anguished but more often blissful testimony
was indispensable to the truthful, multifaceted presentation of (a
female) self.

Finally, I want to suggest that the scenario concluding *Adventures of Rivella* functions on various levels as a feminized and
eroticized version of the political vision we see in Manley's Tory
tracts, with its valorization of peace, its praise of a collective social
network that triumphs over divisive self-interest, and its nostalgic
yearning for a society free of the crass commercialism and posses-
sive individualism promoted by England's capitalist development
after the Glorious Revolution. The sexual generosity displayed by
Rivella contrasts strikingly with the selfish lusts (for wealth,
power, and furtive pleasures) that the tracts ascribe to the Marlboroughs and other Whig leaders. By the same token, Rivella,
preparing for the rites of love in a pastoral setting that privileges
nature over artifice and ostentation ("her Pillows neatly trim'd
with Lace or Muslin, stuck round with *Junquils,* or other natural
Garden Sweets, for she uses no Perfumes" [119]) is the antithesis
of Belinda at her toilet, undergoing the "sacred Rites of Pride" by
adorning herself in the opulent spoils of England's imperialistic
ventures abroad. As opposed to the sexual (and self-) objectification shown in the Popeian passage, Manley's scenario, stressing
women's erotic subjectivity, rejects the forces of sexual commodi-
fication produced by the newly emergent capitalist system, where
women circulate as objects of exchange and pieces of property.
True, it can be argued (as Janet Todd has done) that the scenario
also implicitly celebrates another form of commercial enterprise
in the newly empowered activities of the published female author,
whose effective manipulation of literary language "yields delight
and money "through its portrayals of male-female relationships."[36]
However, the memoir's concluding scene emphasizes verbal

rather than written expression. Through her mastery of the varied techniques and pleasures of "conversation," shown to be equally necessary for bedroom and drawing-room communication (and we may recall here that Manley's epitaph specifically notes that her birth, education, and wit "Made her conversation / Agreeable to All who knew her"[37]), Rivella comes to occupy a prominent role in a world of orality that constitutes a forceful critique of the very middle-class print culture that afforded her creator a considerable degree of professional recognition, and which in reality permeated every aspect of Manley's life as the long-time companion of the printer John Barber, whose financial exploitation of Manley's literary labors ironically mirrored the very system these labors sought to expose. The memoir's shifts in generic register, from the realism of Rivella's recounted personal and professional adversities to the romance of her fantasized bower of bliss, allow Manley to explore the actual conditions of women's plight in society while at the same time offering a utopian vision of a world uncontaminated by war-mongers, stock-jobbers, and misogynistic oppressors.

It would appear, then, that if Tory ideology was broad enough to accommodate Swift's anarchic tendencies and his anticolonialist sentiments, it was also sufficiently inclusive (or contradictory) to accommodate Manley's feminist perspective and her sympathies for the underdog. If the two writers' shared status as "premature anticapitalists" has produced critical confusion over the years as far as ideological definition is concerned (centuries later, an even more tumultuous fate would befall "premature antifascists" in this country, perhaps suggesting a fundamental problem in the way we attempt to understand forms of resistance that have had the misfortune to occur before their "proper" time), this is all the more reason to study them jointly: to explore all the ways in which their lives, outlooks, and textual productions were intertwined and mutually illuminating. This is not to say that the situations of the two writers should simply be conflated, however, for in the course of studying them together it behooves us to ponder the many ways in which Manley's relationship to Swift, as a "fellow" satirist and political propagandist, would inevitably have been treated differently by her contemporaries and subsequently reconfigured in the official story of literary history, "*if* [to pursue Rivella's own persistent line of inquiry] *she had been a Man.*"

Notes

1. Ehrenpreis, 2:644, 471.
2. J. A. Downie, *Jonathan Swift: Political Writer* (London: Routledge and Kegan Paul, 1983), 185.

3. Peter Stallybrass and Allon White, *The Politics and Poetics of Transgression* (Ithaca: Cornell University Press, 1986), 108.

4. See, e.g., the introductory remarks in Swift, *Poems* 1:148. Constance Clark characterizes the poem as a "vitriolic satire" on Manley in her study, *Three Augustan Women Playwrights,* American University Studies Series 4, English Language and Literature No. 40 (New York: Peter Lang, 1986), 131.

5. Manley, *The History of Rivella: Memoirs of the Life of Mrs. Manley* (1717; reprint, New York: AMS Press, 1976), 110, 114; hereafter cited in text.

6. See Fidelis Morgan, *A Woman of No Character: An Autobiography of Mrs Manley* (London: Faber and Faber, 1986), 76, 80.

7. Clark, *Three Augustan Women Playwrights,* 181.

8. See, e.g., Manley's comments to "The Reader" at the beginning of *Secret History of Queen Zarah and the Zarazians,* ed. Malcolm J. Bosse, Foundations of the Novel (1705; reprint, New York: Garland, 1972).

9. *The Novels of Mary Delariviere Manley,* ed. Patricia Koster, 2 vols. (Gainesville, Fla.: Scholars' Facsimiles & Reprints, 1971), 2:1.

10. M. M. Reese, ed., *Gibbon's Autobiography,* Routledge English Texts (London: Routledge and Kegan Paul, 1970), 119.

11. Dale Spender, *Mothers of the Novel: 100 Good Women Writers Before Jane Austen* (London: Pandora Press, 1986), 67.

12. See Reese, *Gibbon's Autobiography,* 38, 22.

13. J. Paul Hunter, *Before Novels: The Cultural Contexts of Eighteenth-Century English Fiction* (New York: Norton, 1990), 100.

14. David Hume, "My Own Life," in *The Letters of David Hume,* ed. J. Y. T. Greig, 2 vols. (Oxford: Clarendon Press, 1932), 1:2.

15. Jerome Christensen, *Practicing Enlightenment: Hume and the Formation of a Literary Career* (Madison: University of Wisconsin Press, 1987), 82.

16. J. G. A. Pocock, *Virtue, Commerce, and History: Essays on Political Thought and History, Chiefly in the Eighteenth Century* (New York: Cambridge University Press, 1985), 99.

17. *Memoirs of Europe,* in *The Novels of Manley,* 2:16–17.

18. Pocock, *Virtue, Commerce, and History,* 99.

19. Gwendolyn B. Needham, "Mary de la Rivière Manley, Tory Defender," *Huntington Library Quarterly* 12 (May 1949): 253.

20. Spender, *Mothers of the Novel,* 91.

21. Manley, *Secret Memoirs from the New Atalantis,* Vols. 1 and 2, ed. Malcolm J. Bosse, Foundations of the Novel (1709; reprint New York: Garland, 1972), 1:21.

22. Morgan, *A Woman of No Character,* 156.

23. Sir John Vanbrugh, *The Provoked Wife,* ed. Curt A. Zimansky, Regents Restoration Drama Series (Lincoln: University of Nebraska Press, 1961), 7.

24. Christopher Hill, *The Century of Revolution 1603–1714* (New York: Norton, 1961), 282.

25. See Isaac Kramnick, *Bolingbroke and His Circle: The Politics of Nostalgia in the Age of Walpole* (Cambridge: Harvard University Press, 1968), 171–72.

26. Manley, *A New Vindication of the Duke of Marlborough,* in *The Works of Jonathan Swift,* ed. Sir Walter Scott, 19 vols. (London: Bickers & Son, 1883), 5:387.

27. Manley, *A Learned Comment Upon Dr. Hare's Excellent Sermon Preach'd before the D. of Marlborough, On the Surrender of Bouchain,* included in Swift, *Prose,* 3:266.

28. Manley, *A New Vindication of Marlborough*, in *The Works of Jonathan Swift*, ed. Scott, 5:385.

29. Ibid.

30. Anne Finch, Countess of Winchilsea, "The Introduction" (1.1), in *The Meridian Anthology of Early Women Writers: British Literary Women from Aphra Behn to Maria Edgeworth, 1660–1800*, ed. Katharine M. Rogers and William McCarthy (New York: Penguin, 1987), 73.

31. Manley, *A Learned Comment Upon Dr. Hare's Sermon*, in Swift, *Prose*, 3:271.

32. *In Honor of that High and Mighty Princess, Queen Elizabeth of Happy Memory* (ll. 78, 49–51), in *The Works of Anne Bradstreet*, ed. Jeannine Hensley (Cambridge: Belknap Press of Harvard University, 1967), 197, 196.

33. Manley, *A Modest Enquiry into the Reasons of the Joy Expressed . . . upon the Spreading of a Report of Her Majesty's Death*, in Swift, *Prose*, 8:188.

34. Jane Spencer, *The Rise of the Woman Novelist: From Aphra Behn to Jane Austen* (Oxford: Basil Blackwell, 1986), 53.

35. Reese, *Gibbon's Autobiography*, 58.

36. Janet Todd, *The Sign of Angellica: Women, Writing and Fiction, 1660–1800* (New York: Columbia University Press, 1989), 98.

37. Morgan, *A Woman of No Character*, 156.

Rage and Raillery and Swift: The Case of *Cadenus and Vanessa*

Claude Rawson

Cadenus and Vanessa is Swift's longest poem and one of his most directly autobiographical. It was published in 1726, the year of *Gulliver's Travels,* but was drafted much earlier, probably around 1713, when Swift became Dean of St. Patrick's.[1] Cadenus is an anagram for Decanus or Dean. Vanessa, a name now widely used but which is said to have been invented by Swift, is the fictional name of Esther Vanhomrigh, a woman with whom (as also with Stella) Swift had a tutorial-erotic friendship whose exact nature has remained unclear. The poem appeared after Vanessa's death in 1723, perhaps after an unauthorized publication forced Swift to produce it. It may never have been intended for publication, and it certainly has a sticky intimacy. But the poem was made public and owned, and it shows in strong relief certain features that are recurrent in some of Swift's other well-known poems.

Cadenus and Vanessa is an elaborately gallant fiction in which the Court of Venus has to hear a plea as to who is more to blame for the modern decline of love: the men, who have ceased to pursue it, or the women, who aren't worthy of the pursuit. Venus decides to test the case by forming a perfect woman, with every beauty and every quality of mind, and Vanessa is the result. The notion that women can and should be admired for the same intellectual qualities as men, instead of being treated as angels or as ornamental dolls, is implicit here, as it is explicit in the "Letter to a Young Lady, on her Marriage" (1723: Swift, *Prose,* 9:83–94) and in the poems to Stella. In that sense, the supposed misogynist Swift comes closer to a rational feminist position, as we might recognize it now, than do Pope, Steele, or Addison, whose more overt friendliness to women took a form of genial quasi-urbane gallantry

---

which Swift contemptuously called "fair-sexing" (*JS*, 2:482 (8 February 1712).

On the other hand, when the poem describes the creation of Vanessa, we learn that Venus can only obtain for Vanessa the intellectual virtues she wants her to have through the cooperation of Pallas, the goddess of wisdom; and that to get that cooperation, she must hide from Pallas the fact that Vanessa is a girl (ll. 185ff.). Pallas is thus duped into sowing into the presumed boy "Seeds long unknown to womankind, / For manly bosoms chiefly fit, / The seeds of knowledge, judgement, wit" (ll. 200ff.) and is furious at the deceit (ll. 250ff.). And when Cadenus, Vanessa's teacher, contemplates her progress, it is with "the master's secret joy / In school to hear the finest boy" (ll. 552–53). In this the poem resembles a passage in the "Letter to a Young Lady," in which Swift reassures her against the fear of joining the derided species "who are commonly called learned Women," on the grounds "that after all the Pains you may be at, you never can arrive, in Point of Learning, to the Perfection of a School-Boy" (Swift, *Prose*, 9:92). It is just possible that Swift's irony here indicates some gap between society's perceptions and his own; or that he is suggesting that the young woman in question is disadvantaged by not having had the schoolboy's years of instruction. But these possibilities don't seem available in the poem, where deities make prior assumptions as to which virtues are appropriate to each sex. For some reason that escapes me, a few feminist critics, conventionally hostile to Swift, have nevertheless taken up this poem as a shining example of ideological correctness on Swift's part,[2] a choice almost as baffling as the current elevation into a feminist hero of the rancid old patriarch Samuel Richardson.

Cadenus and Vanessa, on any reading, precipitates some questions about Swift and women. But I think that this poem raises even more fundamental issues which have to do with Swift's relations with himself, and which inevitably bear on his relations with others: with women of course, and lovers, but also with readers and that animal called man. I shall be arguing that *Cadenus and Vanessa* is vitiated by a kind of bad faith, which afflicts many of the most admired autobiographical poems, including the *Verses on the Death*. And at the heart of this bad faith is a species of irony, a coy self-derision, which is frequently referred to as "raillery" but which functions in specialized ways. To clarify what I mean, I must first say a few general things about raillery and about the quality frequently paired or contrasted with it, rage.

Rage and raillery are traditionally associated with Swift, and of the two "rage" probably holds sway in the popular imagination as the more characteristically Swiftian. We need not go to Thackeray's "furious, raging, obscene" and their analogues. The customary and in itself accurate recognition of Swiftian "intensities" more naturally, or more commonly, evokes rage than raillery, except to those critics who deny the "intensities" as such and think of Swift as a sober-sided moderate from the Land of the Golden Mean. Against this stereotype even Thackeray should be welcomed with relief. We have not fully acquired a critical language which recognizes that intensities may coexist with a studied refusal of the language of intensity, and perhaps rage with a commitment to the language of raillery. Hence the stubborn tradition of a Juvenalian Swift, in the face of Swift's insistent denial of a "lofty style" (described in *Cadenus and Vanessa*, ll. 804–5, as something "which he had taught her to despise," and more elaborately repudiated in the epistle *To a Lady*, ll. 148, 230), and his declared preference for "that Kind of Satyr, which . . . gives the least Offence . . . [and] instead of lashing, laughs Men out of their Follies, and Vices; and is the Character that gives *Horace* the Preference to *Juvenal*."

This remark, we recall, is made à propos of the *Beggar's Opera*: a relatively genial work, to which the Horatian half of the antithesis will seem broadly appropriate, remembering however that Swift is not well known for his concern that satire should give the least offense; and also that he spoke, in the same essay, of Gay's opera as having "placed Vices of all Kinds in the strongest and most odious Light."[3] The discriminations thus seem a little unfocused, not quite true of the opera or consistent with one another: unfocused in the manner of much of Swift's writing on Gay, perhaps because he is so much given, on that particular topic, to throwing himself back into his own personal obsessions (on matters of preferment and careers as much as on problems of writing style). We get some refinement of essentially the same distinction in *To a Lady*, which speaks of lashing and smiling (l. 147) as simultaneous and not, as in the *Intelligencer* essay, as mutually opposed, and of scorning rather than hating because scorn torments the victim more than spite does (ll. 152–54). *To a Lady* also amplifies Swift's famous remark to Pope about vexing the world in an image of making the victims "wriggle, howl, and skip" (l. 190), of setting their "spirits all a-working" (l. 218), while he would hang them if he could (l. 180). In these formulations, Horace is again in Swift's mind (ll. 210ff.):

It is well observed by Horace,
Ridicule has greater power
To reform the world, than sour.

The total profile may not greatly resemble the smooth urbane
Horace of some English Augustan mythologies, or of some recent
attempts to demythologize the mythologies, and it is arguably
closer to the Roman poet than is Pope's more polished version.
But when Swift's refusal of the lofty style is glossed as a matter
of not wanting to "make a figure scurvy" (l. 231), the result, as
I have argued elsewhere, is neither Horatian nor Juvenalian. It
is Swiftian.

The salient fact about it is that it is declared, quite specifically,
to be a matter of inhibition. And such self-regarding constraint is
an essential ingredient of Swift's manner, a source of strengths
as well as of weaknesses, and seldom openly admitted in this fashion, as though constraint was to be activated in, or imposed on,
the very avowal of constraint. But *dis*avowal of "lofty style," of
"rage," of "anger": *that* is a characteristic stance, the positive projection of inhibition, the active guard erected in negation (characteristically, as many would say, after Leavis).[4] We have not learned
to read it right. There are still those who understood the famous
letter to Pope about Swift's not hating mankind—"it is vous autres
who hate them because you would have them reasonable Animals,
and are Angry for being disappointed"—in a simple literal sense,
despite decades of pointing out by a succession of readers that the
disavowal of hatred or anger continues with the words "I am no
more angry with ——— Then [than] I was with the Kite that last
week flew away with one of my Chickins and yet I was pleas'd
when one of my Servants Shot him two days after."[5] "Drown the
World, I am not content with despising it, but I would anger it if
I could with safety," he says earlier in the same letter, much as
To a Lady declares that, for all his apparent merriment, "it must
be understood, / I would hang them if I could." The denial of
anger, the refusal to concede rage, is a tease, a form of concealment through raillery, which proclaims anger by denial: it's part
huffy, quarrelsome (as though saying *I'm* not angry with them,
they're beneath *my* anger, and so on), and part rhetoric of the "I
am no orator as Brutus is" variety. But it is also the denial of a
manner rather than a substance. "This great foundation of Misan-
thropy (though not Timons manner)"[6] may in fact mean hatred
without railing, protective of the speaker's cool, preventing the
figure scurvy, getting in first with the tease. And as a tease, it

carries the characteristic expectation that some people will be taken in (and modern critics, like Irish bishops and old sea captains, frequently oblige); and also the expectation that the rest should ask "if he's not angry what is he?", registering the question as a rhetorical bind. That is, saying he's not angry is also saying that he's not not angry, while keeping his guard and disturbing the reader's. Sometimes, as in Swift's other displays of pseudo-coolness (most notably in the *Modest Proposal*), the tease is heightened by deadpan utterance, the verbal equivalent of the clown's straight face. It's a case of substantive "rage" coming over in the guises of "raillery," Swift's true refusal being not so much of "rage" as of "rail*ing*."

There is an opposite, or I prefer to say a complementary process, where the forms of rage are indeed loudly in evidence (as in the relatively rare cases of *Traulus* or the *Legion Club*), not disguised by denials but partially undercut or disarmed by their own excess. It would I think be possible to show how Swift in these late, overtly vitriolic denunciations gave himself over to some primitive routines of ritual cursing that go back to ancient flyting traditions and to Irish bards who rhymed men dead. In *The Legion Club* (1736), drumming imprecation,

> Tom, halloo boy,
> Worthy offspring of a shoe-boy,
> Footman, traitor, vile seducer,
> Perjured rebel, bribed accuser,
>
> (ll. 67–70)

comes over in a syncopated rhetoric of magical chanting, the primitive incantation played for all it is worth in a high-spirited exercise which is part angry indulgence and part bravura mimicry, heaving with ritual question-and-answer routines, with strenuous feats of rhyming, with perfectly timed slapstick defilements:

> Such a triplet could you tell
> Where to find on this side hell?
> Harrison, and Dilkes, and Clements,
> Souse them in their own ex-crements,
>
> (ll. 183–86)

(the last word is studiously hyphenated),[7] and the whole poem is introduced by a witty proleptically Byronic or Audenesque informality:

> As I stroll the city, oft I
> Spy a building large and lofty,
> Not a bow-shot from the college,
> Half the globe from sense and knowledge.

(ll. 1–4)

Here a playfulness is delightfully evident, in a context where no suspicion could possibly arise that there was any lack of rage in the emotional package. It's a sophisticated defense in the very teeth of a certain kind of lofty style, a "low" lofty style if you like, but charged with indignant denunciation. It is, in a sense, aestheticized: the game of ritual cursing is not merely entered into, it is played self-consciously for all it is worth, and it is the suggestion of this, in the *diablerie* of full-scale performance, that acts as a reticence of overstatement, whereas in "I do not hate mankind" we have an opposite reticence of disavowal or mock-disavowal.

This is a trick Swift practiced in other contexts, where there was a risk of appearing emotionally overcommitted. In the so-called poems of body-hatred, it is widely recognized that whatever Swift may have felt about the thought that Celia shits, the Strephons who overreact to it are the subject of much comic exposure. But in the horrors of "A Beautiful Young Nymph Going to Bed" there are no such obvious opportunities for self-disengagement through a pointed display of "raillery." The poem is dry and relentless in its listing of scabrous particulars. By the end of his life, even Irvin Ehrenpreis had stopped believing that all of this was just a matter of a conscientious clergyman warning against fornication. But in the early essay in which Ehrenpreis propounded this view, he also demonstrated that one of the things Swift was doing in this poem was working on a traditional formula in which a fine woman or handsome man are disassembled of what turns out to be a succession of mechanical parts.[8] What he did not say was that Swift went beyond most of the analogues in the listing of scabrous particulars, and that arguably there seems to be a poker-faced impulse to outdo the competition in cheeky perfectionist bravura, playing the gimmick for all it is worth. Here there is a variation on the manner of *Traulus* and the *Legion Club*: the excess gets dry and deadpan formulation, as in the *Modest Proposal*, rather than an exuberantly animated one. But it is the same kind of excess, a "raillery" that qualifies the display of "rage" (or other shocking disclosure) and by doing so enables its release.

Like "I would hang them if I could," he does not strictly speaking mean it and does not not mean it either.

The bravura exercise of outdoing suggests at once that he can play the game with the best and that he is not imprisoned within it. The figure he makes remains secure, not scurvy. Raillery becomes a means of saying that even when most apparently in Timon's manner, the manner isn't quite Timonic, though the substance *is*. This needling defensiveness is one source of Swift's strong aggressive power. Viewed from a certain moral perspective, it is also potentially a kind of bad faith: a bad faith that perhaps, from some romantic or postromantic perspectives (the perspective, for example, of Herbert Read), attaches to all or most radical displays of irony. It is the emotional dishonesty which makes Swift give himself, in the *Verses on the Death*, all the praises of a traditional *apologia*, but remove the responsibility for this to an impartial commentator, conveniently invented by himself (this, by the way, is something which even the self-regarding Pope did not usually feel the need to do).

Cadenus and Vanessa has in common with the *Verses on the Death* a note of light raillery which enables certain self-regarding obliquities to take over. It consists of setting up a front designed to disguise or neutralize embarrassment at poetic acts of self-celebration or self-justification.

This long poem about his friendship with Esther Vanhomrigh shares many features with Swift's other group of autobiographical love poems, those to Stella, which seem to me splendid; but, unlike the Stella poems, it displays an uneasy solipsistic coyness. The ideological postures are similar. The arguments, against romantic love and in favor of more soundly based friendship, are given more elaborate utterance, and Vanessa is praised for having (in addition to beauty and grace) all the moral and intellectual qualities for such friendship. But the poem shows her developing a romantic passion for Cadenus because those very qualities make her uninterested in, and superior to, the common forms and customary objects of courtship. Swift is not only the embarrassed object of her passion, but is shown to have aroused it by teaching her those high intellectual standards that made it possible for her to fall in love with him. And she is indeed made to declare that the very lessons he taught her made her love him (ll. 606ff., 682ff.). Compounding this situation are the barely concealed boast of an older man at being beloved by a young and beautiful woman and his pretense of being above such things, itself conveyed through a

mock-pretense of being beneath them, unworthy, and so forth.
The fussy registering of these ironic consequences of the teacher/
pupil relationship may be contrasted with the passionate forth-
rightness of Eloisa's casuistry in Pope's "Eloisa to Abelard":

> Guiltless I gaz'd; heav'n listen'd while you sung;
> And truths divine came mended from that tongue.
> From lips like those what precept fail'd to move?
> Too soon they taught me 'twas no sin to love.
> Back thro' the paths of pleasing sense I ran,
> Nor wish'd an Angel whom I lov'd a Man.
> Dim and remote the joys of saints I see,
> Nor envy them, that heav'n I lose for thee.
>
> (*TE*, 2:304, ll. 65–72)

Part of the difference has of course to do with the different emotional pitch of the two poems and with the fact that Eloisa's words
are spoken in the grimly distressing circumstances which readers
know to have befallen the lovers (the piquantly unhappy outcome
of Vanessa's story in real life, or the mythologies surrounding it,
are not in the same way a known factor in Swift's poem, which
was written, though not published, before Vanessa's death).[9] The
essential awkwardness of *Cadenus and Vanessa* resides principally
in Swift's curious posture as both the retailer of her feelings *and*
the object of her passion. In this context, the mincing self-
exculpations of the narrator become exceptionally unpleasant:

> *Cadenus,* who could ne'er suspect
> His lessons would have such effect . . .
>
> (ll. 734–35)

The autobiographical exposure is barely disguised by the ostensible distancing or formality suggested by the latinized names.
Indeed their transparency (Cadenus an anagram of Decanus or
Dean, Vanessa obviously derived from the surname Vanhomrigh)
flauntingly neutralizes the disguise, adding to it a flavor of self-
exhibition, teasingly insistent in its effect as the overt use of real
names, or alternatively of frankly fictitious ones, would not have
been. The enterprise lacks the clear and open tenderness, the
delicate blend of romantic gallantry and jokeyness, which inform
Swift's use of the name Stella. The montage of romanized fancy
dress is sustained by the whole pseudo-mythology in which
Vanessa's beauty, good sense, and fatal passion are made to appear
as products of a complex divine imbroglio, and in which Venus,

Cupid, and Pallas manipulate the human agents to their own purposes. The decorative indirection heightens rather than depersonalizes the febrile embarrassment. And when Venus's Court of Love at the end condemns all men because a perfect creature like Vanessa "never could one lover find" (l. 875), the gallantry with which Swift takes the blame to himself, implicitly becoming one with the foolish beaux who cannot love a clever woman, leaves a sour taste. Voiture, who taught Swift "that irony which turns to praise," has turned to vinegar.[10] Swift has traditionally been a target for feminist attacks, but, as I have already noted, some recent defenses of this poem have been mounted on feminist lines: and if this is to be the fate of such displays of male self-regard, one may be justified in asking, with such enemies who needs friends?

Throughout the poem, Swift goes through the motions of a frank self-analysis whose implication is that only he is at fault. He is old, unworthy of her, "understood not what was love" (l. 547). The latter claim, unlike similar remarks to Stella, again carries a simpering note of self-exculpation. Swift makes Cadenus return to it (ll. 776–77, 794), not only with the alternative promise of "gratitude, respect, esteem" (l. 795) and of more rational and durable pleasures, but with an admission that Cadenus was aware of his own special pleading, as well as of being flattered by Vanessa's love:

> So when Cadenus could not hide,
> He chose to justify his pride . . .
>
> (ll. 770ff.)

These luxuries of self-exposure are, in various ways, ironic. But the irony is part of the exhibition, self-mockery—as in Sterne or Byron—adding a further coil to complex indirections of display, though less "openly" than in Sterne or Byron. Sterne's self-irony is simultaneously a freely indulged self-cherishing, however, and where he criticizes himself within it he seems less dedicated to the substantive censure than to the piquant complexities of the censuring self. If an indecorum or embarrassment results, it will in turn be taken up, freely played with, ritualized in the whole rich exhibition of introspective personality. Such indulgence Swift could not admit, even to himself: it is an important target of the anti-"modern" satire in A Tale of a Tub. But all the face-value lucidities of his self-critique in the poem do in practice go a long way towards protracting the embarrassment, without taking Sterne's final step of making the embarrassment itself part of the

game. What results is an uneasy and unintended "modernism,"
not parodied in a figure whom Swift ostensibly rejects outright,
as in the *Tale*, but emanating from a character who (even more
than Sterne's Tristram) is a confessed projection of the real author,
as the name Cadenus makes clear. The fact throws light on the
strange kinship of Swift to his satiric butt in the *Tale*, but the
latter's self-expression is protected by fictional concealments, re-
leasing energies of mimicry which are free from official authorial
self-involvement.

This protection is lacking in *Cadenus and Vanessa*. In one passage, however, omitted from some early editions, a radical concealment does occur, the reader being told that he or she will never
learn the outcome of the story:

> But what success Vanessa met,
> Is to the world a secret yet:
> Whether the nymph, to please her swain,
> Talks in a high romantic strain;
> Or whether he at last descends
> To live with less seraphic ends;
> Or, to compound the business, whether
> They temper love and books together;
> Must never to mankind be told,
> Nor shall the conscious muse unfold.
>
> (ll. 826–35)

The last line is a tease of the same kidney as Tristram Shandy's
simpering secret about his relations with his dear, dear Jenny.[11]
Did Vanessa end up talking in "high romantic strain" in order "to
please her swain" (the point being that Cadenus had in fact
"taught her to despise" the "lofty style," ll. 804–5)? And did Cadenus finally lapse to "less seraphic ends," like the philosopher in
the *Mechanical Operation,* "who, while his Thoughts and Eyes
were fixed upon the *Constellations,* found himself seduced by his
lower Parts into a *Ditch*" (Swift, *Prose,* 1:190)? Swift puts himself
potentially on a par with all the canting moderns and hypocritical
Puritan zealots, but it is presumably because the poem will not
tell us what really happened that Swift allows himself the luxury
there of openly inviting the speculation. He is saved from confes-
sional excess by a simpering confession of unwillingness to confess. The objection is not, of course, to any unwillingness to tell,
but to the whole ostentatious production of the not telling.[12]

Two-thirds of the way through the poem, Cupid, in search of a

man likely to be acceptable to "A nymph so hard to be subdued"
(l. 496), discovers Cadenus:

> "I find," says he, "she wants a doctor,
> Both to adore her and instruct her;
> I'll give her what she most admires,
> Among those venerable sires.
> Cadenus is a subject fit,
> Grown old in politics and wit;
> Caressed by ministers of state,
> Of half mankind the dread and hate.
> Whate'er vexations love attend,
> She needs no rivals apprehend.
> Her sex, with universal voice,
> Must laugh at her capricious choice."
>
> (ll. 498–509)

Here the paraded self-depreciation takes the form not of concealment, half-hinting at a sexual lapse, but of acknowledgments of
unlovability, to be countered by the bewildering *fact* of Vanessa's
passion. Mock-incomprehension readily resolves itself into a fond
self-praise, not only in the intrinsic nature of the situation, but
through complimentary additives to do with Swift's sagacity, his
prowess in politics and wit, the power (political or satiric or both)
which makes him "Of half mankind the dread and hate." Formally
Cupid is speaking, not Swift, but he's scripted by Swift on the
subject of Swift. Nothing would more clearly illustrate the bankruptcy of traditional persona criticism than a pedantic disen-
gagement that failed here to register appropriate interactions
between speaker and author. The two are not, of course, identical,
but it is the nature of an author's investment in the persona, and
not the latter's separate character, that demands sensitive
recognition.

Cupid's words are variously revealing about Swift's modes of
self-projection. And the characterization of Swift in the middle—

> Cadenus is a subject fit,
> Grown old in politics and wit;
> Caressed by ministers of state,
> Of half mankind the dread and hate,

—highlights the fact that in the atmosphere of self-regarding
obliquity which disfigures this poem, it is not women who are at
issue, but Swift's own sense of himself. These lines are an exam-

ple of a mode of eloquence, common in Swift's poems about himself, which has many admirers. The gingerly, quasi–ironic
indulgence of the "lofty style" he ostentatiously disavowed
achieves quotable felicities of self-description, offering critics a
pleasant shorthand for affectionate tributes, the more so, perhaps,
because the solipsistic overtones are less obvious outside the context of the poems in which they first appear. Among the best-
known examples are the following lines from "The Author upon
Himself," probably written in 1714, the year after *Cadenus and
Vanessa* was drafted, which are not only often quoted but have
provided the title of a standard book on Swift's poems. Like the
lines from *Cadenus and Vanessa,* they contain some vaunting of
his influence with ministers:

> Swift had the sin of wit, no venial crime;
> Nay, 'twas affirmed, he sometimes dealt in rhyme:
> Humour, and mirth, had place in all he writ:
> He reconciled divinity and wit.
> He moved, and bowed, and talked with too much grace,
> Nor showed the parson in his gait or face;
> Despised luxurious wines, and costly meat;
> Yet, still was at the tables of the great.
> .   .   .   .
> And now, the public interest to support,
> By Harley Swift invited comes to court.
> In favor grows with ministers of state;
> Admitted private, when superiors wait:
> And, Harley, not ashamed his choice to own,
> Takes him to Windsor in his coach, alone.
> At Windsor Swift no sooner can appear,
> But, St. John comes and whispers in his ear;
> The waiters stand in ranks; the yeomen cry,
> "Make room," as if a duke were passing by.

(ll. 9ff., 27ff.)

Swift could laugh at his childish vanities, as in the charming
"Panegyric on the Dean" (1730), purportedly spoken by "a Lady
in the North" (Lady Acheson):

> Envy must own, you understand your
> Precedence, and support your grandeur . . .

(ll. 45–46)

This lighthearted grace is relatively infrequent in the poems about
himself, though he often sought to achieve it: the frequent ges-

tures of ironic undercutting are in a sense its clumsy trace. A blurring of commitment to the praise, in the choice of proxy speakers, is evident even in the "Panegyric." In "The Author upon Himself," where the tone teasingly hovers between what gossip might be supposed to be saying ("'twas affirmed") and what the author himself would say in his ironic perspicacity, makes the self-regard come over as somewhat furtive, fraught with a self-vaunting of which the author seems anxious to wash his hands, without really giving up its satisfactions. This is also true, perhaps especially so, of the most famous of the poems about himself, the *Verses on the Death*.

Notes

1. For a summary of the composition and publication details and for biographical information see Rogers, 658–59, 938; also Swift, *Poems*, 2:683–86.

2. See Ellen Pollak, *The Poetics of Sexual Myth* (Chicago: University of Chicago Press, 1985) 128–58, and Margaret Anne Doody, "Swift among the Women," *Yearbook of English Studies* 18 (1988): esp. 75–77.

3. Review of the *Beggar's Opera* in *Intelligencer*, No. 3 (1728), in Swift, *Prose*, 12:33, 35.

4. F. R. Leavis, "The Irony of Swift," in *The Common Pursuit*, London: Chatto and Windus, 1952) 73–87.

5. Swift to Pope, 26 November 1725, *Corresp.* 3:118.

6. Swift to Pope, 29 September 1725, *Corresp.* 3:103.

7. The hyphen does not appear in Rogers, 555, which modernizes and normalizes Swift's text. For the original old-spelling version, see Swift, *Poems*, 3:837.

8. Irvin Ehrenpreis, *The Personality of Jonathan Swift* (Cambridge: Harvard University Press, 1958) 38–49; for the change of emphasis, see Ehrenpreis, 3:103–7, 691–95, 695, n. 3.

9. See Rogers, 658–59, 938.

10. "To Mr. Delany" (1718), l. 34, Rogers, 180.

11. *Tristram Shandy*, 1:xviii; ed. Melvyn New and Joan New, Florida Edition of the Works of Laurence Sterne (Gainesville: University Presses of Florida, 1978–84) 1:56. Tristram's Jenny recurs from time to time in the novel, and Tristram is impotent with her in a well-known later episode (7:xxix, ed. New, 2:624. On the possible autobiographical aspects of the allusions to Jenny, see 3:87–88.

12. For a different reading, and valuation, of this passage, see Pollak, *Poetics of Sexual Myth*, 130ff.

Concurring Opponents: Mary Wollstonecraft and Jonathan Swift on Women's Education and the Sexless Nature of Virtue

David F. Venturo

Mary Wollstonecraft and Jonathan Swift are almost always classified by critics today as ideological opponents on the subject of women's issues.[1] The reasons for this classification are not hard to fathom: Wollstonecraft, after all, has a well-earned reputation as one of the founders of modern feminism. She has been hailed as "the first major feminist" and her *Vindication of the Rights of Woman* praised as "the feminist declaration of independence."[2] Swift, by contrast, has achieved considerable notoriety in some feminist circles as a prime example of "Augustan misogyny." The author of the Celia poems has been labeled an "antifeminist" along with his Scriblerian friends Pope and Gay and accused of writing corrosive, unconstructive satire. As one critic complains, Swift "criticized female manners and the vogue of mawkish sentimentality with which women were newly regarded without advocating any serious reform of their education."[3] Sandra Gilbert and Susan Gubar in *The Madwoman in the Attic* go so far as to declare that Swift's treatment of women was viciously destructive and deeply disturbed—that Swift believed that "all women were inexorably and inescapably monstrous, in the flesh as well as in spirit."[4] Mary Wollstonecraft herself set a precedent of sorts for twentieth-century feminist attacks, accusing Swift in *A Vindication of the Rights of Woman* of "petulant acrimony" for his censuring of women in "The Furniture of a Woman's Mind" for acts that she believes are the result of their education, or lack thereof, rather than of any conscious moral failure.[5]

Such a dichotomous approach to Swift and Wollstonecraft tends to encourage simple, reductive contrasts while it ignores evidence of beliefs that these authors held in common. In fact, Swift's and Wollstonecraft's views on the sexless quality of virtue, the moral capacity of women to achieve virtue, and the importance of education in the pursuit of this goal are in many ways surprisingly similar. The commonality of their beliefs is more than coincidental: not only do Swift and Wollstonecraft write out of the same humanist tradition, which insists on the moral equality of men and women, but Wollstonecraft was quite familiar with Swift's works in verse and prose. Moreover, she was willing, on occasion, to cite Swift as an ally in her arguments that women should be educated in the same fashion as men and held to the same, sexless standards of virtue. Thus Wollstonecraft reprinted several of Swift's poems in her anthology designed for the instruction of women, *The Female Reader*.[6] Unfortunately, in the "Whig" or "Progressive" interpretation of feminist history,[7] it has become fashionable to simplify such figures as Wollstonecraft and Swift into mere furtherers or impeders of the movement for women's rights, instead of addressing the complexity of their attitudes toward women, women's education, and eighteenth-century standards of virtue.

In spite of Wollstonecraft's criticism of Swift in the *Vindication of the Rights of Woman,* she and Swift are both moralists who share a common humanist desire to reform women through education. While Wollstonecraft complains in the *Vindication* of the "sarcasms" of Swift's poem "The Furniture of a Woman's Mind," Swift is far from Wollstonecraft's chief opponent in the book (*VRW*, 187). The primary targets of Wollstonecraft's criticism, as she makes clear in chapter 5 of the *Vindication*, are sentimentalists such as Rousseau and Dr. James Fordyce, author of *Sermons to Young Women*, who render women objects of men's pity and encourage them to use emotional and sexual manipulation rather than reason to achieve their ends. Such behavior is precisely what Swift attacks in *Gulliver's Travels, A Letter to a Young Lady on Her Marriage* (a personal letter written to Deborah Staunton in 1723 to advise her on her education and conduct upon her marriage to Swift's friend John Rochfort), and *On the Death of Mrs. [Esther] Johnson* (a brief memorial and character sketch of his friend, Stella, which Swift wrote shortly after her death in 1728, although it was not published until 1765).[8] In the *Letter,* for example, Swift urges the young lady to reject any advice on how to manipulate her husband by emotional means; to avoid those "Arts by which you may discover and practice upon his weak Sides; when to work by Flattery and Insinuation; when to melt

him with Tears; and when to engage him with a high Hand"
(Swift, *Prose*, 9:88). Indeed, Swift and Wollstonecraft are both
antiromantics who offer the classical humanist virtues of reason
and friendship as alternatives to the rising tide of sentimental
celebrations of passion and romantic love between the sexes.

There remain, of course, significant differences that distinguish
Swift's and Wollstonecraft's critiques of female behavior, and of
human behavior generally. Wollstonecraft, born a decade and a
half after the death of Swift and Pope, shares to a large extent the
distrust of satire that characterizes the Age of Sensibility. Thus, in
articles written for the *Analytical Review*, Wollstonecraft censures
what she calls "yahoo satires" and complains of the "painful sensa-
tion of disgust, and even distrust of Providence, which Gulliver's
Travels never fail to excite in a mind possessed of any sensibility."[9]
At the same time, Wollstonecraft is no mere sentimentalist. She
recognizes the ideological dangers inherent in associating women
with the sentimental or the beautiful, as she makes clear in her
attacks in the *Vindication of the Rights of Men* and the *Vindication of the Rights of Woman* on Edmund Burke's equation of masculinity with the sublime and femininity with the beautiful in his
*Philosophical Enquiry into the Origin of Our Ideas of the Sublime
and Beautiful* and *Reflections on the Revolution in France*.[10] In
addition, Wollstonecraft, like William Godwin, subscribes to a version of the "Doctrine of Necessity," a precursor to the twentieth-
century liberal belief that environment is the predominant factor
in the shaping of character.[11] By means of this doctrine, which is
outlined in chapter 6 of the *Vindication of the Rights of Woman*,
"The Effect which an Early Association of Ideas Has upon the
Character," she absolves women of the moral responsibility for
much of their behavior, blaming perceived affectations instead on
the pervasive influence of a sexist society that prevents women's
development into independent, rational, moral beings: "till women
are led to exercise their understandings, they should not be satirized" for conduct that "appears to be the inevitable consequence
of their education" (*VRW*, 188). Swift, on the other hand, was
never a modern liberal. The kind of casuistical thinking (I use the
term nonpejoratively[12]) central to modern liberal thought, which
assumes that circumstances can determine, explain, and even ex-
cuse behavior, is congenial to such authors raised in the Dissenting tradition as Defoe, Godwin, and Wollstonecraft, but not to
the Anglican Swift. Because eighteenth-century Dissenters believed that they were compelled to deal with a hostile and coercive
establishment in church and state, they were much more likely

to view casuistry sympathetically than their Anglican contemporaries. Swift, despite occasional misgivings, felt little compunction about satirizing women's behavior since he assumed that they were free agents and thus bore ultimate moral responsibility for their conduct.[13]

Despite these differences, both Swift and Wollstonecraft strongly believed that virtue has no sex and that, consequently, men and women should be held to the same standards of virtuous conduct. "I am ignorant of any one Quality that is amiable in a Man, which is not equally so in a Woman. . . . Nor do I know one Vice or Folly, which is not equally detestable in both," avers Swift in the *Letter to a Young Lady* (*Prose*, 9:92–93). Wollstonecraft's sentiments on this subject in the "Author's Introduction" to the *Vindication of the Rights of Woman* are very similar to Swift's. She urges on her female readers "the imitation of manly virtues, or, more properly speaking, the attainment of those talents and virtues, the exercise of which ennobles the human character" regardless of sex (*VRW*, 74). As one critic has recently observed, "In keeping with the assumptions of Enlightenment tradition, Wollstonecraft aspires beyond sex altogether. Her pervasive emphasis upon reform in the education of women aims ultimately at restoring their full—and sexless—humanity. . . . Wollstonecraft subordinates the female to the human in order to assert the equality of reason and therefore [of] right."[14]

Consequently Wollstonecraft shares Swift's exasperation with affectations that were countenanced and even encouraged in women, but that would have been regarded as contemptible in men, such as the affectation of fear and weakness. "In the most trifling danger," she writes in the *Vindication,*

> [women] cling to [men's] support, with parasitical tenacity, piteously demanding succour; and their *natural* protector extends his arm, or lifts up his voice, to guard the lovely trembler—from what? Perhaps the frown of an old cow, or the jump of a mouse; a rat, would be a serious danger. In the name of reason, and even common sense, what can save such beings from contempt; even though they be soft and fair? (*VRW*, 131).

Because Swift also believes that "the same Virtues equally become both sexes," he expresses similar puzzlement in *A Letter to a Young Lady on Her Marriage* that while

> Women profess their Admiration for a Colonel or a Captain, on Account of his Valour; [that] they should [nevertheless] fancy it a very graceful becoming Quality in themselves, to be afraid of their own Shadows; to scream in a Barge, when the Weather is calmest, or in a

Coach at the Ring; to run from a Cow at an Hundred Yards Distance;
to fall into Fits at the Sight of a Spider, an Earwig, or a Frog.
(*Prose*, 9:93).

Swift was especially proud of the bravery of his lifelong friend
Esther Johnson, whom he nicknamed "Stella," perhaps in reference to the title character of Sir Philip Sidney's sonnet sequence,
perhaps merely as a Latin play on "ester," the Hebrew word for
"star." Swift firmly believed that Esther Johnson's strength of
character gave the lie to the notion of inherent female cowardice.
In *On the Death of Mrs. Johnson*, Swift recalls an incident during
which Stella displayed "the personal courage of a hero":

> She . . . having removed [her] lodgings to a new house, which stood
> solitary, a parcel of rogues, armed, attempted the house, where there
> was only one boy: She was then about four and twenty: And, having
> been warned to apprehend some such attempt, she learned the man-
> agement of a pistol; and the other women and servants being half-
> dead with fear, she stole softly to her dining-room window, put on a
> black hood, to prevent being seen, primed the pistol fresh, gently
> lifted up the sash; and, taking aim with the utmost presence of mind,
> discharged the pistol loaden with the bullets, into the body of one
> villain, who stood the fairest mark. (*Prose*, 5:229–30)

Stella's self-possession and courage on this occasion so impressed
the duke of Ormonde that afterwards "he often drank her health
to [Swift] upon that account" (Swift, *Prose*, 5:230). This courage
is also reflected in Stella's stoical self-restraint. As Swift notes in
the last of his birthday odes, even under the "tort'ring Pain" (l.
49) of advanced breast cancer Stella refused to complain.[15] Surely
Stella exemplifies what Wollstonecraft terms in chapter 3 of the
Vindication of the Rights of Woman the "fine woman," whose intellectual and moral accomplishments inspire not the protective
tenderness of Burkean pity but "more sublime emotions" of respect and admiration (*VRW*, 116).[16]

Indeed, Wollstonecraft implicitly endorses Stella as an example
for other women by reprinting two of Swift's poems to Stella in
her anthology, *The Female Reader*, compiled, according to the subtitle, "For The Improvement of Young Women."[17] Not surprisingly,
one of the poems, "To Stella, Visiting me in my Sickness," lauds
Stella for a courage that transcends sex:

> She thinks that Nature ne'er design'd
> Courage to Man alone confin'd:
> Can Cowardice her Sex adorn,
> Which most exposes ours to scorn?
>
> (*Poems*, 2:725, ll. 65–68)

The other, "Stella's Birth-day. Written A.D. 1720–21" (*Poems,*
2:734–36), notes how "Men of Sense" (l. 57), admire Stella for
her moral qualities, her "Breeding, Humor, Wit, and Sense" (l.
25), rather than for any distinctly sexual attributes. That Wollstonecraft anthologizes two of Swift's lesser-known poems indicates not only substantial familiarity with Swift's works, but a
willingness to employ Swift as an ally in her arguments on behalf
of sexless virtue and expanded educational opportunities for
women.

Swift and Wollstonecraft both firmly believed in holding men
and women to a uniform code of private conduct that transcends
the limits of sex. Hence Wollstonecraft's ideal marriage is based
not on erotic passion but on friendship—that is, on the mutual
modesty, tolerance, and respect of its partners. She insists that
marriages based on sexual passion alone lack "durable interest"
and thus will likely fail the test of time (*VRW,* 74). "Friendship,"
she writes," . . . is founded on principle, and cemented by time.
The very reverse may be said of love" (*VRW,* 142). Swift had expressed nearly identical views in the 1720s and 1730s: in the
Letter to a Young Lady (1723), he warns his charge not to found
her marriage on "Youth and Beauty," but on "more durable Qualities" (*Prose,* 9:89). Likewise, after the comic, scatological antics
that comprise most of the mock-epithalamium "Strephon and
Chloe" (1731), the narrator offers some serious marital advice in
the closing lines:

> Rash Mortals, e'er you take a Wife,
> Contrive your Pile to last for Life;
> Since Beauty scarce endures a Day,
> And Youth so swiftly glides away;
> Why will you make yourself a Bubble
> To build on Sand with Hay and Stubble?
>   On Sense and Wit your Passion found,
> By Decency cemented round;
> Let Prudence with Good Nature strive,
> To keep Esteem and Love alive.
> Then come old Age whene'er it will,
> Your Friendship shall continue still:
> And thus a mutual gentle Fire,
> Shall never but with Life expire.
>   (*Poems,* 2:593, ll. 301–14)

Wollstonecraft's attacks on female immodesty often echo the
sentiments, though not the explicit language, of some of Swift's

"unprintable poems." Wollstonecraft devotes the whole of chapter 7 of the *Vindication* to the subject of modesty, insisting that "cleanliness, neatness, and personal reserve" are "the graces that ought to adorn beauty" (*VRW*, 198). Like Swift, Wollstonecraft calls for cloacinal reserve and even expresses strong disapproval of some women's forwardness to "obtrude on notice" the topic of their menstruation, a process that she describes with some distaste as "that part of the animal oeconomy, which is so very disgusting" (*VRW*, 198).

It should be noted, however, that Wollstonecraft carefully points out that "personal reserve . . . has nothing sexual in it, and that . . . it [is] *equally* necessary in both sexes" (*VRW*, 198). Neither men nor women are exempt from treating one another with modesty and respect (*VRW*, 66). Swift, who had expressed similar sentiments, extends the rule of personal reserve and uniform good manners out of the bedroom and into the semi-private arena of the drawing room. He recalls how Stella once silenced a man who was indulging in double entendres that the other women present pretended either not to hear or to understand. "'Sir,'" she said,

> "all these ladies and I understand your meaning very well, having, in spite of our care, too often met with those of your sex who wanted manners and good sense. But, believe me, neither virtuous, nor even vicious women love such kind of conversation." (*Prose*, 5:234)

Stella's willingness to correct this man instead of ignoring him or waiting for a man to do so, pointedly indicates that he has violated not a sexual, but a human code of manners. Indeed, Swift himself was known to rise and leave the room when others indulged in vulgarity or profanity.

Because they believed that virtue transcends sex and results from the capacity to make informed decisions, both Swift and Wollstonecraft considered it crucial to cultivate women's as well as men's minds. Wollstonecraft's plans for the education of women are much more ambitious and systematic than Swift's, but they differ more in degree than they do in kind. Gulliver approvingly recalls that in the utopian schools of Lilliput, "the young Girls of Quality are educated much like the Males," with only minimal "Difference[s] in their Education, made by their Difference of Sex." As a result, there is no clear moral "double standard" in Lilliput and thus "the young Ladies there are as much ashamed of being Cowards and Fools, as the Men."[18]

Wollstonecraft's educational proposals are much more detailed and ambitious, but their moral objective is similar to Swift's. She hopes that by founding a system of national coeducational day schools, boys and girls, having been taught to live according to the same moral standards, will grow into men and women who treat one another as equals, regardless of sex. In chapter 9 of the *Vindication*, Wollstonecraft even looks ahead to a time when women will benefit society by entering professions heretofore exclusively male. She predicts that women will one day pursue careers in business and medicine, and that having achieved a "civil existence in the State," they will enter politics as well (*VRW*, 218–19).

Swift's hopes for women are much more modest. Instead of imagining women as beings capable of achieving independent political and economic status, he conceives of them still largely as supportive partners in what Lawrence Stone has called "companionate marriages."[19] Swift's *Letter to a Young Lady* advises, "the grand Affair of your Life will be to gain and preserve the Friendship and Esteem of your Husband" (*Prose*, 9:89). Yet Swift also thinks it important for women to have knowledge of history, philosophy, and the public sphere. In the *Letter to a Young Lady on Her Marriage*, Swift laments that women, by custom, are too often excluded from knowledge and discussion of these topics: "it is a shame for an *English* Lady not to relish such Discourses, not to improve by them, and endeavour by Reading and Information, to have her Share in those Entertainments; rather than turn aside, as it is the usual Custom, and consult with the Woman who sits next her, about a new Cargo of Fans" (*Prose*, 9:91). In the memorial to Stella, Swift proudly outlines the extent of Esther Johnson's knowledge of history, anthropology, moral philosophy, government, and religion:

> She was well versed in the Greek and Roman story, and was not unskilled in that of France and England. She spoke French perfectly, but forgot much of it it by neglect and sickness. She had read carefully in all the best books of travels, which serve to open and enlarge the mind. She understood the Platonic and Epicurean philosophy, and judged very well of the defects of the latter. . . . She understood the nature of government, and could point out all the errors of Hobbes, both in that and religion. (*Prose*, 5:231)

In addition, Swift countenanced none of that affected modesty that, according to Wollstonecraft, kept women in the eighteenth century from learning about the biological sciences (*VRW*, 192–

93): Stella "had a good insight into physic, and knew somewhat of anatomy" (*Prose*, 5:231).

If Swift cannot generally conceive of women as economically independent, he nevertheless admires Stella's economic independence, born of her frugality. He describes how after some youthful extravagance she learned to manage her household economy so well that even with a small annuity she was able to supply her own needs and give generously to the poor. She could do so because, like Wollstonecraft, she preferred "simple garb" (*VRW*, 199) to the costly, fashionable wear of fine ladies. As Swift explains, "She bought cloaths as seldom as possible, and those as plain and cheap as consisted with the situation she was in" (*Prose*, 5: 233).

Swift also praises Stella for her public-spiritedness and patriotism: he notes that in contrast to many of the Anglo-Irish absentee landlords of her day, Stella not only professed to love Ireland, but actually lived there and invested her fortune in the Irish funds; and when she died she left the bulk of her estate, about one thousand pounds, to Dr. Steevens's Hospital, then under construction in Dublin, to provide the stipend for a chaplain (*Prose*, 5:235–36).[20] Swift admires Stella not merely for her interest in the public welfare of Ireland or for the skillful management of her estate, but for the way in which her prudent private economy allowed this woman to have an effect on the public condition of Ireland.

Although Mary Wollstonecraft had some reservations about Jonathan Swift's satirical treatment of women, the supposedly neat ideological division between her and Swift is narrower and more complicated than scholars commonly assume.[21] Swift may never have envisioned the universal public education of women, but he nevertheless believed in their education and in holding men and women to the same moral standards. He had taken, as he says with ironic understatement, "some share" in Esther Johnson's education from the time she was eight years old, and Swift believed that Stella stood as living proof that women's moral and intellectual capacity was equal to men's (*Prose*, 5:227).[22] As Felicity Nussbaum notes, "For Swift, Stella's values of honor, sense, wit, and friendship are noble goals, and he urges both sexes to seek them."[23] Wollstonecraft builds upon the humanist belief in the personal moral equality of the sexes, espoused by Swift, among others, when she argues for the public and political equality of men and women. To vilify Swift as a hater of women whose ideas are antithetical to those of Wollstonecraft is to distort the historical record and to ignore important aspects of the lives and literary careers of both authors.

Notes

1. I would like to thank Donald Mell and my wife, Jeanne Conerly, for their encouragement and advice as I wrote and revised this essay.

2. Miriam Brody Kramnick, introduction to *A Vindication of the Rights of Woman* by Mary Wollstonecraft (New York: Viking Penguin, 1985), 7.

3. Ibid., 36.

4. Sandra M. Gilbert and Susan Gubar, *The Madwoman in the Attic:The Woman Writer and the Nineteenth-Century Imagination* (New Haven and London: Yale University Press, 1979), 31.

5. Mary Wollstonecraft, *A Vindication of the Rights of Woman,* in *A Vindication of the Rights of Men; A Vindication of the Rights of Woman; Hints,* vol. 5 of the *Works of Mary Wollstonecraft,* ed. Janet Todd and Marilyn Butler (London: William Pickering, 1989), 93n; hereafter cited as *VRW.*

6. See below, note 17.

7. One can draw a parallel to those nineteenth- and twentieth-century "Whig" or "Progressive" interpreters of British history who simplified figures from the era of the English civil wars, Interregnum, and Restoration into "heroes" who fought for "progress" and the institutions of parliamentary government, and "villains," who supported the king's prerogative. For more on this subject see Herbert Butterfield, *The Whig Interpretation of History* (New York: W. W. Norton and Co., 1965).

8. On the history of *A Letter to a Young Lady on Her Marriage,* see Jonathan Swift, *Irish Tracts 1720–1723 and Sermons,* vol. 9 of Swift, *Prose,* xxvii; hereafter cited in the text. On the history of *On the Death of Mrs. [Esther] Johnson,* see Jonathan Swift, *Miscellaneous and Autobiographical Pieces, Fragments and Marginalia,* vol. 5 of Swift, *Prose,* xxv–xxvi; hereafter also cited in the text.

9. Mary Wollstonecraft, *On Poetry and Contributions to the Analytical Review,* in *The Works of Mary Wollstonecraft,* 7:104, 479.

10. Steven Blakemore, *Burke and the Fall of Language: The French Revolution as Linguistic Event* (Hanover, N. H., and London: University Press of New England for Brown University Press, 1988), 49–55.

11. William Godwin, *Enquiry Concerning Political Justice,* ed. with introduction by Isaac Kramnick (Baltimore: Penguin Books, 1976), 96–115, 335–60, 632–33.

12. For further reading on the history of casuistry in England, see G. A. Starr, *Defoe and Casuistry* (Princeton: Princeton University Press, 1971), and Camille Wells Slights, *The Casuistical Tradition in Shakespeare, Donne, Herbert, and Milton* (Princeton: Princeton University Press, 1981). For the history of casuistry in Europe, see Perez Zagorin, *Ways of Lying: Dissimulation, Persecution, and Conformity in Early Modern Europe* (Cambridge: Harvard University Press, 1990).

13. I say "despite occasional misgivings" because in his "Hints" for an essay on the "Education of Ladyes," Swift observes, "Women I own do often want balast &c. but it is often through ignorance or half knowledge." See Jonathan Swift, *Irish Tracts, 1728–1733,* vol. 12 of Swift, *Prose,* 308.

14. Paul Youngquist, "*Frankenstein: The Mother, the Daughter, and the Monster*," *Philological Quarterly* 70 (1991): 339–40.

15. Swift, *Poems*, 2:765; hereafter cited in the text.

16. See Blakemore, *Burke and the Fall of Language*, 51–55.

17. Mary Wollstonecraft, *Thoughts on the Education of Daughters; The Female Reader; Original Stories; Letters on the Management of Infants; Lessons*, in *The Works of Mary Wollstonecraft*, 4:308–10, 319–20.

18. Jonathan Swift, *Gulliver's Travels, 1726*, vol. 11 of Swift, *Prose*, 62.

19. Lawrence Stone, *The Family, Sex, and Marriage in England, 1500–1800*, abridged ed. (New York: Harper Torchbooks, 1979), 217–24.

20. Ehrenpreis, 3:547.

21. Indeed, Mary Wollstonecraft's desire to defend women from the criticism of others while criticizing them herself is quite similar to Swift's proprietary treatment of the Irish, whom he likewise defends from the attacks of others while criticizing them himself.

22. Ehrenpreis, 2:68.

23. Felicity Nussbaum, *The Brink of All We Hate: English Satires on Women, 1660–1750* (Lexington: University Press of Kentucky, 1984), 115–16.

Premium Swift: Dorothy Parker's Iron Mask of Femininity

Ellen Pollak

> To be happy one must be (a) well fed, unhounded by sordid
> cares, at ease in Zion, (b) full of a comfortable feeling of superi-
> ority to the masses of one's fellow men, and (c) delicately and
> unceasingly amused according to one's taste.
>
> —H. L. Mencken

> If artists and poets are unhappy, it is after all because happi-
> ness does not interest them.
>
> —George Santayana

> It is true that Mrs. Parker's epigrams sound like the Hotel
> Algonquin and not like the drawing-rooms and coffee-houses
> of the eighteenth century. But I believe that, if we admire, as
> it is fashionable to do, the light verse of Prior and Gay, we
> should admire Mrs. Parker also. She writes well: her wit is the
> wit of her time and place; but it is often as cleanly economic
> at the same time that it is as flatly brutal as the wit of the age
> of Pope; and, within its small scope, it is a criticism of life. It
> has its roots in contemporary reality.
>
> —Edmund Wilson

IN November 1927 Dorothy Parker, one of the most trenchant
satirists of modern times, published a short review in the *New
Yorker* entitled "The Professor Goes in for Sweetness and Light."
Her subject was a book called *Happiness* by William Lyon Phelps,
a Yale Professor of English well known as a women's club lecturer
and a molder of public opinion. Affectionately known in Yale circles as "Billy the booster" because of the inimitable capacity of
his endorsements to create best-sellers overnight, Phelps would
become popular in the 1930s as "tastemaker of the airwaves"
through his weekly radio appearances on the "Swift Hour" variety
program; hence his recent dubbing by author Joan Shelley Rubin
as "Swift's Premium Ham."[1]

The purpose of this essay, whose title playfully adapts Rubin's already playful epithet, is to suggest an intertextual relationship between Parker's review of Phelps and the writings of Jonathan Swift, especially his two early prose works *The Battle of the Books* (1704) and *A Tale of a Tub* (1704). Such a relationship cannot be established with empirical certainty, since Parker makes no direct reference to Swift either in her review or elsewhere in her work. She left no library in which to forage for editions of Swift's writings, no letters, no memorabilia, nor any complete, firsthand inventory of her clearly voluminous reading. Emily Toth records her impression of a general, though not necessarily direct, Swiftian influence in Parker's satire and biographer Leslie Frewin testifies to Parker's delight in and admiration for Swift, whom he claims that "she adored" and whose work "she loved reading."[2] But more compelling as evidence of Parker's deployment of Swift as an operative point of reference in "The Professor Goes in for Sweetness and Light" is a careful reading of the text itself within both its immediate and extended cultural and political contexts. Such a reading strongly suggests that Parker not only knew Swift but meant to invoke him—at least in the minds of some educated readers.

Parker's attack on Phelps is scathing enough without the added force of blows delivered through her sly intertextual triggering of Swift's texts; it does not require an educated reader. Reading Swift in her satire, nevertheless, helps one to apprehend "The Professor" with a richer, more plural sense of its layered ironies. For despite its slight length, barely over a thousand words, "The Professor Goes in for Sweetness and Light" is more than a local critique of a current best-seller; it is also a devastating analysis of the gender, class, and ethnic biases inherent in the social and intellectual values of the Ivy League. Parker uses Swift both to level an attack on Phelps as a modern "hack" and to articulate her own problematic status as a woman writer positioned simultaneously inside and outside the historically male-dominated traditions of literary criticism and satire.

"The Professor" takes the form of a mock-defense, one of Swift's favorite satiric strategies. Assuming the voice of a female speaker at a women's club luncheon—perhaps addressing the sort of audience Phelps himself often addressed—Parker begins by enlarging upon the magnificent simplicity of Phelps's diminutive work:

Professor William Lyon Phelps, presumably for God, for Country and for Yale, has composed a work on happiness. He calls it, in a word,

Happiness, and he covers the subject in a volume about six inches tall, perhaps four inches across, and something less than half an inch thick. There is something rather magnificent in disposing, in an opus the size of a Christmas card, of this thing that men since time started have been seeking, pondering, struggling for, and guessing at.[3]

While one might assume that Parker here merely indulges in satiric hyperbole to belittle Phelps's book, the material object itself testifies both to her narrator's literal-mindedness and to the accuracy of her own physical account. A gift item on the scale of, say, Charles Schulz's 1960s best-seller, *Happiness Is a Warm Puppy,* Phelps's *Happiness* in fact neatly fits the dimensions given in Parker's text.

Parker's narrator is deferential and a bit inept. She digresses, but is unable to explain the logic of her own peregrinations. Her mode of argument appears less rational than impressionistic and heavily anecdotal. Phelps's book, she remarks with self-effacing dismissiveness, reminds her

> though the sequence may seem a bit hazy, of a time that I was lunching at the Cap d'Antibes (oh, I get around). I remarked, for I have never set up any claim to being a snappy luncheon companion, that somewhere ahead of us in the Mediterranean lay the island where the Man in the Iron Mask had been imprisoned.
>
> "And who," asked my neighbor at the table, "was the Man in the Iron Mask?"
>
> My only answer was a prettily crossed right to the jaw. How expect one who had had a nasty time of it getting through grammar school to explain to him, while he finished the rest of his filet, an identity that the big boys had never succeeded in satisfactorily working out, though they gave their years to the puzzle?
>
> Somewhere, there, is an analogy, in a small way, if you have the patience for it. But I guess it isn't a very good anecdote. I'm better at animal stories.
>
> (461–62)

What is the analogy that the reader is being asked—under the guise of the narrator's self-deprecating evasion—to have the patience for? What is the point, if there is one, of Parker's anecdote? Why does she say she is better at animal stories? Unlike Phelps, this narrator does not presume to compete with the "big boys." The definition of happiness is a puzzle for greater minds than hers, an historical enigma as inscrutable as the Man in the Iron Mask, that mysterious prisoner whose identity remained concealed behind a mask of black velvet throughout his life and who eventually died unnamed in the Bastille in 1703. This "little woman" is in no position to take on such a daunting task; she will stick to bedtime stories.[4]

At another level, though, the narrator's reference to animal stories is misleading. For beneath her display of humility and authorial incompetence lurks both an erudite allusion and an intellectual savvy glimpsed only in that worldly aside where she cynically assures the reader that she "gets around." Wasn't it a fictionalized version of that renowned animal fabler Aesop, after all, who coined the phrase "Sweetness *and* Light" in his long descant upon an argument between a spider and a bee in Swift's mock-epic history of *The Battle of the Books*?[5]

Phelps is a professor, a learned man; Parker's narrator is merely an uneducated woman, an American tourist in France with enough of a smattering of European popular culture to make dinner-table conversation but with an utter lack of intellectual authority. When her male luncheon companion asks a stupid question, disclosing his lack of knowledge of the "identity" of The Man in the Iron Mask ("Who *was* the man in the Iron Mask?"), it is her inability to respond rather than the ignorance prompting his question that becomes the object of self-deprecating humor. This is quintessential Parker. The narrator's self-mockery is, of course, disingenuous—an exposé of the social hypocrisy of gender relations masquerading as an attack on female vacuity. Regardless of the facts, the mask of male superiority remains intact—as unyielding as iron or as the narrator's seemingly inescapable mask of velveteen femininity.

But the full force of Swift's ghostly presence is not felt until somewhat later in Parker's text, when readers learn that the magnitude of Professor Phelps's arrogance, like that of the narrator's male luncheon companion, is directly proportionate to his ignorance. In his lack of indebtedness to his literary and philosophical forbears, he is more like Swift's self-generating and self-sufficient modern spider, who "*scorns to own any Obligation or Assistance from without,*" than like the diligent, ancient bee whose "*infinite Labor*" and far-ranging pursuit of beauty and truth bring home "Sweetness *and* Light" (*Battle,* in Swift, *Tale,* 234–35):

> The professor starts right off with "No matter what may be one's nationality, sex, age, philosophy, or religion, everyone wishes either to become or to remain happy." Well, there's no arguing that one. . . .
>
> "Hence," goes on the professor, "definitions of happiness are interesting." I suppose the best thing to do with that is to let it pass. Me,

I never saw a definition of happiness that could detain me after train-time, but that may be a matter of lack of opportunity, of inattention, or of congenital rough luck. If definitions of happiness can keep Professor Phelps on his toes, that is little short of dandy.

We might just as well get on along to the next statement, which goes like this: "One of the best" (we are still on definitions of happiness) "was given in my Senior year at college by Professor Timothy Dwight: 'The happiest person is the person who thinks the most interesting thoughts.'" Promptly one starts recalling such Happiness Boys as Nietzsche, Socrates, de Maupassant, Jean-Jacques Rousseau, William Blake, and Poe. One wonders, with hungry curiosity, what were some of the other definitions that Professor Phelps chucked aside in order to give preference to this one. (462–63)

Promptly the well-informed reader of Swift starts recalling one definition Professor Phelps has either dismissed or overlooked. "What is generally understood by *Happiness*," observes Swift's narrator in *A Tale of a Tub*," . . . will herd under this short Definition: That, *it is a perpetual Possession of being well Deceived.* . . . The Serene Peaceful State of being a Fool among Knaves" (Swift, *Tale,* 171–74). Parker may indeed be a victim of lack of opportunity and congenital rough luck, but inattention seems to be a trait more peculiar to "Billy" Phelps, that privileged son of Yale. We begin to understand what Parker means when she implies that her professor does not always "go in" for sweetness and light; like the peripatetic bee, she is indeed the one who "gets around."

Does Parker considerately prime the reader for an allusion to Swift by including her own tale of a tub? "[T]here is this to be said for a volume such as Professor Phelps's *Happiness*," she remarks off-handedly,

It is second only to a rubber duck as the ideal bathtub companion. It may be held in the hand without causing muscular fatigue or nerve strain, it may be neatly balanced back of the faucets, and it may be read through before the water has cooled. And if it slips down the drain pipe, all right, it slips down the drain pipe. (462)

Admirers of her work may well object that since Dorothy Parker did not attend college—according to one biographer, her formal education ended when she was only fourteen[6]—she would be unlikely to have read Swift, especially not such rarified works as *The Battle of the Books* and *A Tale of a Tub*. Although first used by Swift in *The Battle of the Books*, the phrase "sweetness and light" became familiar only later, when Matthew Arnold appropriated it in his 1869 treatise *Culture and Anarchy,* a work Parker was more likely to have known. As Rubin has documented in her recent study, *The Making of Middlebrow Culture,* Arnold's program of diffusing "sweetness and light" through the dissemination of "the best that has been thought and said in the world" sustained currency and ongoing cultural significance in the efforts of early-twentieth-century culture-makers to define literary standards and sensibility within a distinctly American and increasingly consumer-oriented context. Living in New York as a staff writer for *Vanity Fair* between 1915 and 1920, Parker may well have known—or known of—Stuart Pratt Sherman's 1917 *Matthew Arnold: How to Know Him,* a work celebrating Arnold's lifelong effort to make "aristocratic taste prevail in a world which was becoming rapidly democratic."[7] And she may have been familiar with the climate of heated criticism and debate surrounding Sherman's subsequent celebration of the Anglo-Saxon Puritan tradition in his 1923 book, *The Genius of America,* which because of its disdain for unassimilated immigrant populations was roundly condemned in *The Nation* by one of her Algonquin set associates, Ernest Boyd, as a brand of "Ku Klux Kriticism" (723).[8]

While neither Swift nor Arnold is mentioned explicitly in "The Professor Goes in for Sweetness and Light," Arnold's express concerns (as well as those of his American followers) do dovetail ironically with those of Parker, whose review provides an indirect commentary on the murder conviction and subsequent execution of the famous anarchist radicals Nicola Sacco and Bartolomeo Vanzetti. The title of Arnold's treatise, *Culture and Anarchy,* neatly epitomizes the sinister connection that Parker's review seeks to expose between what she views as Phelps's disturbing cultural elitism and the political scapegoating and persecution of two working-class Italian immigrants who had been tried and found guilty of the murders of a factory paymaster and guard in South Braintree, Massachusetts, on 5 April 1920. In Boston on 10 August 1927 (when, after almost seven years of legal maneuvering, Sacco and Vanzetti were scheduled to die), Parker had been arrested, jailed overnight, and fined five dollars for participating in a demonstration advocating a stay of execution. Late in her review, moreover, she expressly invokes Sacco and Vanzetti's cause through a reference to Harvard University President Abbott Lawrence Lowell and his role on the Fuller Committee, which had investigated the fairness of their trial but ultimately found in favor of the court. Sacco and Vanzetti died in the electric chair on 22 August 1927—on Dorothy Parker's thirty-fourth birthday. Matthew Arnold's concern with the relationship between culture and anarchy, though with an ironic twist, was Parker's too.

It would appear, then, that in criticizing Phelps, Parker was using Arnold's idea of "culture" ironically to debunk the inherent hypocrisy of an educated American elite who, under the guise of democratizing learning, sought to homogenize and purify American intellectual life by reconciling genteel, Arnoldian values with the demands of an increasingly commercialized publishing industry. In doing so, she participated in an already well-established intellectual tradition of criticizing the politics of American middle-brow culture-makers, the so-called merchants of light.[9]

Still, while Arnold may have held more influence in Parker's day, there is no reason to assume her ignorance of Swift. As Parker once remarked for a newspaper interview during her tenure in the early 1960s as Distinguished Visiting Professor of English at California State College in Los Angeles, "Because of circumstances, I didn't finish high school. But, by God, I read."[10] Indeed, while there remains disagreement among biographers as to how many years Parker actually spent at Miss Dana's finishing and college preparatory school in Morristown, New Jersey, where she followed a standard course of study including Latin, English, the Bible, and history, all seem to agree that the young woman who would later become known to *New Yorker* readers as "The Constant Reader" did in fact read constantly. According to Frewin, Parker had already sampled an impressive array of British authors before she arrived at Miss Dana's, largely in spite of the curriculum at Blessed Sacrament Academy, where she attended elementary and secondary school. Included, in addition to Swift, were works by Pope, Dickens, Hardy, Carlyle, Shakespeare, and Thackeray (whom she claimed to have first discovered at age eleven).[11] At Miss Dana's she also became acquainted with Horace, Virgil, Catullus, Aristotle, Socrates, Goethe, Montaigne, Martial, and La Rochefoucauld; in addition, scholars have commented on the subsequent influence of classical poetry on her work.[12]

By 1927, moreover, Parker had maintained close, longtime working friendships with Harvard graduates Robert Benchley and Robert Sherwood, whom she had first met in May 1919 and with whom she regularly lunched in the early 1920s at the famous Algonquin Round Table with such other notable literary types as Heywood Broun and Edna Ferber. In such an atmosphere of sophistication and educated wit, itself resembling the ambiance of the Scriblerians, it would hardly be frivolous to speculate that Swift might have come up. According to his son Nathaniel, Robert

Benchley had resolved at one point to write a history of the humorists in the age of Queen Anne and by 1927 had "a growing collection of books about the Queen Anne period, of which he finally gathered about a hundred."[13] Parker, who had intimate knowledge of Benchley's intellectual pursuits, would have had access not only to his thoughts during this period but also to his library. Nor would there have been any paucity of editions of Swift's work generally available to her. A volume of *Selections from the Prose Writings Of Jonathan Swift,* edited with notes and an introduction by Cornell University Professor F. C. Prescott, was published in New York in 1908, and another New York edition of *A Tale of a Tub, The Battle of the Books and Other Satires* was brought out by E. P. Dutton & Co. in 1909 with three subsequent reprintings (in 1911, 1916, and 1920). In addition to Humphrey Milford's 1919 Oxford edition of *Gulliver's Travels, A Tale of a Tub, and The Battle of the Books,* two editions of *Gulliver's Travels* with introductions and notes followed in 1925 and 1926.[14]

The conspicuous absence of direct reference to Swift in Parker's review would perfectly suit her satiric purposes. Since Parker undertakes to lodge her critique of the professor through the medium of a distinctly "feminine" (and thus not well-educated) persona, it makes eminent sense for her to mask her debt to Swift, even as her allusive context enables Swift's own words to deliver the crowning blow to Phelps. That she slyly omits explicit mention of Swift in her ironic inventory of representative "Happiness Boys" seems less a sign of his irrelevance than a way of pointing through parody to the dismissiveness and incompleteness of that version of intellectual history represented by Phelps's own privileging of the "modern" genius of Timothy Dwight (a Yale professor like himself, no less) over the wisdom of diverse continents and ages. In a gesture of ironic narration that might be characterized as Swiftian in its complex handling of masks, Parker manages simultaneously to perform a masquerade of "femininity" and, through an indirect display of erudition, to demolish Phelps's claims to cultural superiority. In the process she blasts Phelps's false presumption that intelligence correlates with cultural privilege, producing a withering political commentary on the disturbing dogma that emanates from the elite American academy. *Happiness,* she demonstrates, is not just a silly book, a diversionary piece of harmless sentimental poppycock: its underlying assumptions are dangerous.

Phelps begins *Happiness,* as Parker's narrator notes, with a number of self-evident and irrefutable assertions. He invokes the universal human desire for happiness regardless of nationality, sex, age, philosophy, or religion, and later he seems to understand that "Happiness is not altogether a matter of luck" but "is dependent on certain conditions" (463). The narrator responds to the first of these pronouncements with characteristically submissive reverence:

> The author has us there. There is the place for getting out the pencil, underscoring the lines, and setting "how true," followed by several carefully executed exclamation points, in the margin. It is regrettable that the book did not come out during the season when white violets were in bloom, for there is the very spot to press one. (462)

Beside Phelps's indelibly printed words the narrator's responses remain tentative and marginal; she uses a pencil and yearns to mark his text by pressing only white violets, whose petals leave no stain. But Parker's moral outrage is never very far from the surface, manifesting itself not only in deadpan assertions like "The author has us there" (which suggest that, to her, Phelps's platitudes have a certain coercive edge), but also in the incongruities created by her narrator's indiscriminate admiration for Phelps, despite his frequent and inadvertent self-contradictions. Parker evidently wants readers to see that even as Phelps expresses truths that seem to recognize the social bases of happiness, he indulges in a blithe obliviousness to the realities of social inequality:

> "Money is not the chief factor in happiness." . . . "I am certain that with the correct philosophy it is possible to have within one's possession sources of happiness that cannot permanently be destroyed." . . . "Many go to destruction by the alcoholic route because they cannot endure themselves." (463)

Against the backdrop of the Sacco and Vanzetti execution, Phelps's assertion that "correct philosophy" can provide "sources" of happiness that "cannot permanently be destroyed" assumes some rather sinister implications. Phelps at one point makes a statement so inanely optimistic that Parker (who by 1927 had weathered a broken marriage, a failed love affair, an abortion, two suicide attempts, and several bouts with alcoholism) cannot refrain from directly addressing it in an aside:

> "Life, with all its sorrows, perplexities, and heartbreaks, is more interesting than bovine placidity, hence more desirable. The more interest-

ing it is, the happier it is." (Oh, professor, I should like to contest that.) "And the happiest person is the person who thinks the most interesting thoughts." (463–64)

Parker establishes her assessment of Phelps's sentimental whitewashing of social reality when she has her narrator extol his book's utter inoffensiveness. By now her use of the term "happily" has acquired a complex layering of ironic resonance:

> Here is a book happily free from iconoclasm. There is not a sentence that you couldn't read to your most conservative relatives and still be reasonably sure of that legacy. . . . I give you my word, in the entire book there is nothing that cannot be said aloud in mixed company. (463)

Here, if only momentarily, Parker cannot resist trading her mask of timid propriety for one of cynical irreverence. There may be nothing in Phelps's book that cannot be said aloud in mixed company, but

> there is, also, nothing that makes you a bit the wiser. I wonder—oh, what will you think of me—if those two statements do not verge upon the synonymous. (463)

A swipe at women? Or at a culture that justifies its own complacence on the grounds that women need protection from the seamy side of life? Wisdom, Parker seems to be saying, resides in exploding lies, in telling the truth about life, even if that means indecorously betraying that men are sometimes self-serving and corrupt or that women have voices, bodies, eyes, and minds.

To Parker, Phelps's offensiveness depends upon his community of readers. When one's greatest catastrophe in life is losing one's rubber duck down the bathtub drain, it may be easy to be happy. But when one is unhappy about the conditions under which one lives, Phelps's denial of human evil and misery, his linking of intelligence and happiness—with its implication that those who are unhappy with their lot in life are neither interesting nor smart, and its unimaginative assumption that people drown their sorrows in alcohol only because they cannot endure themselves may seem offensive. Such readers might be happier with Parkeresque irreverence.

It becomes increasingly apparent as Parker proceeds that what initially may have seemed a relatively lighthearted attempt to ridicule one foolish Brahmin of higher education is actually a serious political critique with wide-ranging social significance. Parker's swipes at Phelps may look like prettily crossed rights to the jaw, playful blows delivered just in fun, but in fact they constitute serious indictments of a male WASP power elite—indictments leveled by Parker not just on her own behalf (as excluded woman and half-Jew), but also on behalf of other politically, culturally, and economically disenfranchised groups (like political anarchists, Italian immigrants, or factory workers). Although Parker's penchant for irony and masks makes it impossible ever to construe her personal gestures as entirely transparent signs, the fact that she left the bulk of her estate, some twenty thousand at her death in 1967, to the Reverend Martin Luther King, Jr. (whom she admired but had never met), with her bequest to King to pass it on to the NAACP at his death seems consistent with the spirit of her review in its material expression both of commitment to the promotion of social justice and of respect for the realities of American cultural heterogeneity.

The final paragraph of "The Professor" registers Parker's bitterness and establishes its political context unmistakably:

> These are the views, this is the dogma, of Professor William Lyon Phelps, the pride of New Haven. And, of course, at Harvard there is now—and it looks as if there might be always—President Lowell, of the Fuller Committee. I trust that my son will elect to attend one of the smaller institutions of higher education. (464)

Parker is disturbed not just by Phelps's inveterate superficiality but also by the brutal complacency of his willful blindness to social injustice. Such blind complacency, she suggests, has become institutionalized in bastions of higher education and has devastating human implications. "The Professor Goes in for Sweetness and Light" is her expression of disgust at the massive immorality of this circumstance, an immorality underscored by the magical immunity that certain individuals, here represented by President Lowell, seem to acquire. Unlike Sacco and Vanzetti who, like white violets, easily (and apparently bloodlessly) bloom and die, leaving no trace behind, Lowell—son of the wealthy and influential Lowell family of Massachusetts—has cultural force and something like institutional permanence: "there is now—and it looks as if there might be always—President Lowell" (464). The intellectual folly of providing facile solutions to difficult problems, whether definitions of happiness or identities for the Man in the Iron Mask, may have political ramifications that take their toll in human terms. Was this the case in identifying the Braintree murderers? In a famous article in *The Atlantic Monthly* published in March of 1927, Felix Frankfurter asserted that the "only issue" at the trial of Sacco and Vanzetti "was the identity of the murderers":

> the killing of Parmenter and Berardelli [paymaster and guard] was undisputed. . . . Were Sacco and Vanzetti two of the assailants of Parmenter and Berardelli, or were they not?
> On this issue, there was at the trial a mass of conflicting evidence.[15]

Would it be possible to say that, given what Frankfurter called the "elements of uncertainty"[16] at their trial, the conviction of Sacco and Vanzetti was, like Phelps's magnificently efficient explication of happiness, based on a mix of arrogance and ignorance? While at the literal level Parker's narrator modestly takes for granted that no son of hers could ever possibly aspire to so much greatness as that embodied by Phelps and Lowell, the irony of her message is quite clear: as a woman with no direct power to prevent the values of such cultural icons from being reproduced, she can only "trust" that her college-bound son will wisely exercise his dubious privilege of choosing whether to pay homage to the "big boys."[17]

But no matter how ugly Parker's prettily crossed rights to the jaw become, they are never as distasteful to her readers as is Phelps's "pretty tribute to what he calls the American cow" to her. This is the "animal story" with which the eminent professor concludes his little book:

> The cow, he points out, does not have to brush her teeth, bob her hair, select garments, light her fire and cook her food. She is not passionate about the income tax or the League of Nations; she has none of the thoughts that inflict distress and torture. "I have observed many cows," says the professor, in an interesting glimpse of autobiography, "and there is in their beautiful eyes no perplexity; they are never even bored." He paints a picture of so sweet, so placid, so carefree an existence, that you could curse your parents for not being Holsteins. And then what does he do? Breaks up the whole lovely thing by saying, "Very few people would be willing to change into cows. . . . Life, with all its sorrows, perplexities, and heartbreaks, is more interesting than bovine placidity." (463–64)

Does "the American cow" represent Professor Phelps's ideal of woman as a vacuous reproductive vessel? One is somehow reminded, though the sequence may seem a bit hazy, of that filet on the plate of the narrator's male companion at Cap d'Antibes, or of those "dams" whose children Swift's modest proposer so relishes the thought of cooking up.[18] Cannibalism notwithstanding, even animal life is not always as happy as it seems.[19] In any event, there is something profoundly disturbing to Parker—something chillingly like Gulliver upon his return from Houyhnhnmland—about a mentality that sentimentalizes cows, femininity, purity, and life (with all its miseries) while tacitly sanctioning the execution of human beings. Swift's definition of happiness thus once more comes to mind. Phelps is not simply a fool, but something much more troubling: a fool among knaves. Parker has produced a portrait of a world turned upside down. But it is not just the categories of wisdom and folly that are reversed in her review, or even those of culture and anarchy. In typical Swiftian fashion, she probes the very order of civilization and savagery and finds that order skewed. A woman needs not only irony but a mask of iron—some self-protective shield against facile knowledge of who and what she "really" is—when she registers so much savage indignation.

"Men seldom make passes / At girls who wear glasses," quipped Dorothy Parker, apparently innocently, in a short poem called "News Item" written in the summer of 1926.[20] Now, more than sixty years later, the aphoristic fame of these lines has superseded popular knowledge of their authorial provenance. Indeed, their anonymous appropriation by recent feminist theory, most notably by film critic Mary Ann Doane, who, in her landmark essay on the female gaze, uses them as the verbal corollary of an important cinematic commonplace, is itself moot testimony that Parker had tapped into a powerful cultural cliché. The image of the woman who wears glasses, argues Doane, "is a heavily marked condensation of motifs concerned with repressed sexuality, knowledge, visibility and vision, intellectuality and desire."[21] When Dorothy Parker, as female critic, scrutinizes the willful blindness of Professor William Lyon Phelps, she assumes a spectatorial stance that paradoxically "womanizes" and desexualizes her. (According to Parker's epigrammatic logic, the girl who wears glasses becomes an intellectual woman but thereby loses her girlish sex appeal.) To protect herself against rejection for her usurpation of the masculine-coded subject position of intellectual womanhood, therefore, Parker must deploy precisely the strategy identified in 1929 by Joan Riviere in her now-classic essay "Womanliness as a Masquerade"; she must produce herself as an excess of girlish femininity, masquerade as a blissfully myopic "little lady" who needs glasses but, like Gulliver, either does not know it or will not wear them, so girlishly smitten is she by seeing only what Swift elsewhere once called "the *Superficies* of Things" (Swift, *Tale*, 174), by being placidly and complicitously well-deceived.[22]

Why would Dorothy Parker be thus inclined to align herself with Swift? One might point to similarities in the way both writers were positioned, or positioned themselves, in relation to major sites of cultural power. Parker shared with Swift an attraction to wealth and power laced with a sense of personal injury at not properly belonging to their ranks, and for both writers, this sense of personal injustice translated into championship of the down-trodden and oppressed. Swift's entire career was defined by a series of social, ethnic, and professional self-divisions. A writer who made his living by the Church, a clergyman who satirized religion, the son of English Protestants living in Ireland yet first seeking refuge in England and then in Ireland, at one time hungry for advancement in English political life and for a deanery in En-gland, at another time champion of the Irish against the English, choosing finally "to be a freeman among slaves, rather than a slave among freemen,"[23] Swift was the living site of multiple and often conflicting loyalties.

Like Swift, Parker moved in circles of wealth and influence where she never felt fully like either an insider or an outsider. Frequenting such offices and homes as those of Condé Nast and Herbert Bayard Swope, she was part of the upper class but not quite of them.[24] In 1917, as the half-Jewish Dorothy Rothschild, she had married the Hartford-born Edwin Pond Parker II, "a de-scendent in the ninth generation of William Parker, who had ar-rived in Hartford from England in 1636."[25] Estranged from her father, Dorothy had long rejected her Jewish roots. But as biogra-pher Marion Meade notes, when Eddie's grandfather, the Rever-end Edwin Pond Parker—Connecticut's "leading Protestant clergyman and one of Hartford's most distinguished citizens"—referred to her upon their first meeting as "a stranger within our gates," she experienced a heightened sense of her own ethnic identity:

> Stupefied at his mean spirit, she was harshly reminded of the chasm separating New England Congregational pulpits and the Lower East Side sweatshops. If she had felt no harmony with the Jews, it was now clear that she had even less in common with these Hartford Brahmins, "toadying, in sing-song, to a crabbed god." [26]

Thus, when Parker later lambasted the New Haven- and Hartford-bred Professor William Lyon Phelps, son of a Baptist minister and descendent of that William Phelps who settled at Windsor, Connecticut, in 1638,[27] she was attacking not only a particular instance of academic folly but also those strongholds of cultural privilege for whose comforts she longed but from whose inner circles she somehow felt constitutionally excluded. Yale, Harvard, and the Massachusetts Lowells were simply institutionalized displacements of her (by that time all-but-former) New England in-laws, bastions of corrupted power that protected private interests in the false name of the larger community.

Parker mounts her critique of Phelps by creating for herself endlessly displaced identities. In poses akin to Swift's alternating masks of the cynic and the naif, she by turns impersonates the "little lady" and the slightly sluttish "woman of the world." In addition, she mercilessly subverts her readers' ability to distinguish fact from fiction by sprinkling her narrative with various "interesting glimpses of autobiography." (She had, for example, actually spent part of the summer of 1926 at Cap D'Antibes at the villa of her new acquaintance, Yale graduate Gerald Murphy, heir of the New York leather goods store Mark Cross.) Historically, critics have all too often mistaken Swift's masks for the man himself, but Swift never goes out of his way as mercilessly as Parker does, misleadingly, to tantalize his readers with incidental autobiographical details. Situating herself only partly in the world of her own experience, Parker heightens our sense of the illusory or invented nature of even her "real" identity, itself always already mediated by culturally constructed versions of womanhood. If femininity is a fiction—a pose or mask behind which this author hides—so too, we are led to understand, is the "real" woman it professes to conceal.

Thus while Parker's use of Swift may illuminate her affinities with him, it also reveals some telling differences. Parker the reviewer and ravenous reader seems in the end to have identified as much with Swift's monstrous female embodiment of literary criticism in *The Battle of the Books*—that malignant deity of the Moderns, Criticism—as she did with Swift himself. A voracious, rotting, self-consuming, maternal presence who lies "extended in her Den, upon the Spoils of numberless Volumes half devoured" as at her "Teats . . . a Crew of ugly Monsters . . . greedily [suck]" (Swift, *Tale*, 240), Criticism is roused from her epic lethargy only by the necessity of preventing the destruction of her worshipers, the Moderns—especially that of Wotton, her favored son. To assist him without dazzling or overwhelming him with her divine repulsiveness, Swift's hungry goddess undergoes a miraculously dematerializing metamorphosis in which she is transformed corporeally from a physically sprawling maternal body into the neatly delimited compass of a male-authored text:

> She . . . gathered up her Person into an *Octavo* Compass: Her Body grew white and arid, and split in pieces with Driness; the thick turned into Pastboard, and the thin into Paper, upon which, her Parents and Children, artfully strowed a Black Juice. . . . In which Guise she march'd on towards the *Moderns,* undistinguishable in Shape and Dress from the *Divine B-ntl-y, W-tt-n's* dearest Friend. (Swift, *Tale,* 242–43)

Having thus disguised herself, Criticism takes "the ugliest of her Monsters" (243), flings it invisibly into Wotton's mouth, and vanishes in a mist.

Parker, one might argue, manages an analogous transformation of active rage into apparently demure textuality when—by means of a narrator also concerned for the well-being of her son—she decorously, though no less cannibalistically, "makes mincemeat" of Professor Phelps. Vaguely anorexic (despite her "hungry curiosity" about definitions of happiness, it is in fact only the narrator's male luncheon companion whom we actually see eat), this narrator's criticism is more admiring than analytic; it has the timidity of pencil marks and the arid innocuousness of pressed white (not purple) violets. Through it, Parker deftly dodges the stigma Swift himself attaches to female rage. (For surely Swift is never quite so repulsed by Gulliver, even in the latter's angriest and most misanthropic moments, as he is by the splenetic Mother of all Gall). By surreptitiously mobilizing Swift's satiric texts, Parker's assaults—like Swift's own monstrous goddess's—are rendered indirect, flung, as it were, into another critic's mouth.

Ironically, nevertheless, it is through this very self-transformation that Parker most compellingly establishes herself as a locus of moral outrage. For it is precisely in her identification with Swift's angry goddess that she is able most pointedly to differentiate herself from Phelps. Parker recognizes Phelps as a fellow literary critic, one whose word—like hers—has the power to make or break a book. But just as there is for Swift a difference between the malicious and protectionist lies produced by Lilliputian or Walpolian hypocrisy and those produced by the elusive masquerading satirist, so too there is for Parker a difference between the sophisticated literary hoaxes she perpetrates in the interest of brutal veracity and the intellectual charlatanry (with its truly brutal consequences) of the "academic" Phelpses of the world. Phelps and Parker may both go in for artificial sweetness, but only Parker's counterfeit invites detection or produces light. Parker's review may be intellectually demanding, may even invite the attention of a certain highly educated class, but ultimately, and with deliberate irony, it is more genuinely "populist" in spirit than Phelps's "popular" little tome of platitudes. Through its appeal to a common sense of human suffering and shared humanity—that of women and Italian immigrants not excepted—it is far more accessible to the general public, if we understand that public in the truest sense to be constituted not by but across lines of class, ethnic, gender, and educational privilege.

Notes

1. Joan Shelley Rubin, *The Making of Middlebrow Culture* (Chapel Hill: University of North Carolina Press, 1992), 281.

2. Emily Toth, "Dorothy Parker, Erica Jong, and the New Feminist Humor," in *Regionalism and the Female Imagination,* ed. Emily Toth (New York: Human Sciences Press, 1985, 71; Leslie Frewin, *The Late Mrs. Dorothy Parker* (New York: Macmillan, 1986), 16 and 17. Frewin's claims remain undocumented.

3. "The Professor Goes in for Sweetness and Light," in *The Portable Dorothy Parker,* rev. ed. (New York: Viking, 1973), 461. All subsequent references to "The Professor," cited parenthetically by page number in the text, will be to this edition.

4. On the Man in the Iron Mask, see Sidney Dark, introduction to *The Man in the Iron Mask* by Alexandre Dumas (New York: Norton, 1955), 11–14. On the topos of the "little woman" in Parker's work and in that of other American female humorists, see Nancy Walker, "Fragile and Dumb: The Little Woman in Women's Humor, 1900–1940," *Thalia* 5, no. 2 (Fall/Winter 1982–83): 24–29.

5. Jonathan Swift, *The Battle of the Books,* in Swift, *Tale,* 233–35. All future references to *The Battle of the Books* and *A Tale of a Tub,* cited parenthetically by page number in the text, will be to this edition.

6. Marion Meade contends that Parker stopped attending classes at Miss Dana's school for girls in 1908 during the spring of her freshman year (*What Fresh Hell Is This?* [New York: Villard, 1988], 27–28). In contrast, Frewin claims that there is solid evidence that Parker remained at Miss Dana's until the fall of 1910 (*The Late Mrs. Dorothy Parker,* 13); John Keats notes that Parker entered Miss Dana's as a member of the class of 1911 and, although he never specifically asserts that she actually graduated, he seems to assume that she did (*You Might as Well Live: The Life and Times of Dorothy Parker* [New York: Simon and Schuster, 1970], 21–28); and Arthur F. Kinney claims that Parker graduated from Miss Dana's in 1911 (*Dorothy Parker* [Boston: Twayne, 1978], 27).

7. Stuart Pratt Sherman, *Matthew Arnold: How to Know Him* (Indianapolis: Bobbs-Merrill, 1917), 1–2.

8. Stuart Pratt Sherman, *The Genius of America* (New York: Scribner's, 1923); Ernest Boyd, "Ku Klux Kriticism," *The Nation* (20 June 1923): 723–24.

Interestingly, Parker's implicit charges against Phelps in her review (charges I attempt to explicate below) echo many of Boyd's charges against Sherman. The following two passages from Boyd's text, which disdain Sherman's hankering after American ethnic purity, seem especially pertinent: "Sinister Jews and Irishmen, apparently in the mistaken belief that they have any rights of self-expression in this great Anglo-Saxon republic, are actively engaged in the damnable work of undermining the Puritan stamina of the American people. Be Anglo-Saxon or be forever silent is, I gather, the exhortation which Mr. Sherman and his colleagues extend to the articulate few in the welter of races, creeds, and traditions which make up the America of today" (723); and "Before Mr. Sherman appeals to the artist on behalf of the community, he will have to make up his mind that the community is something vastly more complicated and less homogeneous than is dreamt of in his Ku Klux philosophy" (724). According to Clare Booth Luce, Boyd was one of Parker's "intimate friends and great admirers" and a member of the Algonquin set (Keats, *You Might as Well Live,* 49).

9. Rubin, *Middlebrow Culture,* chaps. 2 and 5. See also Daniel Aaron's "Merchants of Light," review of Rubin's book in *The New Republic,* 6 July 1992, 34–36.

10. Meade, *What Fresh Hell Is This?,* 28.

11. Frewin, *The Late Mrs. Dorothy Parker,* 12–14.

12. Kinney, *Dorothy Parker,* 103ff.

13. "He left a standing order at the Holliday Bookshop that any book about that period, or any book relating to it in any way, should be sent to him, and he read them all as they came in. . . . After he had done a monumental amount of reading, beginning with all the works of the all the humorists, he came to the reluctant conclusion that not one of them was funny" (Nathaniel Benchley, *Robert Benchley, a Biography* [New York: McGraw-Hill, 1955], 190).

14. H. Teerink, *A Bibliography of the Writings in Prose and Verse of Jonathan Swift D.D.* (The Hague: Martinus Nijhoff, 1937), 146–48.

15. Felix Frankfurter, "The Case of Sacco and Vanzetti," *The Atlantic Monthly,* March 1927, 410.

16. Ibid., 415.

17. Parker in fact did not have children.

18. *A Modest Proposal,*" in Swift, *Prose,* 12: 110. It is perhaps germane here to quote a passage from Phelps's book that Parker regrettably omits from her review. Phelps is in the process of ruminating on the American cow: "After eating for an hour or so . . . she begins to chew the cud. Her upper jaw remains stationary, while the lower revolves in a kind of solemn rapture; there is on her placid features no pale cast of thought; the cow chewing the cud has very much the expression of a healthy American girl chewing gum. I never see one without thinking of the other. The eyes of a cow are so beautiful that Homer gave them to the Queen of Heaven, because he could not think of any other eyes so large, so lustrous, so liquid, and so untroubled" (William Lyon Phelps, *Happiness* [New York: E. P. Dutton, 1927], 45–47).

19. Parker's love of animals was well known. "That inveterate dislike of her fellow creatures which characterizes so many of Mrs. Parker's utterances is confined to the human race," wrote Alexander Woollcott. "All other animals have her enthusiastic support. . . . [A]ny home of hers always has the aspect and aroma of a menagerie. Invariably there is a dog. There was Amy, an enchanting, wooly, fourlegged coquette whose potential charm only Dorothy Parker would have recognized at first meeting. For at that first meeting Amy was covered with dirt and

a hulking truckman was kicking her out of his way. This swinish biped was somewhat taken aback to have a small and infuriated poetess rush at him from the sidewalk and kick him smartly in the shins ("Our Mrs. Parker," in *While Rome Burns* [New York: Viking, 1934], 151).

20. *The Portable Dorothy Parker,* 109.

21. Mary Ann Doane, "Film and the Masquerade: Theorising the Female Spectator," *Screen* 23 (1982): 82.

22. Joan Riviere, "Womanliness as a Masquerade," in *Formations of Fantasy,* ed. Victor Burgin, James Donald, and Cora Kaplan (London: Methuen, 1986), 35–44. Riviere's article was originally published in *The International Journal of Psycho-Analysis* 10 (1929): 303–13. According to Frank Crowninshield, who as the editor of *Vanity Fair* had published a number of Parker's early works, Parker herself "wore horn-rimmed glasses, which she removed quickly if anyone spoke to her suddenly" (quoted in Frewin, *The Late Mrs. Dorothy Parker,* 29). "She wore glasses at work because she was badly nearsighted," writes biographer John Keats. "But she always took them off when anyone stopped at her desk, and she never wore them on social occasions" (*You Might as Well Live,* 86). Donald Ogden Stewart, Dorothy Parker's longtime friend and Algonquin Round Table compatriot, later reminisced about the Dorothy Parker of the 1920s. "Every girl has her technique," he observed, "and shy, demure helplessness was part of Dottie's—the innocent, bright-eyed little girl that needs a male to help her across the street" (Frewin, *The Late Mrs. Dorothy Parker,* 66).

23. Swift to Alexander Pope, Dublin, 8 July 1733, Swift, *Corresp.,* 4:171.

24. Kinney, *Dorothy Parker,* 43–44. "I hate almost all rich people," Parker once remarked, "but I think I'd be darling at it" (Marion Capron, "Dorothy Parker," in *Writers at Work: The "Paris Review" Interviews,* ed. Malcolm Cowley [New York: Viking, 1958], 80).

25. Meade, *What Fresh Hell Is This?,* 38.

26. Ibid., 41.

27. *Current Biography* (1943): 582, s.v. "Phelps, William Lyon."

Swift and the Woman Scholar

Nora F. Crow

Why are you not a young fellow, that I might prefer you?
—Swift, *Journal to Stella*

[H]e has appointed me an hour on Saturday, when I will open my business to him; which expression I would not use if I were a woman.
—Swift, *Journal to Stella*

If she had been a Man, she had been without Fault: But the Charter of that Sex being much more confin'd than ours, what is not a Crime in Men is scandalous and unpardonable in Woman, as she her self has very well observ'd in divers Places, throughout her own Writings.
—Delariviere Manley, *Adventures of Rivella*

In her ground-breaking essay "Swift among the Women," Margaret Anne Doody raises the question whether the Dean, in the eyes of his contemporary detractors, was "too womanly a man."[1] After quoting the hostile accusations of Lord Orrery and Lady Mary Wortley Montagu (1689–1762), which imply that Swift was "too fond of women,"[2] Doody turns to the admiring appraisal of Laetitia Pilkington (1708–50). This Swiftian protégée recorded, without disparagement, an event that appeared to support the censorious Lady Mary and Lord Orrery:

The Bottle and Glasses being taken away; the Dean set about making the Coffee, but the Fire scorching his Hand, he called to me to reach him his Glove, and changing the Coffee-pot to his Left-hand, held out his Right one, ordered me to put the Glove on it, which accordingly I did; when taking up Part of his Gown to fan himself with; and acting in Character of a prudish Lady, he said, "Well, I don't know what to think; Women may be honest that do such things, but, for my Part, I never could bear to touch any Man's Flesh—except my Husband's, whom, perhaps," says he, "she wish'd at the Devil."[3]

222

This "little riff of sudden mimicry," as Doody calls it, is indeed characteristic of Swift and reminiscent of his poetic impersonations in "The Humble Petition of Frances Harris" (1700), "Mary the Cook-Maid's Letter to Dr. Sheridan" (1718), and "A Panegyrick on the Dean in the Person of a Lady in the North" (1730).[4] In "To a Lady WHO DESIRED THE AUTHOR TO MAKE VERSES ON HER IN THE HEROIC STYLE" (ca. 1733), Swift supplies both the charge and the defense—the accusations and explanations in his own voice and the rebuttal in Lady Acheson's. Deborah Baker Wyrick discusses at length what she calls Swift's "transvestitures," among which she includes tropes of sexual transformation in *The Battle of the Books* (ca. 1697–98), *A Tale of a Tub* (1704), the *Drapier's Letters* (1724), and *A Proposal for the Universal Use of Irish Manufacture* (1720). She speaks of Swift as Arachne, as Penelope, as Philomela, and as Pallas Athena.[5] To scholars like Doody and Wyrick, Swift is not just a friend to women: his protean sensibility gives him empathic knowledge of what women are like.

Of course, shape-shifting is everywhere in Swift; and it crosses all boundaries. In the *Drapier's Letters,* Swift breaches class lines. "The Beasts' Confession to the Priest" (1732) crosses the line between species. In *A Modest Proposal* (1729), the reformer talks like a lunatic. In the *Digression . . . concerning Madness*, the lunatic talks sense. In *The Last Speech and Dying Words of Ebenezor Elliston* (1722), the solid citizen appropriates the criminal mind. In "On the Day of Judgement" (1733?), the divine Jove speaks in the accents of the human satirist. In all his incarnations, I am convinced, Swift bears out the truth of Irvin Ehrenpreis's observations in *"Personae"* (1963):

> As long as a man's character is alive, it is trying out roles in language, in conduct. At the same time, although one "self" does continually displace another, each remains a form or mode of revelation of the real person. It is not illusory appearances that the real person sets before us: it is visible effluences, aspects, reflections—however indirect—of an inner being that cannot be defined apart from them.[6]

More recently, in his essay in this volume, Claude Rawson seems to espouse a similar view. The subject is Cupid's obliquely laudatory speech about Cadenus:

> Formally Cupid is speaking, not Swift, but he's scripted by Swift on the subject of Swift. Nothing would more clearly illustrate the bankruptcy of traditional persona criticism than a pedantic disengagement that failed here to register appropriate interactions between

speaker and author. The two are not, of course, identical, but it is the nature of an author's investment in the persona, and not the latter's separate character, that demands sensitive recognition.[7]

We might extend Ehrenpreis's and Rawson's remarks to conclude that when Swift is playing the part of a prudish lady, he is not so much acting as revealing the woman within him. The poses he assumes and the way he speaks strike us as marvelously accurate. He is, for a moment, the real thing. If his contemporary critics found him "too womanly," it may be that his willingness to abdicate a male role suggested a dangerous fluidity.

For Swift, apparently, a woman's sexual identity was as fluid as his own. Just before Pilkington reports his behavior as a prudish lady, she records a curious conversation in which Swift seems to forget her sex:

"Pray, Madam," says he, "do you smoak?" "No indeed, Sir," says I; "Nor your Husband?" "Neither, Sir": "'Tis a Sign," said he, "you were neither of you bred in the University of *Oxford;* for drinking and smoaking are the first Rudiments of Learning taught there." . . .[8]

In a moment of heady play, Swift has offered Pilkington the exhilarating fantasy of indulging herself in both a vice and an education that are not available to her. He has at the same time set her and her husband upon an equal footing. Indeed, on other occasions, Swift arranges contests in which she excels Matthew Pilkington and wins a chance for the training she covets so much: "'Pox on you for a Dunce,' said he; 'were your Wife and you to sit for a Fellowship, I would give her one sooner than admit you a Sizar.'"[9] Matthew was not pleased to hear his wife's intelligence praised. When he remarried after her death, he chose a woman who, though "ferociously ugly" in his son's opinion, was "divinely domestic" in his own.[10] Nonetheless, even Matthew bowed to the Dean's eccentric treatment of sexual identity:

The Gentlemen guessing at my Circumstances, by my decreasing Face, and increasing Waist, were so over-obliging to know what I liked best; that at last I told the Dean, I wish'd I was a Man, that I might be treated with less Ceremony: Why, said the Dean, it may be you are: I wish, Sir, said I, you would put the Question to the Company, and accordingly to their Votes let my Sex be determined. I will, said he; Pilkington, what say you? A Man, Sir: they all took his Word; and, in Spite of Petticoats, I was made a Man of after Dinner: I was obliged to put a Tobacco-pipe in my Mouth. . . .[11]

Thus, a woman pregnant and in petticoats is transformed at Swift's whim, by her own wish, and with her husband's acquiescence into a man smoking a pipe. At a stroke Pilkington has been freed of the gentlemen's unwelcome attentions to her emphatically female "Circumstances."

Pilkington's metamorphosis will hardly surprise scholars familiar with Swift's praises of Stella and Vanessa. In "Cadenus and Vanessa" (1713), Venus tricks Pallas into mistaking Vanessa for a boy. The goddess of wisdom then endows the child with virtues "For manly bosoms chiefly fit / The seeds of knowledge, judgement, wit" (ll. 204–5). Cadenus's delight in Vanessa's progress "Was but the master's secret joy / In school to hear the finest boy" (ll. 552–53).[12] In a letter to Vanessa, dated 1 June 1722, Swift tries to allay her passion by enjoining her to "talk and act like a man of this world."[13] Responding on 18 November 1711 to a letter from Swift, Anne Long implies that he has remarked on the masculine qualities of her second cousin, Esther Vanhomrigh: "But how can I pretend to judge of anything, when my poor cousin is taken for an hermaphrodite. . . ."[14] Now this is Stella's case in fact:

> Say, Stella, was Prometheus blind,
> And forming you, mistook your kind?
> No: 'twas for you alone he stole
> The fire that forms a manly soul . . .
>
> (ll. 85–88)

In this poem, "To Stella, Visiting Me in My Sickness" (1720), the "manly" Stella nurses an ailing Swift, who gives way to "unmanly" (l. 99) laments.[15] Swift jokingly exempts MD from his dislike by unsexing them: "I don't like women so much as I did. [MD you must know, are not women.]"[16] And throughout the *Journal*, he refers to MD as "sirrahs," "lads," and "boys."[17]

For a man who does not like women, Swift is uncommonly egalitarian. His "LETTER to a Young LADY, on Her MARRIAGE" (1723), which is almost curmudgeonly enough to justify the opprobrium sometimes heaped on Swift, is redeemed by its evenhanded description of the virtues and vices: "I AM ignorant of any Quality that is amiable in a Man, which is not equally so in a Woman: I do not except even Modesty, and Gentleness of Nature. Nor do I know one Vice or Folly, which is not equally detestable in both."[18] Characteristically, Swift counsels the young lady to eschew finery and improve her mind: her studies will inspire her husband with those feelings of "Esteem" and "Friendship" that Swift valued so highly in his own relationships.[19] The fragment "Of the Education of Ladies" (1765) appears to be an abortive *Modest Proposal* for cultivating in women good sense; wit and humor; facility in their own language; a taste for history, for books of travels, and for "moral or entertaining discourses"; and solid judgment in poetry.[20]

In the first and the last parts of *Gulliver's Travels* (1726), Swift presents a utopian vision of women educated alongside men. The Lilliputians, who here represent ideal citizens, educate their young women in virtue and knowledge: "Thus the young Ladies there are as much ashamed of being Cowards and Fools, as the Men; and despise all personal Ornaments beyond Decency and Cleanliness; neither did I perceive any Difference in their Education, made by their Difference of Sex, only that the Exercises of the Females were not altogether so robust. . . ."[21] The Houyhnhnm master thinks it "monstrous" to give females a different kind of education from that provided to males.[22]

Although Swift did not conceive a detailed proposal for educating women, his agenda seems in harmony with those of Mary Astell (1666–1731) and Mary Wollstonecraft (1759–97). In fact, in another essay in this volume, David Venturo has pointed to the similarities in Swift's and Wollstonecraft's ideas about women's education and the nature of virtue.[23] (Did Wollstonecraft develop a belated affection for the author she decried in *Thoughts on the Education of Daughters* [1787] and *A Vindication of the Rights of Woman* [1792]? On 3 November 1796 she wrote to William Godwin, her suitor and a great admirer of Swift's: "I will come to you in the course of half an hour—Say the word—for I shall come to you, or read Swift."[24]) Like Astell's and Wollstonecraft's, Swift's plans for educating women appear considerably more enlightened than those of his detractor, Lady Mary. Although she is solicitous about her granddaughter's education, she endorses a policy of concealment. Writing to her daughter, Lady Bute, she says: "The second caution to be given her (and which is most absolutely necessary) is to conceal whatever Learning she attains, with as much solitude as she would hide crookedness or lameness. The parade of it can only serve to draw on her the envy, and consequently the most inveterate Hatred, of all he and she Fools. . . ."[25] Swift might have agreed with her assessment of the consequences, but he held, with Vanessa, "That common forms were not designed / Directors to a noble mind" (ll. 620–21).[26] He was proud of his pupils.

Doody's essay provides short accounts of Swift's mentorial influence over his circle of female friends—mostly writers and mostly Irish. Besides Pilkington, there were Mary Davys (1674–1732), Mary Barber (1690–1757), Constantia Grierson (ca. 1704–32), and Delariviere Manley (ca. 1663–1724). Mary Leapor (1722–46) learned techniques and attitudes from Swift, as did Mary Jones (d. 1778), and—somewhat later—Fanny Burney (1752–1840) and Hester Lynch Thrale (1741–1821). Swift's circle of female friends was discussed disdainfully, then and now. In our own time, Carole Fabricant has quoted, critically, J. A. Downie's insistence upon keeping Swift and his friend Manley in separate categories. "[Richard Steele] explicitly added insult to injury," writes Downie, "in dealing with the new Dean of St. Patrick's in the same manner in which he would deal with scribblers of the kidney of Delariviere Manley. . . ."[27]

This kind of comment has a long history. Orrery began the very peculiar tradition of trivializing the abilities of the women who were drawn to Swift while casting aspersions on his sexuality. He writes: "It is true, my friend, the Dean kept company with many of the fair sex, but they were rather his amusement than his admiration. He trifled away many hours in their conversation, he filled many pages in their praise, and by the power of his head, he gained the character of a lover, without the least assistance from his heart."[28] Swift was no lover, Orrery implies, and the women with whom he wasted his time were unworthy of any feeling but amusement. What is the object of this paradoxical attack—the worthless women or the heartless Swift? Orrery continues:

> You see the command which SWIFT had over all his females; and you would have smiled to have found his house a constant seraglio and very virtuous women, who attended him from morning till night, with an obedience, an awe, and an assiduity, that are seldom paid to the richest, or the most powerful lovers; no, not even to the Grand Seignior himself.
> To these Ladies SWIFT owed the publication of many pieces, which ought never to have been delivered to the press. He communicated every composition as soon as finished, to his female senate. . . . [29]

The image of an ignominious senate may come from Pope's lines about Addison: "Like *Cato*, give his little Senate laws, / And sit attentive to his own applause."[30] Pope's portrait also contains a Turkish motif—"Bear, like the *Turk*, no brother near the throne" (l. 198)—that may recall Lady Mary's discussion, in her Turkish Embassy Letters, of an emperor deposed and poisoned by his brother.[31] A "seraglio" of "very virtuous women" is (outside a ha-

rem) a contradiction in terms. Orrery suggests that the women
were sexually vulnerable to Swift, were at his disposal, but that
Swift remained a mentor rather than a lover. The idea fills Orrery
with contempt.

Lady Mary read Orrery's *Remarks on the Life and Writings of
Swift* in June 1754 and found herself "extremely entertain'd."[32]
From her travels in Turkey she was familiar with the customs of
the seraglio and with the habits of the Grand Seignior, the Sultan.
Writing in her commonplace book, she improved upon Orrery's
description of Swift: "Dr. S[wift] in the midst of his Women, like
a master E[unuch] in a seraglio."[33] Swift's female friends are,
again, kept women, though the castrated Swift can make no use
of them. This analysis of the Dean's reasons for befriending
women, for only *befriending* them, is one of Lady Mary's favorite
conceits. In her verses "The Reasons that Induced Dr S[wift] to
write a Poem call'd the Lady's Dressing room" (1733?), the "Reverend Lover" rationalizes his impotence by blaming it on his
whore's stinking person and quarters.[34] Swift's relinquishing of
male sexual privileges unfairly calls his very sexuality into question. For these contemporary critics, sex is the only conceivable
reason for a man's having female friends. Their petrification of
sexual roles stands in contrast to Swift's fluidity.

In the nineteenth century, Leslie Stephen toyed with the language of sexuality while he described Swift as a sultan and deni-
grated his female friends:

> His dominion was most easily extended over women; and a long list
> might be easily made out of the feminine favourites who at all periods
> of his life were in more or less intimate relations with this self-
> appointed sultan. From the wives of peers and the daughters of lord
> lieutenants down to Dublin tradeswomen with a taste for rhyming,
> and even scullery-maids with no tastes at all, a whole hierarchy of
> female slaves bowed to his rule, and were admitted into higher and
> lower degrees of favour.[35]

Stephen finds it almost incredible that Swift could have resisted
having sex with Stella: "[I]t is singular that a man should be able
to preserve such a relation. It is quite true that a connexion of
this kind may blind a man to its probable consequences; but it is
contrary to ordinary experience that it should render the consequences less probable."[36] His first attempt at explaining this mys-
tery leads him to a speculation previously entertained by Lady
Mary: "If Swift constitutionally differed from other men, we have
some explanation of his strange conduct."[37] Swift is still a eunuch:

the imputation is simply more polite. Some of the women have no taste at all.

Just as feminist attitudes have many manifestations, antifeminist viewpoints come in different varieties. I suppose that Orrery and Lady Mary would be surprised to be numbered among the detractors of women, but the evidence suggests that they belong there. In 1949, in a book called *The Conjured Spirit; Swift: A Study in the Relationship of Swift, Stella, and Vanessa,* the scholar Evelyn Hardy evinced another kind of antifeminism. She ruefully described the deplorable consequences of Swift's misconceptions about gender:

> For since the male and female sides of his nature were so pronounced, and intermingled so completely, they bred in him an outer confusion and lack of discrimination. He responded readily to the demands made upon him by both men and women, and he identified himself profoundly with the demands of each in turn: yet in some extraordinary way he did not distinguish between the sexes fundamentally, but laid down laws and axioms for their behaviour irrespective of their structural and emotional divergencies.[38]

Hardy quotes Swift writing to Sheridan and Swift writing to Vanessa and somberly notes: "The tone to the woman is the same as that to the man, with no shade of difference."[39] The pitiful Swift, according to Hardy, "hated his fellow-creatures for being able to act in a manner distasteful to him." The footnote to this sentence elucidates the overactful prose: "See Swift's ferocity concerning the fiddler to be hanged for rape, whose pardon he prevented. . . . And *Poems,* II, p. 516: 'An Excellent New Ballad, or the True English Dean to be Hanged for a Rape.'"[40] Rape, alas, was distasteful to Swift; and what is more, he wasn't "able" to rape anyone. The old canard has returned in a new guise. This time it is accompanied with sympathy rather than scorn. The sympathy extends to Swift's benighted habit of treating men and women in the same way, a habit no doubt due to the fatal admixture of male and female in his own nature.

In her book *Feminism in Eighteenth-Century England* (1982), Katharine M. Rogers has argued that Swift's age required from women a winning softness, timidity, and subordination. She comments thus: "If femininity is to be identified with weakness and inferiority, the feminist will demand that women be like men."[41] Swift, then, will qualify as a feminist who deserves the accolades of modern readers. But the matter is not so simple. Some modern women scholars detect misogyny in Swift.

In the Winter 1977 issue of the feminist journal *Signs*, Susan Gubar excoriates Swift for creating female "monsters" that inhibit women "from attempting the pen."[42] In the Spring 1978 issue, the feminist scholar Ellen Pollak rebuts Gubar courteously but firmly: "[I]f Swift creates mad or obsessive visions of women in his verse, he does so quite self-consciously and, finally, only to expose the inadequacies of such perspectives."[43] In 1979, in *The Madwoman in the Attic: The Woman Writer and the Nineteenth-Century Imagination*, Sandra M. Gilbert, collaborating with Gubar, repeats the accusation that Swift creates female monsters and demeans female arts.[44] Doody joins the many other critics who dissent from Gilbert and Gubar: "The effect of Swift's humour is not to silence the woman but to force her into utterance."[45] As Pollak points out in her essay about teaching Swift, "Swift among the Feminists" (1992), "It is a far cry indeed from Gubar's view . . . to Doody's argument. . . . But a feminist pedagogy need not impose more consensus on its students than feminism expects even from itself."[46]

The dialogue among women scholars nonetheless provokes some smirks. Writing in the Autumn 1993 issue of *The Scriblerian*, the editors thus begin a review of Erin Mackie's article on the excremental poems: "Rejecting Susan Gubar ('The Female Monster in Augustan Satire') and Felicity Nussbaum (*The Brink of All We Hate*), Ms. Mackie lines up with Ellen Pollack [sic] (*The Poetics of Sexual Myth: Gender and Ideology in the Verse of Swift and Pope*) and Deborah Wyrick (*Jonathan Swift and the Vested Word*) whose 'hermeneutic tools of poststructuralist discourse produce more historically vivid readings of Swift.'"[47] The sentence is snidely convoluted, but the complexity is justified by the debate. The feminists Gubar and Nussbaum, according to this review, have discovered Swift's perfidy, while the feminists Mackie, Pollak, and Wyrick are convinced he is an ally. In the volume of *Eighteenth-Century Studies*, for Winter 1993–94, the controversy continues. Carol Barash politely disagrees with Carol Houlihan Flynn's conclusions in *The Body in Swift and Defoe* (1990). Barash first quotes Flynn's analysis of Swift (which is antipodal to my own):

Unlike Defoe dreaming Moll's escape from Roxana's nightmare, Swift cannot even begin to imagine women from the inside. Keeping his ironic distance, he flails and strips "the sex" to get at the truth of its loathsome condition. The knowledge he produces is always external and judgmental. For reasons cultural as well as psychological, Swift defines women according to a physicality that is gross, filthy, and lasting.[48]

Diffidently, Barash offers her objection to this view: "I know this remains a minority position in feminist criticism of Swift, but I continue to find Swift's grotesque and disfigured female bodies compelling, even heroic in their dismemberment. . . . And, as Margaret Doody has shown in 'Swift among the Women,' eighteenth-century women writers certainly found much to love and imitate in Swift."[49]

It may be, however, that Barash is not in the minority after all. Both historically and at the present time, many distinguished women scholars have chosen Swift as their primary subject of study and have passionately committed themselves to his life and works. These scholars include feminists who may not always approve of Swift's views, but who nonetheless are intensely engaged in the field. More often than not, even the feminist critics find redeeming qualities in Swift; and among these, I would argue, is Felicity Nussbaum, whom the editors of *The Scriblerian* consign to the other camp.

To explain why Swift, so frequently condemned as a mysogynist, should be the focal point of many women scholars's lives, let me return for a moment to the three quotations with which I began. Swift's rhetorical question to Stella—"Why are you not a young fellow, that I might prefer you?"—suggests that a world of opportunities, now denied to Stella, might be open to her if she were a man. Her best friend is frustrated in his wish to promote her interests. At the same time, the word "prefer" carries the slightest hint of ambiguity. The second of Swift's quotations— "which expression I would not use if I were a woman"—suggests the plethora of restrictions on an eighteenth-century woman's conduct, and in particular on her use of language. In the quotation from Manley's *Adventures of Rivella,* I hear a yearning to be free of the moral constraints peculiar to women, to be a man of good character rather than a woman of ill repute: "*If she had been a Man, she had been without Fault. . . .*" It is almost as if, by a change of sex, she would be absolved of sin. This yearning to partake of the bounty available to males is not confined to the eighteenth century. In their recent book, *Failing at Fairness: How America's Schools Cheat Girls* (1994), the educators Myra and David Sadker examine sexual bias in schools. As part of their study, they asked girls and boys, "Suppose you woke up tomorrow and found you were a member of the other sex?" The girls were intrigued; but "For boys the thought of being female was appalling, disgusting, and humiliating."[50] Swift's fluidity about gender offers women—though only in fantasy—a moment of freedom from conventional restraint and a chance to enjoy opportunities, even vices, without stint and without reprisal. Women of earlier ages can, like Pilkington, be men and go to university—or smoke tobacco-pipes. Such privileges have their modern counterparts.

For eighteenth-century women and, perhaps, for women even now, the practice of publishing—if not writing—and the pursuit of knowledge were especially tainted activities. Having read the first volume of Mrs. Pilkington, Elizabeth Montagu (1720–1800), Queen of the Bluestockings, thus described the dangers attendant on female intelligence: She has a

> pretty genius for poetry, a turn of wit & satire, & vanity. . . . It is often said that wit is a dangerous quality; it is there meant that it is an offensive weapon that may attack friend as well as Enemy, & is a perilous thing in Society; but wit in Women is apt to have other bad consequences; like a sword without a Scabbard it wounds the wearer, & provokes assailants. I am sorry to say the generality of Women who have excelld in wit have faild in chastity; perhaps it inspires too much confidence in the possessor, & raises an inclination in the Men towards them without inspiring an esteem, so that they are more attacked & less guarded than other women.[51]

Speaking of Aphra Behn (1640–89) and Eliza Haywood (1693?–1756), Katharine Rogers goes even further than Montagu did: "The women were attacked as if they supported themselves by prostitution (which would have been an easier way than writing)."[52] Swift rose above the prejudices of his age to encourage women both to write and to study. He believed they were just as competent and just as deserving as men—no more and no less. The way his female friends, particularly the writers, benefited from his company helps explain why large numbers of women scholars have always chosen to work on Swift. In our own time the catalogue includes an impressive array of distinguished names besides those I have already mentioned: Rachel Trickett, Miriam Starkman, Kathleen Williams, Rosalie Colie, Marjorie Nicolson and Nora Mohler, Mackie Jarrell, Louise K. Barnett, Hopewell Selby, Laura Brown, Jenny Mezciems, Melinda Alliker Rabb, Barbara McGovern, and Ann Cline Kelly. These scholars have not consistently focused on Swift's attitude toward women, but (with a few exceptions) it has clearly not repelled them.

In fact, women's readings of Swift, especially when he touches upon the issue of gender, have been and continue to be valuable complements to those of men. For culturally determined reasons, women bring to the interpretation of Swift certain gender-specific advantages over men. Women have cause to be more grateful for Swift's emphasis on the lasting qualities of mind and spirit. They are more sensitive to the humor and intelligence that Swift, by his raillery, attributes to his female friends. They are more alert to the hints of aggression and the withholding of personal commitment implied by this means of compliment. They are better able to penetrate his curmudgeonly poses and more susceptible to his quirky kind of flirtation. They recognize with special appreciation Swift's habit of shaping a human ideal while seeming to describe a standard for women alone.

One might think that, for women scholars, the excremental poems would prove an insuperable obstacle to appreciating Swift. But that is not the case. With the exceptions of Susan Gubar and Carol Houlihan Flynn, women commentators seem to be more accepting of these poems than some of their male counterparts. I have consistently found that, in the classroom, male students are (or feel they must pretend to be) appalled by the poems, while women tend to be amused. Ricardo Quintana may have been right: "The same piercing eyes which saw delusion in romance, *ennui* in marriage, and indignity in the necessities of the body, saw also the chief, if hidden, attribute of cultivated women—her realism."[53] Ellen Pollak devotes her book, *The Poetics of Sexual Myth: Gender and Ideology in the Verse of Swift and Pope* (1985) to contrasting Swift's healthy attitude toward gender with Pope's misconceptions: "Swift was committed in his poems to exploding certain bourgeois sexual myths that Pope's verse insistently worked to justify. . . ."[54] Whatever the editors of *The Scriblerian* may say, Nussbaum also exempts Swift from the charge of misogyny. She endorses Pollak's views and adds, "Swift made the best of what was available to him and used the scatological tradition for original, but not primarily misogynist, purposes."[55] In 1966, in *The Troublesome Helpmate: A History of Misogny in Literature*, Katharine Rogers writes lengthily of Swift's aversion to women, and then adds a coda proving that his attitudes toward women were astonishingly enlightened for his time.[56] In 1982, in *Feminism in Eighteenth-Century England*, Rogers reverses the process. She writes almost a whole section on Swift as a feminist, and ends with three paragraphs of qualification.[57]

In *Ends of Empire: Women and Ideology in Early Eighteenth-Century English Literature* (1993), Laura Brown comments thus

on Rogers's *volte-face:* "The difficulty Swift presents for a feminist
reading is suggested by the fact that Rogers's first book presents
Swift as a misogynist . . . and her second as a feminist . . . on
identical evidence."[58] Brown herself, perhaps the most radical of
Swift scholars, uses a circuitous (and rather bizarre) argument
to rescue her author at the last moment: "Swift's misogyny is
appropriately understood in the context of mercantile capitalism. . . . [T]he structure of that misogyny opens up a critique of
the treatment of racial difference essential to Swift's strategy in a
crucial part of *Gulliver's Travels*. . . . [T]he unpromising materials
of misogyny enable us to perceive the critique of racism."[59] By the
penultimate paragraph, Swift has become a "positive model," not
a "negative lesson."[60] The vindications of Swift differ from scholar
to scholar, but almost all female Swiftians argue in his defense.

Flynn, one of the few women scholars who see Swift as hostile
to women, accuses him of lacking empathy, of being unable "to
imagine women from the inside." I would argue that, on the contrary, Swift's pervasive empathy is responsible for some critical
confusion. In the passage from Pilkington's *Memoirs*, where he
perfectly imitates the prudish lady, Swift is disturbingly knowl-
edgeable about female gestures, idioms, and attitudes. He does
not, however, approve morally of the husband-hating hypocrite
whose mind and body he has assumed. As Pilkington represents
it, he shifts from the lady's viewpoint to his own "outside" judgment within half a sentence: "but, for my Part, I never could
bear to touch any Man's Flesh—except my Husband's, whom,
perhaps,' says he, 'she wish'd at the Devil.'" In his other mono-
logues spoken by female figures, he exhibits the same uncanny
knowledge. And again, that intimacy with the female figure does
not necessarily carry moral approbation. In his many manifestations, including his female creations, Swift shows himself master
of a skill Keats would later describe: he can suppress his ego
sufficiently to inhabit the body of another being of his own creation. Keats would point out that Shakespeare knew Iago from the
inside, that temporarily he was Iago; and no moral sense intruded
to spoil the verisimilitude.[61] For Swift, the moral judgment preceded or succeeded the impersonation, but it was never suspended
for long.

Swift's capacity for empathy unaccompanied by moral approval
may explain why critics—men and women—are so divided over,
say, "A Beautiful Young Nymph Going to Bed" (1731). The poem
begins and ends in bitter contempt and visceral revulsion. But
some critics—for example, John Aden, J. A. Downie, and Felicity

Nussbaum—have chosen to focus on the middle of the poem, where Swift seems to take on himself the prostitute's fear and pain. The poet vividly describes her physical torment, the result of venereal disease, and the mental torture she endures even in her dreams. As she awakens to find her paraphernalia in disorder, he adopts her values and her way of speaking:

> Corinna wakes. A dreadful sight!
> Behold the ruins of the night!
> A wicked rat her plaster stole,
> Half ate, and dragged it to his hole.
>
> (ll. 57–60)[62]

Aden, Downie, and Nussbaum interpret such passages as conveying Swift's sympathy for the whore.[63] My students tend to believe, rather anachronistically, that Swift is condemning the society that renders prostitution necessary. My own opinion is that the ending is morally definitive: "Corinna in the morning dizened, / Who sees, will spew; who smells, be poisoned" (ll. 73–74).[64] Swift has entered Corinna's mind only to make his mockery more devastating. It is a cruel maneuver, and scholars who like Swift cannot always believe he is cruel.

Empathy without approval is one reason that Swift is the focus of passionate debate. The disagreement over "The Beautiful Young Nymph" is, however, only a vista in the panorama of critical controversy over Swift. Conflict is endemic to Swift studies. We must remember that even the division between the "hard" school and the "soft" school over *Gulliver's Travels* is not a phenomenon peculiar to our own time. In the eighteenth century, as in the twentieth, some critics could not believe that Swift was as cruel as he is. Here is William Godwin, writing in *The Enquirer: Reflections on Education, Manners, and Literature* (1797):

What is the tendency of Gulliver's Travels, particularly of that part which relates to the Houyhnmhns [sic] and Yahoos? It has frequently been affirmed to be, to inspire us with a loathing aversion to our species, and fill us with a frantic preference for the society of any class of animals, rather than of men. A poet of our own day [Hayley], as a suitable remuneration for the production of such a work, has placed the author in hell, and consigned him to the eternal torment of devils. On the other hand it has been doubted whether, under the name of Houyhnmhns [sic] and Yahoos, Swift has done any thing more than exhibit two different descriptions of men, in their highest improvement and lowest degradation; and it has been affirmed that no book breathes more strongly a generous indignation against vice, and an ardent love of every thing that is excellent and honourable to the human heart.[65]

Understanding Swift, or attempting to do so, is difficult work requiring the application of many kinds of intelligence. Each of us brings to the interpretation of Swift a set of assumptions that very much affects how we read him. Women's scholarship on Swift is, at present, a particularly active and exciting field. But women's views (diverse as they are) cannot displace men's any more than American and English views can displace German, Irish, Scottish, Welsh, Canadian, and Australian. In this enterprise, we are all partners.

Notes

1. Margaret Anne Doody, "Swift among the Women," *Yearbook of English Studies* 18 (1988): 70.

2. Ibid., 69.

3. *Memoirs of Mrs. Laetitia Pilkington* (Dublin: For the author, 1748), 1:47–48, as emended for A. C. Elias, Jr.'s forthcoming edition at the University of Georgia Press. Quoted in Doody, "Swift among the Women," 71. I am deeply grateful to Dr. Elias for his encouragement and for his generous sharing of ideas and materials.

4. These poems are mentioned in Doody, "Swift among the Women," 71.

5. Deborah Baker Wyrick, *Jonathan Swift and the Vested Word* (Chapel Hill and London: University of North Carolina Press, 1988), 128–66.

6. Irvin Ehrenpreis, *"Personae,"* in *Restoration and Eighteenth-Century Literature,* ed. Carroll Camden (Chicago: University of Chicago Press, 1963), 31.

7. Claude Rawson, "Rage and Raillery and Swift: The Case of *Cadenus and Vanessa.*" See above, p. 189.

8. Pilkington, *Memoirs,* 1:46.

9. Ibid., 1:96.

10. Iris Barry, introduction to *Memoirs of Mrs. L[a]etitia Pilkington, 1712–1750,* ed. J. Isaacs (New York: Dodd, Mead, 1928), 19. For the original sources of this remark, see Matthew Pilkington's will (1754) as transcribed by F. Elrington Ball, *N&Q,* 11th ser., 6 (27 July 1912): 65–66, and his son Jack's comment in *The Real Story of John Carteret Pilkington. Written by Himself* (London, 1760), 9–10.

11. *The Third and last Volume of the Memoirs of Mrs. Laetitia Pilkington* (London: For R. Griffiths, 1754), 148–49, as emended for the forthcoming Georgia edition.

12. Rogers, 144.

13. *Vanessa and Her Correspondence with Jonathan Swift,* ed. A. Martin Freeman (Boston: Houghton Mifflin, 1921), 135.

14. Ibid., 63.

15. Rogers, 203, ll. 85–88 and l. 99.

16. *JS,* 1:90.

17. See, for example, *JS,* 2:387 and 425.

18. Swift, *Prose,* 92–93.

19. Ibid., 9:89. For other instances where Swift advocates friendship and esteem between man and woman, see "Stella's Birthday" (1725) in Rogers, 286, ll. 29–32, and "Strephon and Chloe" (1731), 463, ll. 309–12.

20. Swift, *Prose,* 4:225.

21. Ibid., 11:62.

22. Ibid., 11:269.

23. David Venturo, "Concurring Opponents: Mary Wollstonecraft and Jonathan Swift on Women's Education and the Sexless Nature of Virtue." See above, pp. 192–202.

24. *Godwin and Mary: Letters of William Godwin and Mary Wollstonecraft,* ed. Ralph M. Wardle (Lawrence: University of Kansas Press, 1966), 45.

25. *The Complete Letters of Lady Mary Wortley Montagu,* ed. Robert Halsband (Oxford: Clarendon Press, 1967), 3:22. Lady Mary seems to have hated Swift almost as much as she did Pope. She ordered her portable commode painted with books labeled "Swift" and "Pope" so that she could have the pleasure of besmirching them every day. See Robert Halsband, "New Anecdotes of Lady Mary Wortley Montagu," in the James M. Osborn Festschrift, *Evidence in Literary Scholarship,* ed. René Wellek and Alvaro Ribeiro (Oxford: Clarendon Press, 1979), 245 (anecdote), 243 (authenticity).

26. Rogers, 146, ll. 620–21.

27. J. A. Downie, *Jonathan Swift: Political Writer* (London: Routledge and Kegan Paul, 1984), 185. Quoted in Carole Fabricant's essay in this volume, p. 154.

28. John Boyle, Earl of Orrery, *Remarks on the Life and Writings of Dr. Jonathan Swift . . . In a Series of Letters . . .,* 3d ed. (London, 1752), 78.

29. Ibid., 83.

30. "An Epistle to Dr. Arbuthnot," *TE,* 4:111, ll. 209–10.

31. Montagu, *Letters,* 1:380, n. 4.

32. Ibid., 3:56.

33. Ibid., 3:56, n. 2.

34. *Lady Mary Wortley Montagu: Essays and Poems and Simplicity, A Comedy,* ed. Robert Halsband and Isobel Grundy (Oxford: Clarendon Press, 1977), 273–76.

35. Leslie Stephen, *Swift* (London: Macmillan, 1898), 120–21; in the *English Men of Letters* series, ed. John Morley (New York: Harper and Brothers, 1894).

36. Stephen, *Swift,* 139.

37. Ibid., 140.

38. Evelyn Hardy, *The Conjured Spirit, Swift: A Study in the Relationship of Swift, Stella, and Vanessa* (London: Hogarth Press, 1949), 244–45.

39. Ibid., 245.

40. Ibid., 238, n. 1.

41. Katharine M. Rogers, *Feminism in Eighteenth-Century England* (Urbana: University of Illinois Press, 1982), 60.

42. Susan Gubar, "The Female Monster in Augustan Satire," *Signs* 3, no. 2 (Winter 1977): 393.

43. Ellen Pollak, "Comment on Susan Gubar's 'The Female Monster in Augustan Satire,'" *Signs* 3, no. 3 (Spring 1978): 730.

44. Sandra M. Gilbert and Susan Gubar, *The Madwoman in the Attic: The Woman Writer and the Nineteenth-Century Imagination* (New Haven: Yale University Press, 1979), 31–34.

45. Doody, "Swift among the Women," 72.

46. Ellen Pollak, "Swift among the Feminists," in *Critical Approaches to Teaching Swift,* ed. Peter J. Schakel (New York: AMS Press, 1992), 75.

47. Unsigned, *The Scriblerian*: 26. 1 (Autumn 1993): 37. To be fair, the reviewer may be reacting, in part, to Wyrick's use of critical jargon.

48. Carol Houlihan Flynn, *The Body in Swift and Defoe* (Cambridge: Cambridge University Press, 1990), 88.

49. Carol Barash, rev. of Carol Houlihan Flynn, *The Body in Swift and Defoe, Eighteenth-Century Studies* 27, no. 2 (Winter 1993–94): 327.

50. Myra and David Sadker, *Failing at Fairness: How America's Schools Cheat Girls* (New York: Scribner's, 1994), 83.

51. Mrs. Montagu to Ann Donnellan, A.L.S. [early 1749?], now in the Hyde Collection. Quoted in A. C. Elias, Jr., "Male Hormones and Women's Wit: The Sex Appeal of Mary Goddard and Laetitia Pilkington," *Swift Studies* 9 (1994): 15–16.

52. Rogers, *Feminism,* 21.

53. Ricardo Quintana, *The Mind and Art of Jonathan Swift* (New York: Oxford University Press, 1936), 171–72.

54. Ellen Pollak, *The Poetics of Sexual Myth: Gender and Ideology in the Verse of Swift and Pope* (Chicago: University of Chicago Press, 1985), 13.

55. Felicity A. Nussbaum, *The Brink of All We Hate: English Satires on Women, 1660–1750* (Lexington: University of Kentucky Press, 1984), 108.

56. Katharine M. Rogers, *The Troublesome Helpmate: A History of Misogyny in Literature* (Seattle: University of Washington Press, 1966), 166–74.

57. Rogers, *Feminism,* 58–62.

58. Laura Brown, *Ends of Empire: Women and Ideology in Early Eighteenth-Century English Literature* (Ithaca: Cornell University Press, 1993), 174, n. 1.

59. Ibid., 199.

60. Ibid., 200.

61. See *The Letters of John Keats, 1814–1821,* ed. Hyder Edward Rollins (Cambridge: Harvard University Press, 1958), 1:386–88.

62. Rogers, 454, ll. 57–60.

63. See John M. Aden, "Corinna and the Sterner Muse of Swift," *English Language Notes* 4 (1966): 28; Downie, *Jonathan Swift,* 311–14; Nussbaum, *The Brink of All We Hate,* 110–12.

64. Rogers, 455, ll. 73–74.

65. William Godwin, *The Enquirer: Reflections on Education, Manners, and Literature* (Philadelphia, 1797), 107. Although Godwin notes here the dispute over Swift's attitude toward mankind, he never doubts that the Houyhnhnms are Swift's ideal.

Notes on Contributors

CARYN CHADEN is associate professor of English at DePaul University, where she also directs the College of Liberal Arts and Sciences Honors Program. In addition to her work on Mary Leapor, she has written articles on Richardson, Goldsmith, and Brackenridge. She is currently working on a study of eighteenth-century representations of Bath.

NORA F. CROW is associate professor of English at Smith College. She is the author of *The Poet Swift* (1977) and coeditor of *The Evil Image: Two Centuries of Gothic Short Fiction and Poetry* (1981). She contributed the master entry on Jonathan Swift to *The Dictionary of Literary Biography, Eighteenth-Century British Poets*. Besides essays on eighteenth-century topics, Crow has written several articles on the subject of literature and medicine.

CAROLE FABRICANT teaches in the English Department at the University of California, Riverside. She is author of *Swift's Landscape* (1982), which has been reissued in paperback by the University of Notre Dame Press, as well as other recent essays on Swift appearing in *The Profession of Eighteenth-Century Literature* (1992), *"Gulliver's Travels": Case Studies in Contemporary Criticism* (1995), and *Walking Naboth's Vineyard* (1995). She has also published articles on Pope, Rochester, country-house tourism, and eighteenth-century landscape.

BARBARA MCGOVERN is associate professor of English at the Ohio State University at Mansfield. She author of *Anne Finch and Her Poetry: A Critical Biography* (1992) and a number of essays on Restoration and eighteenth-century writers, as well as the forthcoming *The Anne Finch Wellesley Manuscript: A Critical Edition*, which she has coedited. She is currently working on a study of religion and early English women writers.

DONALD C. MELL is professor of English at the University of Delaware. He is author of *A Poetics of Augustan Elegy* (1974), *English*

Poetry, 1660–1800: A Guide to Information Sources (1982), and coeditor of *Contemporary Studies of Swift's Poetry* (1981) and of *Man, God, and Nature in the Enlightenment* (1988). The author of numerous articles on Restoration and eighteenth-century literature, he reviews widely for journals of the period.

ELLEN POLLAK is a member of the English Department at Michigan State University, where she teaches eighteenth-century literature and feminist literary theory. She has published articles on Swift, Pope, Defoe, Behn, and feminist criticism, and is author of *The Poetics of Sexual Myth: Gender and Ideology in the Verse of Swift and Pope* (1985). She is currently writing a book on representations of incest in British prose fiction of the Restoration and eighteenth century.

MELINDA ALLIKER RABB is associate professor of English at Brown University. She has published on a variety of eighteenth-century topics and writers, including the canon, satire, fiction, Swift, Pope, Fielding, Richardson, Godwin, Sterne, Sarah Scott, and Manley. She currently working on a critical study of the works of Delariviere Manley.

CLAUDE RAWSON is George M. Bodman Professor of English at Yale University and Chairman of the Yale Boswell Editions. His books include *Henry Fielding and the Augustan Ideal under Stress* (1972, 1992), *Gulliver and the Gentle Reader* (1973, 1992), and *Order from Confusion Sprung* (1985, 1993). His most recent publications are *Satire and Sentiment 1660–1830* (1994) and a volume of essays by various hands, *Jonathan Swift: A Collection of Critical Essays* (1995).

VALERIE RUMBOLD is a senior lecturer in the English Department at the University of Wales, Bangor. She is the author of *Women's Place in Pope's World* (1989) and of articles on eighteenth-century women writers. Her current project is an edition of Pope's *Dunciad in Four Books* (1743).

PETER STAFFEL, an assistant professor at Wheeling Jesuit College, has read and published papers on Dryden, Pope, and Sterne. Presently he is working on a study of Dryden's *Fables Ancient and Modern*. In this book he tries to solidify the "unitarian" position, which considers the work to be Dryden's summary comment on epic poetry and human comedy.

Linda Veronika Troost is an associate professor of English at Washington and Jefferson College, where she teaches classical literature in translation, eighteenth-century British culture, and drama. She has published on the satirists Samuel "Hudibras" Butler, Richard Brinsley Sheridan, and W. S. Gilbert, has written several articles for the *New Grove Dictionary of Opera,* and is now working on musical comedy in late-eighteenth-century London.

David F. Venturo, assistant professor of English at Clark University in Worcester, Massachusetts, has published articles on Swift, Johnson, and eighteenth-century prosody and poetics. He recently completed work on a study of the poetic career of Samuel Johnson entitled *Johnson the Poet.* He is presently working on a project dealing with the closing years of the literary careers of Milton, Dryden, and Swift.

Index

This index was compiled by Margaret Pyle Hassert with the help of Sara Barnett and under the supervision of Donald C. Mell.

Boldface type indicates extensive discussion of author or work.